"Richard Manning is the most significant social critic in the northern Rockies. We're fortunate to have Dick Manning as he continues his demands for fairness while casting light on our future."
—William Kittredge, author of *The Last Best Place: A Montana Anthology* and *The Next Rodeo: New and Selected Essays*

#

"Richard Manning's work has always been something special, distinguished by its intense passion and its penetrating insights.
—George Black, author of *Empire of Shadows: The Epic Story of Yellowstone*

#

"Richard Manning is at the head of his class."
—Larry McMurtry, author of over two dozen books, including *The Last Picture Show* and *Lonesome Dove*

#

"Richard Manning is the West's greatest journalist. Read this book, and then read everything else he has written, and everything he will ever write."
—Rick Bass, author of *Why I Came West* and *The Traveling Feast*

If It Sounds Good, It Is Good

Seeking Subversion, Transcendence, and Solace in America's Music

Richard Manning

If It Sounds Good, It Is Good: Seeking Subversion, Transcendence, and Solace in America's Music
Richard Manning
© 2020 PM Press

ISBN: 978–1–62963–792–1 (print)
ISBN: 978–1–62963–806–5 (ebook)
Library of Congress Control Number: 2019946087

Cover by John Yates / www.stealworks.com
Interior design by briandesign

10 9 8 7 6 5 4 3 2 1

PM Press
PO Box 23912
Oakland, CA 94623
www.pmpress.org

Printed in the USA

CONTENTS

FOREWORD

Rick Bass

I'll be brief. At its mediocre worst, an introduction or foreword can rush the reader and give away the goods. Why attempt in three pages to speak for the author who for the last many years has relentlessly pursued the subject with depth and, inhabiting the dream of the book into which the reader is about to descend? There's no answer, really. I'm reminded of the anecdote regarding James Joyce and the publication of *Ulysses*. When someone complained jokingly that it might take a year or longer to read it, he is reported to have replied, "Well, it took me fourteen years to write it, so it can take you fourteen years to read it." This is a roundabout way of saying that three pages can in no way capture 250.

My hope for readers of this book is that they come to it as I did—sitting back and just listening, as if to a campfire round of expert picking: runs and riffs, progressions, harmonies, melodies, and improvisations that expand and then dissolve boundaries. I don't think I'm negatively influencing the forthcoming reading experience by revealing that this book, like so many of Manning's works, travels confidently from one major thought or subject to another, whereas another writer might require separate books to cover that same ground.

Fascinating to me is Manning's reminder that music, alone among the senses, requires no central processing in the brain: it reverberates against the cilia of the inner ear and simply *is*, without any translation or interpretation, no chemical transfer required, no synapses, catalysts, enzymes or other neural mechanisms. It's as primal and real as a drum.

It's as much a part of our physiology as is breathing or the pumphouse contractions of the heart.

This being a book by Richard Manning, of course you'll encounter a concise exploration of not just American music history and culture, but also genetic appropriation and germplasm. Everything is as connected in a book by Manning as it is in real life—food, water, craft, religion, wild nature, family, politics.

Why do humans make music? Because we are human, and our brains have, like so many other radiations from the tree of life—including the brains of birds—evolved to absorb, and be moved by, sound waves.

One comes to understand, reading this book, that when the individual is hearing (or creating) music that the brain is most in harmony with, is most congruous with, its time-fitted self. (The philosopher David Rothenberg mines parallel veins in his book *Survival of the Beautiful*, exploring how birdsong and other "art" does not necessarily translate into either sexual selectivity for the singers or survival skills such as reduced mortality. Instead, art, or what we often call beauty, appears to exist simply, or not so simply, because the brain has been made to absorb it. Because we fit beauty.)

Why do humans make music? "Because the world and our body desire it" is perhaps not the most satisfying answer—but in Manning's narrative, this fact is shown to be both true and inescapable.

Where would we be as a species without emotion? Certainly, there are downsides, but here we are, nonetheless, with it, for better or worse. It is who we are and how we got here. It's an interesting question, though. The social, cooperative animals tend to traffic in it quite heavily. Whether as reward or punishment, praise or criticism, and manipulative, no matter: it, emotion, like music, amplifies the brain's activity and therefore power, or potential.

An active brain is, well, a brain that fits the dynamic world in which it evolved.

Music feels *good*. Beyond this, I think music heals.

Manning describes wonderfully this phenomenon as dramatized in Charles Frazier's novel *Cold Mountain*, where the Civil War deserter, Stobrod—otherwise a seemingly irredeemable ne'er-do-well—picks up a fiddle and, in due time, begins to reconstruct not only himself but also his war-damaged compatriots: balm and salve in a hard time.

Manning discusses also the common observation that many if not most musicians seem to hurt a great deal. Does their art push them into estrangement or is it the other way around? It is likely as unanswerable as chicken-or-egg, but I think it is fair to say that all species and populations experience and grow from pain, that it is transformative, and that this is one of the evolutionary advantages of, and reasons for, the existence of, music.

Not that all things must, in the moment, have utility to be valuable. I believe also that beauty matters, on its own. But how wonderful to see the care and fittedness with which the larger world tries to make a place and a space for us, even now, in these crowded, tempestuous, and often solipsistic times.

Because this is a Manning book, music doesn't just define culture and evolution, doesn't just rescue species, individuals, and populations; here, the human, Manning, rescues a guitar.

It occurs to me at this point that it might be easier to describe what scant little might be left out of this book, rather than introducing some of the elements that a reader will encounter within it.

The brain, beautiful though it is, and natural, can be, we are reminded, "a prison of the self," as the philosopher Barbara Ehrenreich writes.

Manning also quotes neuroscientist Walter Freeman concerning the essence and identity of music: "Here in its purest form is a human technology for crossing the solipsistic gulf. It is wordless, illogical, deeply emotional and selfless in its actualization of transient and then lasting harmony between individuals."

It—music—pours into us, it pours out of us. It gives us avenues to step away from the lovely prison, for a little while.

Again, as with all of Manning's books, the same effect is accomplished by reading. Fill your bookshelf with each of his books. Build a new shelf if necessary. Keep a copy of this latest work for yourself, but buy plenty to share with all the musicians—and music lovers—you know.

1

DELIA WAS A GAMBLIN' GIRL

This exactly was the beginning of my life's obsession:

> Delia was a gamblin' girl, she laid her money down.
> Delia was a gamblin' girl, she laid her money down.
> All the friends I ever had are gone.

Decades after, I still can't say why this obsession persists, so this is founding question and my purpose here in this book—not Delia, but exploring this eccentric passion for her and for those like her that swelled when I first heard this verse. Oddly, though, I am not alone. This very Delia surfaces in odd venues, pursued by disparate characters. She is regarded by seemingly rational, respectable, credentialed people as if their lives were as smitten as mine is. What's happening here? It's just a song. The answer lies not in Delia's details but in the nature of song.

Begin by knowing that Delia herself was real. She lived. Not for long, but she lived. In one version, she is introduced abruptly: "Delia cursed Curtis on a Saturday night." This is a fact, confirmed by research. So too is her abrupt death in the very next verse. "Cutty" (his name in my version of the song and in most others, a corruption of "Curtis," and even this was an alias) was fourteen or fifteen years old, and Delia herself fourteen. The printed, official record, the history, is silent on her gambling habits, but this same record makes it pretty clear she was a whore and that Cutty/Curtis was in a brothel when, in the song's telling, "He shot poor Delia down with a flamin' forty-four."

The songs arose—there were multiples, even from the beginning—and spread nationwide almost immediately after Delia died. Five or six decades later, the various versions gained some currency, widely recorded and performed (Bob Dylan, Johnny Cash, Dave Van Ronk, David Bromberg) standards of the mid-twentieth-century boom in folk music. Only later did we learn that the lyrics were fairly close to what really happened.

John W. Gordon wrote a letter in 1928 mentioning some research he had done for the Library of Congress, where the several songs of Delia had already been collected and entombed. Gordon concluded but didn't verify that Delia had been real. Another researcher, John Garst, seized on Gordon's seventy-year-old hunch in June 2000, rifled a newspaper morgue in Savannah, Georgia, found accounts that outlined the story, then fleshed it out in court archives of sworn testimony. The murder had occurred in a "poor, black and violent" Yamacraw section of Savannah at about 11:30 p.m. on Christmas Eve of 1900 when Moses "Coony" Houston shot Delia Green. (The spelling of "Coony" varies in the record, but no matter the spelling, it was still considered okay in 1900 to refer to a young black man that way in print, but not so in mid-century when he became "Cutty.") She died the next day of a wound to her "groin." Houston was tried, convicted, and drew a life sentence (the song's account: "Judge said, 'Poor boy, you got ninety-nine'") but served only twelve and a half years. Delia had indeed "cursed" Cooney. Court testimony reconstructed their conversation that night:

> COONEY: My little wife is mad with me tonight. She does not hear me. She is not saying anything to me. (To Delia:) You don't know how I love you.
> DELIA: You son of a bitch. You have been going with me for four months. You know I am a lady.
> COONEY: That is a damn lie. You know I have had you as many times as I have fingers and toes.
> DELIA: You lie!

Or as the song has it in a verse usually delivered last, the verse delivered in Cooney's voice, from his point of view:

Delia, oh Delia, how can it be?
You loved all those other men, you never did love me.
All the friends I ever had are gone.

This is more or less as I first heard the song on a January night in 1973 in a stately Victorian house serving then as a coffeehouse, the Ark in Ann Arbor, Michigan. I was not then—as were most of the rest crowded into the repurposed parlor that night—a folkie, dyed in the literal wool. I could have been more accurately described as a hick kid, or more accurately still, a misfit, so I fit in this crowd. I would have slipped unnoticed into the heap of flannel plaid shirts, bell-bottomed jeans, tan leather lace-up work boots, print skirts, sideburns and flopping mops of hair, background notes of marijuana and Camel cigarette smoke, fresh-baked whole grains and Ripple wine lingering in unwashed and faded natural fibers of our clothes. We spent a good bit of that night laughing, which is why one came to hear U. Utah Phillips, the Golden Voice of the Great Southwest, a man who in his own telling aspired to be "a rumor in his own time," and I think he accomplished this.

He had not yet risen even to the level of rumor in my reckoning then. I'd never even heard of him and was only there at the urging of a friend of mine, Peter Bowen, a performer in his own right, a gifted songster blessed with a voice that seemed to come from somewhere deep in his chest or the mid-nineteenth century. Bowen was then a hero of mine. A few years older than I was, he had made it a point to oversee my informal education. Later we had a more complicated relationship defined in equal parts by his rampant alcoholism and towering intelligence, but then he was just someone I looked up to. He was from Montana, tall, thin then, a crag of a man with a drift of strawberry blond hair, blue, taut laser eyes, a fine arts student. In fringed buckskin jacket—and he was known to wear exactly this—he could have stood in for George Armstrong Custer in tintype. Just a few months before that night at the Ark, Bowen had listened, drunk, to a recording of Don McLean's "Vincent," a song about Vincent Van Gogh, which inspired him to unfold the high-carbon steel blade of his Buck Hunter model knife and carve flesh canyons on the pale skin side of his forearms. He had bled dangerously before friends marched him off to be stitched up. I had been told all the fine detail of this event and still admired the knife and had to have one. My then-wife gave me the exact duplicate for my twenty-first birthday. I still have it and used it to gut an elk I shot last season.

Bruce "Utah" Phillips, who did indeed achieve a level of fame, knew Bowen and later recorded one of his songs, "Feather Ben," about a battered, aging cowboy from Montana where Bowen and I both live now. Bowen's oater of a song was a natural fit for Phillips, whose own songs rattled all through with the empty and wind of open range. There's a line in one of Phillips's songs about a hobo—a lot of his work was about used-up bums—that says, "All you could see in his soft prairie eyes was the wind and the grass and the snow." This is Phillips. Like Bowen, an escarpment of a man, lambchop sideburns, leather vest, and plaid flannel.

In 1973, Phillips had already made a considerable mark as a folksinger, part of a cohort that orbited the Caffe Lena in Saratoga Springs, New York. But what he was equally known for then and up until he died, was his humor—topical, rustic, biting, Twainish, seditious, a line of bullshit and banter that he used to string together songs of hoboes, trains, and Baptist hymns retooled as Wobbly ballads. One such shaggy-dog story, the venerable "Moose Turd Pie," chewed up a good five minutes between tunes. He told it that night in Ann Arbor, at least this is the way I remember it, a recollection reinforced by the fact that the same story made it onto one of his albums. So too did some of his jokes directed at his sideman both that night in Ann Arbor and on a recording for Philo Records released that year. Martin Grosswendt was eighteen years old and already a brilliant guitar player, studio musician for Philo, sent touring with Phillips.

"When he was a kid, his parents gave him a drum and told him to beat it. But he really wanted to play the violin, but his parents wouldn't let him. Didn't want the neighbors to know they were Jewish," Phillips said of Grosswendt.

Phillips took a break that night and gave the stage over to his sideman, who all evening had been playing not conventional guitar but a Dobro, which is a resonator guitar recognizable by what looks to be a big shiny inverted chrome pie plate centered in its top. Such guitars are often played lap style and not fretted but stopped with a metal bar slide that allows the sounding of notes between standard pitches, an oscillating, woozy effect that can range anywhere from cartoonish to ethereal, depending on the player. Alone on stage, Grosswendt swapped his Dobro for a conventional guitar to play "Delia," not cartoonishly, not a bit.

The conventions of my trade demand that at this point I conjure (or invent) a fully formed description of that performance to snag you on this, the thread of my story. I am, after all, asserting that this simple song as played that very night was life-changing, and it was. The stark truth of the matter is that I remember none of it. Only that it happened.

I do, however, remember this about that night, that Bowen knew Grosswendt, he introduced me to him, and the three of us stood in the darkness of the Ark parking lot after the show and drank a pint of whisky I had brought along. Bowen later marveled at Grosswendt's rendering of "Delia," calling it the best performance of the song he had ever heard, and by that point he had heard lots. I knew that, and I, the studious apprentice, noted his praise as important. I knew that much. Then Grosswendt disappeared, and I never heard of him again, just a memory that popped up when I'd play Phillips's recordings and hear him mentioned on them. I recollect a performer, an itinerant song-ster and a kid younger than I was who became a model. I thought he was cool, and he was, or at least he was in the version of him that my memory made. Not long after, Bowen mostly disappeared too, but not completely.

###

I share my fascination with the song "Delia" with the historian Sean Wilentz, who in one of his books details an interesting lineage of the tune that offers some hint of why we might be so taken with it. Its cur-rency in the '60s was actually an echo of an earlier flourish. It had been recorded many times before Dylan and Cash by predecessors both famous and obscure. Early on, it split to two versions, a development wholly analogous to biology's speciation, the slow drift of error in copying DNA, invention, mutation, and survival of invention that sustains biological change. This is the first and axiomatic rule of folk songs. They are not written so much as they evolve. Evolution is the creator. The song split, and one branch migrated to the Caribbean Islands, where it lived and changed, then returned to the mainland as an almost wholly separate song. (The attention of any biologists in the audience ought to be piqued by this factoid; island populations of biological species play an outsized role as drivers of evolutionary change.) Easy to spot the Caribbean version now; when you hear the chorus, "One more round, Delia's gone, one more round." This is its genetic marker.

This is not the version I first heard and eventually learned to play on my guitar. I learned Grosswendt's and Bromberg's version, almost note for note taken from the great blind gospel and blues guitarist the Reverend Gary Davis, as he had learned it, most likely in North Carolina in the 1920s or '30s. Bromberg was a student of Davis's in New York City. Both Dylan and Van Ronk knew this great man well. In no way, however, does this particular lineage give my version any special claim to authenticity, a folkie's pedigree. Tedious debates over authenticity have given the music a bad name and locked it in endless cycles of academic bickering. I am more interested here in how the music touches a life, which is why I am interested in Wilentz's thread of the discussion.

In Wilentz's telling, "Delia" originally was one of four songs, all of which came into being at the same time, shortly after 1900, all of which recount actual events, that is, could have been written and likely were written out of newspaper accounts. They share common lyrics (something that happens often in blues material—the common phrases are called "floaters" because they seem to float from song to song) but also common musical elements. All four songs remain with us today largely intact, and in fact Dylan recorded three of the four on a single album, which is why Wilentz became engaged with them.

Wilentz writes: "The identities of the bards who wrote 'Delia' and 'White House Blues' as well as when precisely they wrote them, remain unknown—although both songs sound as if they could be rearrangements of 'Stagolee' and 'Frankie and Albert.'"

All four are murder ballads, accounts of "gun violence," as we might put it today in a debate that assumes this is solely a present-day problem. Three of the four are essentially barroom killings. The victims were a black teenager who was probably a prostitute, two pimps, and in the case of "White House Blues," President William McKinley. Ground zero for this little burst of creativity—and we are probably tracing here the birth of the blues—was in the nation's dead center in St. Louis, where the events that inspired "Frankie and Albert" and "Stagolee" both occurred, and both of those songs were probably creations of a single songwriter, a street singer named Bill Dooley. Those two songs spread very rapidly before radio and recordings, through performance, and probably got reworked to "Delia" and "White House Blues" when they bumped into these shootings elsewhere, but it is this wildfire spread that intrigues me now. The blues, yes, a catchy musical form related to the wildly popular ragtime of the day, easy to see how it might do some traveling and show some endurance. But also these stories rooted in race and politics, pistols and poverty, radiating outward from the center of the nation, from the edge of the divide between north and south and east and west at the height of tensions from that period of turmoil that was Reconstruction. Lots to unpack here. Wilentz, Dylan, and the rest of us latch on to these not so much because they are catchy tunes and easy to dance to, but because they capture something about what it means to be human and American. They deliver knowledge of ourselves that is unavailable elsewhere. That syncopated cadence is the backbeat of our story.

That night at the Ark in 1973, Phillips would have summoned up a tune then known as "Cannonball Blues" on the big blonde Gibson J-200 he played, the same make and model favored by the Reverend Gary Davis. Of course he played "Cannonball" that night. The tune had become Phillips's theme song by then, a background vamp of fingerpicking, a steady cardiac thrum of alternating bass notes and filigree of treble that the audience would ride along on as he set up another joke:

"The Unitarians got mad at me and burned a question mark on my front lawn."

"The vice president's library burned down and he lost both books. Hadn't even finished coloring one of them."

"Cannonball Blues" came from the Carter Family, the first family of country music, but was not, like most of A.P. Carter's tunes, even remotely original. "Cannonball Blues" was a straightforward rip-off of "White House Blues." It all weaves together in a song.

I was twenty-one years old on that January night and did not realize it then, but only a couple of weeks away from one of my life's watershed decisions. I was a senior at the University of Michigan, three months from wrapping up three routine papers for three routine courses that would grant me a bachelor's degree in political science. It was no small feat from where I came from; no one in my extended family of farmers and carpenters, no one in my lineage, had ever earned a college degree. I was on a glide path, carrying a 3.0 and never breaking a sweat. A month or so later, I stopped going to classes and never went back, did not finish my degree.

More than forty years on, I am not about to try to pass the night at the Ark off as a complete and credible account of the reasons for this decision. I have thought about it way too much all those years since to the point that I probably know nothing about it now. Still there is a particular conversation that looms in my memory, and I think it happened. An instructor of mine, a professor, a political scientist, something of a malcontent himself, advised me in unmistakable terms not to pursue a degree in that discipline at Michigan. His rationale was clear. Michigan in particular and the field in general were then dominated by those who believed academic legitimacy for social scientists could only be gained by masquerading in white lab coats and fondling slide rules and computers, pretending to be actual scientists. They believed the human endeavor could be adequately accounted for through statistical analysis of data sets built of toggle-switch responses to survey questions. They were quantifiers. They were protos in a lineage that would eventually give us Cambridge Analytica. Quants for short, a label I now mouth as an epithet. These very people today rule our world. They are my villains, antithetical to the story that will unfold in the following pages.

This is not a small issue—not then, and even more crucial now in this age of information and dominance of data in every private corner of our lives. The deeper implications of this argument are intricate and sweeping, having much to do with the very fundamentals of our brain, that we are literally, each of us, of two minds on this matter. The ever-widening gulf in our collective thought, and literally within the folds of our brains, has left us unable to understand who we are. We are in real danger of surrendering the living of our lives to computers. This book will come back to this point, but for now, in the beginning, know that even as a kid, I had managed to summon a visceral, adamant, and correct response to the matter that would shape my life. The question itself was beginning to dig a hungry hole in the center of my mind, which became habitat for music. I mean to say in the coming pages that music is essential, and that one of its essential functions is to rescue our lives from data sets and algorithms. That's what this is really about.

My way into this at the time, though, was doubt. My professors in my formal courses offered a story, an account of people, especially then of Americans, of poor, working Americans, that I knew to be inadequate and benighted, because I came from poor, working Americans. I was ready to flee and forget the ignorance and poverty that had raised me (isn't that what universities were all about?), so one would assume I was fully primed to latch on to the story they were telling, but I couldn't. They simply failed to explain the people who had raised me. Folk songs were better at this.

Then came "Delia." And so what? It's a song like hundreds, thousands even, a murder ballad, maudlin and tawdry. The sort of event this song describes was common as dirt when Delia died, just as it is now, repeated a hundred times a day in trailer courts and pissy-smelling cracker box meth shacks in every village and town. Why should this single event carry a teenage whore through decades to strike so hard in subsequent lives?

Where does this song get the power to endure and to frame a life? I know literally hundreds of songs. Yet I can't tell you where I was or what I was doing, or when or why I listened to any of them. Only this one. I first heard it sung on either January 19 or 20, 1973, at the Ark in Ann Arbor, a happenstance performance by an obscure sideman, a teenager, a kid younger than I was, named Martin Grosswendt.

Of course no single explanation is adequate or even satisfying to the larger task of understanding a life, and this one I have been telling you about a student in Ann Arbor and rebellion and sweeping realization is not much better. It's a rationalization, an intellectualization, the sort of story a professor might tell. I promised myself I wouldn't write it that way this time, not this time around.

This rationalization is nonetheless true, at least as far as it goes, and that's what matters here, that this neat account indeed only scratches the surface of this issue, but the surface here is worth scraping, that the layer that comes up first has resins and sediments that tell us something, that our story, our collective story is layered with bums, presidents, porn stars, addicts, pimps, and gamblers, and they are us, and that we have not faced who we are until we sing the songs that have endured. "Delia" is such a story, but it is not really a story in the sense we have come to expect. Stories, we think, have authors, identifiable. Authors are authority. Not Delia. We have no idea who wrote this song, but authorship is not the point, that once written, it took on a life of its own, like a living being, a biological being complete with fungible DNA, generation to generation. It is not so much a story as it is a collective memory, given then the ability to tell something about, not the writer or even about Delia, but about the people who remembered it and kept it alive. It is, like the hand that rules biology, creation without a creator.

I am not sure I even heard "Delia" that night. What I heard was Bowen's high opinion of it amplified by my then high opinion of him. This was enough to nurture recall and steer me back to the song years later when I had become capable of hearing some of what was layered within, a process that continues even now, every time through, a bit deeper in. But in the beginning, I heard what lies beneath, the thrum of a fingerpicked, steel-stringed guitar, backbeat, syncopation. That's really what I heard, music. It was music that sent me on. I bought a guitar and learned to play it, then, now, and forever, I hope, a simple act of subversion.

###

Elvis Costello is usually credited for the relevant aphorism. He said that writing about music is like dancing about architecture, and how could it be any other way in matters of transcendence, by definition, ineffable? Yet here I am at the beginning of a project of writing about music, trying to eff the ineffable.

There is a subset of this conundrum immediately apparent as I begin this project. Being a lifelong journalist, my normal method in writing about anything is to ask people smarter than I am relevant questions and then string together the answers in a coherent account. There is absolutely no shortage of people smarter than I am about music, but one soon learns that it is almost impossible to ask them questions, at least not important ones. This has much to do with the nature of counterculture and the difficulty of asking the questions I find most interesting of the people I find most interesting. What these people know does not lend itself to linear description on the printed page any more than music can be captured by notation. This is why a book cannot sing.

This is an overly analytical way of saying the people who inhabit this subculture tend to be eccentric. Take my friend Greg Boyd, for instance. Early in the process of thinking about the challenges of this book, I decided I would need to consult various oracles, and Boyd was first on my list. So I made a drive across our town to see him in his garage, a place I know well. I noticed something odd about his garage a few years ago, that it is one of the few places on earth where I might sit quietly without agenda or purpose and pass time settled, at peace, awash in the sense of belonging. It is sanctuary. I imagine that I inhabit this odd space in the same spirit that a little old Italian lady might inhabit the candle-lit Catholic church. But then this is not an ordinary garage. Greg is a major-league, international dealer in vintage and handcrafted guitars, banjos, and mandolins. I have walked into that garage and been handed rare-as-hen's-teeth Martin guitars worth $100,000. He deals worldwide from a website out of his garage converted to a store, which also serves as a sort of social hub for local and traveling musicians. Sit there long enough and listen, and you hear this story assemble itself. And so from time to time have I.

I've known Greg for almost thirty years, and I don't think he has changed a bit in all that time—still the same boyish grin and wide-open face, a side-swept shock of blond hair, baggy khakis, overweight, and always on the verge of doing something about it. A forester by training, he came north from Jackson, Mississippi, in the '70s to fight forest fires and ended up staying in the northern Rockies.

But questions are useless in the garage. Boyd's knowledge of the stringed instruments would overrun the memory of a forty-acre computer server farm, and any conversation leaves you feeling as if you will hear much of his knowledge unspool right now in a single endless sentence. Facts pour forth in a disjointed stream undomesticated by any line of logic or order. Ask about the weather and a few sentences later you will be discussing fire frequency in northern Rockies conifer forests, the virtues of recent-issue BMW motorcycles, the perfidy of Republicans, and why Gibson guitar body styles were so vexingly variable in the transition from the L1 to the L0.

Yet I know he knows something of what I need to know. I have concluded from years of hearing Boyd's meandering monologues that he and characters like him—and they are common in the netherworld of music we are about to enter, misfits, eccentrics, obsessives—are the sources of this story. So I listen. Even try to herd him in a usable direction every now and again with a question. And when I do, off we go on like bees flitting flower to flower: first a debate on the merits of hard maple banjo bridges, then a discourse on using mammoth ivory for guitar nuts and saddles and an examination of the evidence as to whether Martin was really using Adirondack spruce during the prewar Golden Age, or did some Sitka spruce make it into the lumber pile.

And then this, a claim of his that he can identify any musician he knows simply by hearing a few bars.

He tells me: It's the same deal as seeing someone you've only just met from behind, seeing just the back of his head, and you haven't really ever seen the back of his head before, but from just that glimpse you can recognize him.

Then he tells me that one time he was playing in a bluegrass band (he's a banjo player primarily) and happened to hear an old recording of a Texas swing tune, and the guys in the band said they hadn't heard it in years and they ought to go back and listen more and learn those licks. And he said there was no point in doing that. If you ever heard a song, it's already in your playing. It's already there, and there's no point in going back and listening to an old recording.

Then he's off on Rupert Sheldrake, a controversial British biochemist and cell biologist who hatched an idea called morphic resonance, which hypothesizes that all natural systems from termite colonies to orchids have an inherent memory of everything that came before. Greg is particularly taken with Sheldrake's analogy of this idea, an idea that Sheldrake says is not mere analogy but literally true. He says that if an ordinary house key is dipped in a stream, one doesn't need to have that key to make a copy. One only needs to properly sample the water downstream and everything pertinent about that key can be read in the stream.

We need to hear from Gillian Welch now. It is one of my bedrock principles that the practice of songwriting ought to have been forbidden for all time beginning somewhere around 1970, which would have saved us from the plague of singer-songwriters that has occurred ever since. Songs are not written; they evolve. Of course I grant exemptions. Welch is one, largely because her work is less bound up in ego and more steeped in open gratitude to the lineage that made it. In her song "Barroom Girls," she wrote:

> The night came undone like a party dress
> And fell at her feet in a beautiful mess
> The smoke and the whiskey came home in her curls
> And they crept through the dreams of the barroom girls

There is a story, or many stories, seductive and redolent, wafting from this pile of clothes on the floor, yet I will need to let them emerge from the tangles of a beautiful mess.

###

The Reverend Gary Davis recorded during the '60s, but the extensive archive does not include a proper performance of "Cocaine Blues." The reason is right there in the title, and it's not the drug reference but wrapped up in the word "blues." Davis took the "reverend" title seriously, and, despite having built a long career playing Piedmont blues on banjo, 12-string guitar, and on his big J-200 Gibson, he refused to perform anything but gospel by the time microphones and tape captured his music. The blues were widely regarded among religious southerners as the devil's music, a fundamental schism not at all unique to Davis or the South or Protestants, or even to Christianity. This cleavage between organized religion and music can and will tell us much as this conversation unwinds. It is, oddly enough, one of the most important folds in the story.

Davis in the '60s was a street singer and a street preacher. He was blind, and he mostly performed on the streets of Harlem. People stole his guitars, and so even in polite company he was notoriously crotchety and protective of his instruments. He carried a pistol and a flask of whiskey and often during performances, even on stage not street, these would come into play in a menacing combination. All of this made him and audiences, for that matter, dependent on a series of what were known as "lead boys," usually young white men who volunteered to guide him to performances but also intervene as necessary during outbursts of preaching and gunplay. At the same time, the lead boys were also apprentices, took formal lessons, days-long lessons from him, and many became important figures in folk music, keepers of the flame, people like Bromberg, Woody Mann, Larry Johnson, Ernie Hawkins, Rory Block, and even Janis Ian. All studied his style, not so much as students, more as acolytes or apostles.

It's because of these followers, not recordings, that we know how Davis originally played "Cocaine Blues," because he believed the prohibition against the devil's music did not apply to teaching, just performing and recording. He would play and sing blues for his students. Nor did he believe that the prohibition applied to speaking the lyrics. Only singing was sacred, so there are recordings of him talking the "Cocaine Blues" through in an easy cadence. Still, it's nothing like hearing his virtuosity in full, glorious roar, when he pulled out all the stops to sing gospel. Hear him explode into "Twelve Gates of the City" or "Pure Religion." Drop to your knees and weep. I do, and I'm an atheist.

There are subtle differences between recordings of "Cocaine Blues" by Van Ronk and others and those of Davis. Same tune. Same chords and melody, but the derivative versions have been squared off some. Davis offers eccentricities, an odd bass pattern and a major seventh chord, which, I think, no one in all of blues, country, bluegrass, and folk has used since. Yet Davis's variations were not the result of a random walk. There is a clear direction back through time. Follow his eccentricities and you will find yourself lured into an infinite regression. Those intoxicating little licks pull you down a rabbit hole. Maybe somebody shows you a trick or maybe one day by accident, really, an unexpected bit of sound comes from beneath your own fingers, and you know immediately you must have more of this. The courses of entire lifetimes have been determined by such moments.

Start playing a song recorded by, say Counting Crows, and soon enough you're tracking it through Dylan and Van Ronk back to Davis or Dock Boggs, Roscoe Holcomb, Blind Willie Johnson, or Clarence Ashley, feeling your way along a pathway dimly lit by flatted thirds and fifths, slides and drone strings. Ever deeper, but also ever simpler and more visceral. You may start with the label "folk music," but as you trace it a ways, you will likely decide the term "roots music" is more accurate. Or "Americana." "Primitive" is better still. Backtrack through folk and blues and you'll wind up in New Orleans, or more likely, Appalachia, and then switch from guitar to banjo then clawhammer banjo, the ancient style of playing that developed among hillbillies and among the Celts, the Scottish and Irish moonshine runners who settled Appalachia by fleeing England's whiskey tax. But it only developed among them. They didn't invent it. The Celts were fiddlers. The banjo itself and the primitive style of playing it came to them from Africans, slaves. The banjo is African. The hillbillies learned it from the Africans. Track it back into their style, and soon enough you'll be taking the synthetic plastic drum-like head off your new banjo and replacing it with a piece of dried calf hide, because you'll be driven to hear something of the way banjos once spoke, not brassy and shiny like modern bluegrass instruments, but ambiguous and dark. Now remove the machined, nickel-plated hardware that gives modern banjos their bite and sting. Regress to simple wood hoops, tacked-on hide heads and gut strings. Then back a step further to banjos made of gourds, the original form, big, hollowed gourds.

Take the strings and neck off this primitive banjo, and now it's just a gourd with skin stretched across it, a drum. Now it drives a dance, not a performance, but a dance, your whole tribe, everyone you have ever known, dancing together in a circle as your tribe does from time to time, who knows why. At center of the circle sits a drummer and a shaman transformed by trance.

This regression sucked me in. At some point I decided I didn't have enough problems and so began to learn to play banjo. There was something of a method to this madness, a story I'll develop later. For the moment, though, a quick set of signposts I spotted on this path might give you an idea of its direction and the quirky turns in the road.

If you are to learn anything about the banjo then the necessary source is a wonderful big, fat illustrated history of the instrument by Philip F. Gura and James F. Bollman, *America's Instrument: The Banjo in the Nineteenth Century*. I read it again and again. But I also played, and as my understanding of the instrument slowly built, I noticed an odd impulse, that somehow I became interested in American transcendentalism, which arose coincident with the flourishing of the banjo, both developments centered in Boston in the mid-nineteenth century. (Yes, indeed. Boston was the center of banjo manufacture.) Still, it seems a big stretch to suggest the banjo has anything whatever to do with transcendentalism, but I did the scholarly thing and found that one of the go-to books about transcendentalism was written by Gura, the exact same guy who wrote the banjo history. Some coincidences are not merely coincidence, an idea that this project has taught me to respect, but for now, know that the banjo is the root of American music and its lineage is African, so like Delia's story, is wound up in slavery and racism and inevitably and relevantly to its political context, syncopation and the pentatonic scale. These matters are inseparable. Or for that matter, that the transcendentalists were the driving force of abolition, just as folksingers wound up in the civil rights movement.

In order to begin to grasp some of this, I had enrolled as a student at a banjo camp in late May 2015 an hour's drive west of Boston. Adults can do that sort of thing now, go off for a week's worth of bad food and sleeping on bunk beds to earn the rare privilege of sitting in classes with the greats, our musical heroes and learning plunk by plunk. Can and do by the thousands every year, middle-aged and not, white-haired, millennials even, hipsters, misfits, and geeks in guitar camps, fiddle camps, hammer dulcimer camps, shape note singing and flatfooting and clogging.

The nice people at the registration desk had shuffled through their lists a couple of times, rifled packets and checked computer print-outs. Every other case-carrying acolyte in the snaking line had passed Saint Peter and been waved on into the camp, but "no," they said to me, somehow they had my registration and confirmation of payment but no bunk, no berth had been set aside. A snafu obviously, but the fixing would require authority above their pay grade, and could I kindly step out of line and go speak with that round-faced, bald, bellied man standing at the end of the table, a genial guy, despite the considerable responsibilities of his office. And so I did, introducing myself, shaking his hand as I read the name tag: "Martin Grosswendt." I forgot about the bunk for a moment and blurted a three-sentence version of the back-story I have given you above, then concluded by saying I was glad to meet the man who had more or less ruined my life, a man I had not seen since a winter's night in Ann Arbor forty-two years before, had not seen or even known he continued to exist. We talked some through the next several days, then he offered me a copy of his latest CD, recorded that year. He autographed it and included a message, that he was glad he had so ruined my life. Track number seven on this, his latest CD, is "Delia."

2

BIRDS DO IT

The French composer Hector Berlioz was once observed sobbing at a musical performance, prompting some sympathy from another in the audience: "You seem to be greatly affected, monsieur. Had you not better retire for a while?" Berlioz snapped back, "Are you under the impression that I am here to enjoy myself?"

This is precisely the same territory traversed by another neuroscientist, Walter Freeman of Berkeley, but is guided by a more specific inquiry, which happens to be the same one that concerns us here. Freeman's analysis anchored a volume of essays called *The Origins of Music*, in which more than twenty scientists from various disciplines ponder the evolutionary basis of the question before us here: Why do humans make music? All humans for all human time. This turns out to be an old question, well-researched and, like many well-researched questions, unanswered. Or answered in a babel of responses such as one finds on any complex, important interdisciplinary question. Freeman tries to slice through the babel by arguing that our thinking on this matter has been blinkered. He correctly notes that the problem is one of categorization, and the thinkers and researchers who have engaged the question have narrowly focused on aesthetics. He writes, "However, these aspects contribute little to understanding raw emotions induced by music in circumstances where beauty is not at issue, but power is."

We are here to enjoy ourselves, but not just to enjoy ourselves. Power is here too. We are here to call down the thunder.

Decades ago I was lucky enough to get to know an interesting man just before he died. By then he was already benighted in dementia. The mental condition caused him to forget what he had just said, so he repeated himself, not necessarily a bad habit for a teacher. Repetition stressed an important idea. Joseph Eppes Brown had spent his life studying the life ways of Plains Indians, as a scholar, but also as an acolyte. Early in his life, he had become close to the Sioux religious leader Black Elk. Brown's understanding of the Sioux hinged on a simple idea he had learned from them, one necessary for our discussion here. They had no use for the categories that Europeans find crucial to thought. Specifically, Brown said, they made no distinction among religion, aesthetics, and utility. The same knife that had religious purposes in ceremony and thus held as holy could be elaborately adorned as a thing of great beauty and still could be used to gut an elk. Sorting out the separate functions was a waste of time because in the end, in the living of a life, they were not at all separate. Your brain and body have no separate pathways, channels, and circuits for awe, beauty, and simply getting by, the elements of survival. Survival. Persistence. These are the sacred elements of evolution.

The debate about the evolutionary role of music has been channeled by categorization that the Sioux would have ignored, and the rest of us ought to. Better that we wander into this idea by tugging at the thread of persistence, by asking why music persists. The rest will come up in the weave.

The artifact that speaks most clearly to persistence of music in the human condition is a bone flute. (Or to the persistence of the discussion of this matter—Darwin himself cited discoveries of Paleolithic bone flutes as evidence that music played a role in human evolution.) In our time, the marker is a particular flute unearthed in 1995 in a cave in what is now Slovenia. The artifact is a peninsula-shaped broken, hollow thigh bone of a cave bear with holes, round holes, clearly carved or drilled and carefully and deliberately spaced to produce notes if someone blew on the bone's end and fingered the holes, notes that would fit with our present-day idea of the musical scale. (And all of this is hard evidence that this scale, unlike the alphabet, is not an idea, not an invention, but a discovery of a force of nature.)

This particular flute is forty-four thousand years old, the most ancient of a series of bone and stone flutes dug up through the years since Darwin. Naturally its antiquity sponsors headlines that declare it the Adam and Eve of music. There is no reason whatever to think this, not at all. It just happens to be the oldest instrument unearthed so far. No reason to think it's the first flute, not the first bone flute and certainly not the first flute. Perfectly good flutes through all of time have been made of wood and still are, and wood leaves no record. Wood works easier, and probably was used for flutes long before the bone versions came along. No reason to think musical instruments began with flutes and so then did music. Sophisticated drums are easily fashioned of hide and wood and still are, and these, like wood flutes, decay and leave no record. Less sophisticated drums can be built of a hollow log. Yet even these instruments cannot date the origins of music, even if they left findable artifacts. The universal musical instrument is the human body, still is, singing and dancing. Who can know when we, ourselves, our own flesh and breath, began to resonate in rhythm and melody? But following this line of precedence suggests that maybe we have this backward, that there was no point where we began to warble and resonate in pitch and meter, but that the resonance and rhythm began us.

There is, in fact, a thoroughly modern event that undermines the whole business of trying to pinpoint a single origin of music. Bernie Krause began his career as a musician back in folk music days but then became fascinated with natural sounds and spent the rest of his life traveling the world and recording sound from nature. In his book *The Great Animal Orchestra*, he delivers an account of some fieldwork he did in 1971 among the Nez Perce people of Idaho. A Native man took Krause into the forest in predawn hours and waited for the wind to pick up. When it did, Krause was overwhelmed with a sound "that seemed to come from a giant pipe organic. ... The effect wasn't a chord exactly, but rather a combination of tones, sighs, and midrange groans that played off each other." The landscape delivered a loud symphony caused by the Venturi effect of wind blowing across a field of hollow reeds broken off at varying lengths. Krause was stunned, but the Native guy walked to the field of reeds, whipped out a knife, cut one off and began playing it as a flute, which it was.

Then he said, "Now you know where we got our music. And that's where you got yours too."

But for the moment, let's use that ancient bone flute as a marker. Drive a stake at its manufacture forty-four thousand years before our time and mark this as the depth. Then to the present and note the unbroken line, continuity from then until now. One dimension. Now set another stake to mark music's breadth, an all-encompassing span that includes all of humanity. Music is what anthropologists call a cultural universal, meaning all humans through all time and all cultures we know one way or another make music. It is a defining characteristic of humanity, all of humanity, singers, dancers, chanters, drum thumpers, always and everywhere among us.

There are not that many cultural universals, shared behaviors across all of humanity, but it's an interesting list and in evolutionary scale and sense of time, the list assembled not bit by bit, but all of a sudden about fifty thousand years ago. Cultural universals include language, tools, visual art, building houses of some sort, ceremony and funeral rites, and a complex diet with developed ideas of cooking and cuisine. That's about it, but it covers a lot. And misses a lot, probably as a result of cultural biases. (I took this list from Chris Stringer, a respected and thorough contemporary evolutionary biologist, yet he doesn't include, as other anthropologists might, communal care of children, shared responsibility for raising offspring. I add this now because it's going to come up again.) It's important to understand, though, that this list is something more than a checklist of universal traits humans developed over time. Each of these traits arose all of a sudden, all at once, really, and they come as a cluster. They are what set us off from other species, not a set of options or add-ons; they define what made humans human.

Of everything on the list, though, two traits tend to run in parallel in the discussion before us: music and language. In fact, some have argued and still do that music was simply an accident or offshoot of our brains, that as evolution developed the neural circuitry for language, the same circuitry just happened to work to produce music. To use the word of one scientist on this issue, Steven Pinker, music is "cheesecake," and his arguments imply that real and serious scientists ought to be far more concerned with the meat and potatoes, that is, language. In this view language is the pinnacle of human brain development because it conferred fitness, was the great innovation of humanity that allowed us to survive, prosper and dominate the planet. I disagree. The evidence is right there on that thigh bone in the Slovenian cave.

Saying that music is a cultural universal across at least forty-four thousand years of human evolution severely understates the case. The larger idea lies in the spacing of those holes on that bone flute, the scale. This steers us straight into a bit of categorization now, and I'll subvert those borders in time, but for a moment, let's accept the categories generally thought of as defining music: melody, harmony, and rhythm. The holes on the bone flute are evidence of melody and, essentially, evidence of the same notes we sing, of pitch. The bone flute carver positioned those holes to achieve a certain pitch of the notes.

In music, the arrangement of possible notes, the collections of separate pitches is called a scale, and anthropologists spend a lot of time considering the cultural preference for certain scales, that the trained ear can tell Middle Eastern music from Chinese and Delta blues in part by the range of notes employed, and that therefore like many aesthetic values, judgments of beauty is in the ear of the beholder, culture-bound, and therefore not innate but learned. This conclusion ignores some important fundamentals. It's right there on the keys of the piano, the blacks and whites, thirteen tones, eight white keys, five black, defining the scale. All music uses these thirteen notes. The culture-bound scales are simply subsets, a choice among the thirteen. There are runs that sound normal to some (one, three, five, six, eight, you'll do fine on *The Lawrence Welk Show* or in bubblegum music with this one) and edgy (one, flat three, five, flat seven—Delta blues) and weird (two, three, six, eight) but each works the same notes. There is no scale that runs one, 3.256, 5.75, 8.5.

The exception that proves this rule is slide guitar, pedal steel, and other instruments capable of working the space between tones like a trombone or violin. But these exceptions work by initiating a note between tones to jerk the listener to attention by the very unsettling nature of the technique and then resolving that tone, sliding to one of the thirteen, back inside the pale, the way that in language irony works by calling its referent to mind. Failing to resolve back to the scale is just plain irritating, which is which is why a fretless instrument like a violin is an instrument of torture in the hands of a novice. A piano can't work between the notes unless it's out of tune, and if it is, it can't resolve, so is annoying to anyone who hears it, including the untrained. This is not learned behavior. It is hardwired and innate.

The foundation of this cultural universal is the very wiring of our brains. The tipoff to this is simple mathematics: that pitch can be described as a frequency, regularly spaced oscillations across a unit of time, and each of these frequencies has single whole-number mathematical relationships to the next, that music—not just rhythm, but each component, melody and harmony too—is sublimely, deeply mathematical at its very core, and it doesn't matter whether you know this, but it suggests why mathematics may be the ultimate religion.

Whatever its basis, though, pitch is deeply rooted in our brains, a relationship I have already oversimplified and understated. The assertion that music is made up of single notes misses most of the music, and it turns out that the more complex side of the story is even more illuminating as to how deeply this is rooted in structure and function of our brains.

When that piano player hits one of those white keys, say an A, the concert pitch, an A note vibrating a 440 beats per second, the now-near-universal anchor of tuning, the listener hears far more than that pristine vibration. Any computer rendering of that sound into visible waves makes this obvious. That 440 pitch is the primary tone, and it simultaneously generates a series of sympathetic vibrations called harmonics at regular intervals in pitch above the primary pitch. This is a big part of what we hear and value in music, what makes it beautiful, but our brains are anchored on the primary, so much so that researchers were able to demonstrate something quite revealing. They electronically excised the primary tones from a piece of music, that is, they erased the anchor of the melody and instead gave listeners only the harmonics, a sort of musical gibberish. But the listeners' brains filled in the primary tones, that is, sensed something was missing, did the math and filled the hole, made the music complete. Not trained musicians, just ordinary brains. Their ears heard gibberish; their brains heard music. Garbage in; music out.

Yet this result seems almost trivial in its consequences for our discussion here when we consider an extension of this same experiment that went far beyond untrained human ears. Some researchers did essentially the same bit of work by playing a recording of the "Blue Danube Waltz," with all primary tones excised, to an owl. What does an owl know of the "Blue Danube Waltz," or music for that matter? Probably more than you might expect.

As with people, one is drawn first to an owl by its eyes, especially when the bird's stare radiates from a feathered head only a foot and a half away, a live wild bird perched on a gloved hand. To gain this vantage, I'd stooped, crawled, and run down a quarter-mile strip of hawthorn bush thicket, a copse furring an otherwise vacant stretch of intermontane grassland in Montana's Mission Mountains. This is habitat of short-eared owls, a common species in the northern Rockies, so named for short tufts of feathers that look like ears at the top of its head, but owls don't really have protruding ears. Just holes. And the species name notwithstanding, one could be forgiven for ignoring the ears altogether. We are, after all, ourselves a species inextricably biased to vision, and there is that burning yellow glower of eyes just an arm's length distance telling you nothing so much as you stare into the depths of an incomprehensible mystery. The biologist I was with, though—it was his work that gave me the excuse for this close encounter with another kind—explained otherwise. This very species of owl makes a living by hunting thickets of thorned trees, shrubs, and brush, by flying through full speed at night and seizing nocturnal prey such as voles and mice. Its vision is not all that useful; it hunts by hearing.

The cocked head with which it was regarding me explains how, the same curious tilt that a dog exhibits when confronting mystery, this tells us something, just as do the ear holes themselves, placed slightly asymmetrically on the animal's head. The two ears form two points and an obstacle or prey the third crucial point to allow triangulation. That is, the owl's brain is measuring and constantly calculating the microsecond deviation in the arrival of a sound at its ears to pinpoint the object's location. The skill is called "echolocation" and works almost exactly like sonar on a submarine. This is one clue to how hearing works to open up a whole different world in the "primitive" animal's brain. Such clues abound if you spend time among animals.

One long night I rode around a stretch of pristine prairie in Montana with a different biologist. We were trying to spot a black-footed ferret, a species once thought extinct but miraculously rediscovered elsewhere and reestablished in the place we were in. We saw no ferrets on that outing, but we watched coyotes hunt through the night. On spotting one a couple of hundred yards off, barely visible in the spotlight, the biologist rolled down his window and rolled his tongue in a clicking *tsk tsk tsk* such as a passive-aggressive human might insert in a conversation when he didn't wish to be heard. I could barely hear it four feet across the seat of the pickup truck yet the coyote lifted its head and ran toward us. The sound the biologist made was a close imitation of the chatter of a prairie vole, a hamster-like creature common in coyote diet. Such is canid hearing. The animal world traffics in sound in ways we can only begin to imagine and probably should.

Yet in matters musical the real wonder is in how those abilities couple to brain, and the "Blue Danube Waltz" tells some of that story. Simply, when experimenters played the recording, the same as with humans, with primary tones removed, only harmonics, musical gibberish, the owl's brain supplied the primary tones, filled in the blanks, just as humans did. But how would the researchers know this? Unlike humans, owls can't report what they hear. No, but the researchers could, and the way they did so is even more revealing. Researchers themselves could hear two versions of the song, the one with the primary tones removed, what they fed to the subjects, but also a completed, restored version. They could hear the latter by monitoring the owls' brain waves and rendering those physical, otherworldly blips as sound. The playback was a sonic analog of the owl's brain waves, the lilt of the "Blue Danube Waltz," primary tones fully restored.

This is possible because sound is unique among the senses in the way it works in your brain. Sensory information from vision or touch or taste is converted to nerve impulses that work by analogy in your brain. When the wavelength of light that corresponds to the color red hits your eyeball, the waves are converted to a series of nerve vibrations that encode red, and those different waves go through a variety of paths to a variety of places in your brain to allow multiple spots to assemble the idea of red. When your ear hears a concert A 440 pitch, that exact same wave reverberates through your brain, 440 cycles per second, readable and hearable with proper amplification. When the primary tone is missing, as was the case with the owl, the brain doesn't simply use knowledge or imagination to fill in the blank. It generates the missing tone, just as a musical instrument might. Owl's brain, your brain—it doesn't matter. Not analogy, but direct vibration, which is why researchers could hear the "Blue Danube Waltz."

#

It seems odd that there remains considerable debate about which came first, music or language, the two human traits that travel together as cultural universals. Language is without precedent in all other species, yet music is relatively common among our fellow animals. It's a bit like debating whether the iPhone or the telegraph came first, against clear and accepted evidence the telegraph had been around for a century or so. Other species make music. Some are quite good at it, birds for instance, as the owl's brain might suggest. Birds are not even closely related to humans on the evolutionary tree. Not all birds make music, and identifying which species makes music and which do not can tell us much, can begin to tell us what we mean by music, music as opposed to noise, or, in human terms, music as opposed to speech and language.

The A 440 helps us here, a sustained pitch or note. Music is made of these, of course, melody, notes or sustained pitches strung together in a pattern, not only as pitch but as pitches or notes delivered in various intervals of time, a timing that when fully developed we would call rhythm. And that the pitches fall into an overarching scheme in relation to each other we might call harmony. In birds, biologists get at this in much simpler and accessible terms by distinguishing between a bird's song and a bird's call. The latter is a quack or croak or chirp or chuckle, maybe in alarm or discovery, an exclamation, simple short and pretty much the same in every bird of a given species. A song is ornate, complex, patterned, and musical.

I realize I just defined music by labeling it "musical," and while that may seem a bit circular, it turns out that's really all we need. Scientists do indeed belabor this point, winnowing the idea into intricate and contested categories designed to separate music from just plain sound or speech. This is wholly unnecessary. The related debate here is one longstanding in neuroscience, that there is no particular evidence that our brains have particular specialization or structures for music. This lack of evidence—until now—generated the hypothesis that the brain processes music by cobbling together various parts of its auditory circuitry used for other purposes such as recognizing speech. Years of use of sophisticated brain scanning techniques failed to locate any brain regions dedicated to music, supporting this hypothesis. This, however, is no longer true.

In 2016, researchers from MIT published work based on a new and accepted method of mathematically summing brain activity, of viewing not just the dots but the layers of dots generated over time, and this method produced a clear and undisputed result. The brain does indeed discriminate and assign all music to one particular site. Good music, bad music, classical, rap, even drum solos, banjos, and accordions, all sorted and sited, everything else, elsewhere. Your brain does indeed have a clear, identifiable, and demonstrable definition of music. You know it when you hear it.

The scientists' definition of music, however, works as well here, as does your brain's innate understanding of bird music. Under either, it's clear that almost all bird species perform calls, but only about half of all species perform songs. Yet some further distinctions are even more telling. There is very little variation in calls among members of a given species. A quack is a quack for all mallards. Songs, on the other hand, share common themes within a species but are still distinctive to individuals, just as vocal styles are distinctive to individual human singers. There is a social element, which corresponds completely to the idea of a regional dialect in human speech. Birds of a given species and locale sing songs distinct and identifiable to their community. But even within communities, there are variations down to the individual level. A trained ear and even a sonogram for that matter can distinguish between meadowlarks from Montana and Colorado, but also between meadowlark 375 and meadowlark 107 in the Montana population. All of this says that calls may indeed be hardwired in the DNA, but songs are learned. A bird's song is influenced by what the bird hears, a product of mimicry and practice. A song is learned; a call is not.

In a longstanding series of experiments, researchers have deafened young birds, and those subjects never learned to sing properly. But in some experiments, they did so after the birds had already heard their community's songs, and still these deafened birds never learned to sing properly; they could not hear themselves practice. Learning does not occur without corrective feedback loops. But it is not all learning. At issue here is the tension between invention and conformity, that bird-songs and human songs for that matter are charged with simultaneously expressing conflicting ideas.

The British writer Helen Macdonald begins to ponder this very matter in her justifiably popular book *H Is for Hawk*, a description of her sustained and deliberate relationship with a single hawk. Her purpose was to actively and deeply engage the otherness of a single grand bird in order to make sense of her life as it was shattered by grief, not so different from our purposes here. In her account she suggests that the very experiments with deafened birds I've cited here are best considered in context of the Cold War in Britain. The line of work began in the 1950s when a researcher, William Thorpe, raised chaffinches in isolation resulting in the subjects' inability to sing.

Writes Macdonald, "It was a groundbreaking piece of research into developmental learning, but it was also a science soaked deep in Cold War anxieties. The questions Thorpe was asking were those of a postwar West obsessed with identity and frightened of brainwashing."

The key word here is identity, individual and group identity. Song is a method of establishing identity—in birds that sing, in all other animals that sing and in humans. In birds it is used primarily by males to stake out territory, that is to ward off other males and at the same time attract mates. Thus it must ride a fine line. The bird needs to announce simultaneously that it is a chaffinch (like all the others) yet is an individual (unlike, in fact better than, all the others).

The conflict is equally reflected in the bird's brain. There is a learned component of song, but it works within a constrained set of possibilities laid out by genetics. The genetics dictate sameness and learning allow variation. This theme plays out over space, and we have known this ever since Thorpe's experiments. Through learning, birds have regional dialects, so that those singing in another dialect become the other and those of the same kin and tribe, all deeply entwined in identity, even in birds. Song is the basis of bird politics. Power. Like us, they bind together when they all sing their version of Kumbaya, and if that seems a bit too warm and fuzzy, remember people have also bound together by singing the Nazi anthem, the "Horst Wessel Song."

This whole matter gets run up a couple of notches when we move closer on the evolutionary tree to humans, to chimps and ape music. Apes—with the standout exception of humans—are not nearly as musical as birds; most, in fact, do not learn songs. But there is a ritual performance of sorts that still ratchets up the complexity a couple of notches. Male chimpanzees tend to hang together in gangs and within their group develop a shared performance of songs called "pant hoots." It is not a unison performance. Each member has a distinctive pattern and pitches and times his own pant hoots to fill in sonic holes in the larger whole. The show opens generally when the group finds an abundant tree full of ripe fruit. The analysis of this has concluded the nature of the chorus has everything to do with reproduction. The chorus is so coordinated as to fill sonic holes because this allows the group as a whole to achieve maximum volume, broadcasting their simian doo-wop routine as far as possible. It serves as an announcement to the female world—mates must be recruited from other groups, distant, hence the need for maximum volume—that these guys know how to find lots of food. Working as a group would seem to dilute any single male's chances of scoring, but that dilution gets offset by a loud and convincing song that recruits more females, a sort of mass seduction. It's hard not to extrapolate to the dominance of male quartets in teenage bubblegum music.

This extrapolation all might seem too pat an explanation to impose on the wild world, but consider: mortality is high among young male chimps, and so death often leaves a hole in the chorus, because each male has a distinctive assigned part in it. But when this happens, a male that had been signing another part, maybe a less important part, learns and begins to sing the dead guy's part. When I learned this, I could not help but think of the famous old-time mountain singer Ralph Stanley, who died at the age of eighty-nine as I was writing an early draft of this book. He began his career as half of a duo with his brother, Carter. There is a long and intense history of singing siblings, kin raised together on music that used it as a bond through life and as a result ended up a lot better at it than most folks. Carter, an alcoholic, died in 1972, but Ralph went on, ever more famous. Yet for the decades of performance after Carter was gone, Ralph could never break a habit, that when a point in a song came where Carter had leaned in for harmony, Ralph still stepped back from the microphone to make room for his dead brother.

The sun rises on a fine summer's day in a wild place, and it is easy enough to imagine that the music you hear is overture, a chorus raising the curtain on a Broadway show—*West Side Story*, for instance. Hold the show. There is no such thing. Birds do not sing in chorus, as humans do, nor do any other animals. This is not to say they do not sing together. The apes were sort of together in their pant hoots, but not in chorus, in synch. The distinction adds another layer to the story.

Far and away the most common form of shared song among animals is male-female duets between mates, almost the only form of shared song. Yet in these duets, the pair does not sing in unison or even harmony, both singing the same song. Rather the form is more a call and response. One mate will trill off a few notes, a bit of distinctive, repeated song, and then leave a hole, and every musician among us at the moment knows what happens with that hole. The mate chimes in and fills it with her own trilled, common yet distinctive song. This is pair bonding and more or less a shared form of male-female duets not just among birds but also among most animals that make music, and these are predominantly, besides birds, apes, whales, and dolphins.

Lying just beneath, though, is a shared pattern in these same animals that predicts the practice of singing duets. Monogamy is a rarity among all animals. So is music, and this is true even within families of animals. Only about half of all bird species learn songs (as opposed to voicing calls) and only about half are monogamous. Turns out it's the same ones, a direct correspondence. The singers are monogamous. Same deal with apes. Among primates, there are twenty-six species that sing, make music, about 11 percent of the total of primate species. All of those are monogamous; all perform male-female duets. Emmylou Harris and Gram Parsons.

This sort of finding excites evolutionary biologists. Out of earshot of peer review and the constraints of the academy, biologists are often blunt and better at explaining their work than the formalities and conventions might otherwise allow. The best example I know of this is a crisp aphorism shared among evolutionary biologists but unpublished elsewhere, and the absence is a shame. It says that all of evolution can be reduced to three questions: Can I eat it? Will it eat me? Can I fuck it?

Accordingly, findings about the correspondence between music and monogamy among animals excites investigation, simply because so much of evolution hinges on reproduction and passing genes. Birds' use of songs to attract mates gathers a disproportionate share of attention for the same reason. This focus is not wrong. Reproduction is important, but our focus on sex obscures deeper layers, and so it is with monogamy, a story that can be teased out with a chemical.

The pioneering work on this issue was done by Sue Carter, a biologist, not on birds or an animal that has anything to do with singing, but the mouse-like prairie vole, which is a rare little mammal that happens to be monogamous. Males and females pair up and stay that way, and the male participates fully in rearing the young, as predictable and loyal as a fully domesticated millennial playground dad. This is interesting in and of itself because monogamy is truly weird behavior among mammals, a glaring exception to the rule, but made even more interesting by a parallel species, the meadow vole, that looks and acts in every regard like a prairie vole except meadow voles are not monogamous, males as caddish as any other. Females too. As a young biologist, Carter focused on this close parallel and finally drilled down to a common bit of brain chemistry, specifically the chemical oxytocin, the same chemical that figures prominently in well-studied matters like childbirth and lactation. She gave doses of oxytocin to the rakes, young meadow voles, and found it magically transformed their behavior to match completely the monogamous prairie vole.

Were we reductionist scientists, we'd come to rest on this simple fact and claim that we have at least a chemical marker for monogamy and maybe even identify a gene responsible for oxytocin and then score a big advance for the nature side of the nature-nurture argument, not to mention the inherent nature of music, but traits like monogamy are far too complex to reveal themselves fully in a single chemical pathway like this, and Carter herself would be the first to tell you this, as she did when I interviewed her.

There is something else here in her research that is more important to our line of thought: understanding what we mean by monogamy. When evolutionary biologists have considered monogamy, they have tended to focus on the male's control and attention to his offspring as a means to make sure he passes on his genes. Sticking around to protect one's young ensures against infanticide by another male trying to reset the genetic game, an extremely common occurrence. Yet this assumption about monogamy is wrong, and we ought to know better because we know humans and know what monogamy means in humans, an institution observed in the breach more than not, a convention, a just-so story shattered in virtually every culture. DNA studies tore this one apart, showing every place it looked that in humans nominal paternity was not in fact always biological paternity.

Carter has spent much of her career observing voles and says they are monogamous exactly as humans are, that the loyal, nurturing, stay-at-home-dad vole as often as not cares for genes that are not his own. Not just voles, but in birds and apes and all the monogamous species. Does this make monogamy meaningless? Not at all, says Carter. But it is not about passing one's genes, as the evolutionary biologists assumed. It is about the social institution of the pair bond that itself confers fitness because it is a successful survival strategy for the pair. It has advantages for the male, but for the female it is a way she can recruit a partner to help pass on *her* genes. If this means signing a song every now and again with the guy, so much the better. Monogamy is in the animal world what it is in the human: an economic institution, a trait of cooperation, solidarity, and cohesion bolstered in much of the animal world by a shared song.

This gets reinforced when we dig a bit deeper into oxytocin. Humans given doses of oxytocin become more cooperative, more gregarious, above all, more empathetic. It is the chemical of sociality, and all of this wraps back into music, that we find the ability to make music and sing duets associated in the animal world with a chemical that enables cooperation and empathy.

The evolutionary debates about the usefulness of music to our survival have focused on reproduction, and I am not saying this is false or even a blind alley. Yes, there are the arguments about rock stars having more children than everyone else, that singing and playing a guitar is a fine way to demonstrate fitness and attract a mate. This may be exactly right so far as it goes, but the discussion gets more satisfying when we trace some threads that have been more or less overlooked since Darwin first pondered a bone flute.

###

Difficult to say what so upset Berlioz during that musical performance. Maybe he just didn't like the music. But I bet not. Just the opposite: he was moved. As a composer, he would know every trick in the book for tugging at feelings and could spot every card being played. Still he was moved. This is the power of music over logic and learning to communicate emotion.

The basic tricks are indeed very simple, that certain harmonies, minor thirds, for instance, have the power to induce sadness or angst, even without narrative or story or even words. The evolutionists' focus on development of language as our primary tool of communication ignores or discounts that music is communication. To a person of my trade, stuck behind the lines of sentences like these, this is a stunning oversight. No trick available in the printed word allows me to summon a predictable emotional response in the combination of two notes in a phrase shorter than a syllable, certainly not across all cultures and all time.

One of the reasons we fail to fully appreciate this power is the bias of Western thought. We of this lineage are all descendants of René Descartes, disembodied minds defining our being by our thinking. This is far more than philosophical rumination. Almost all of the long line of thinking on this matter regards communication solely as the symbolic content of language, that the power of communication derives from our ability to construct sentences like: "Sales in the third quarter were flat." There is indeed power in the specificity. We need this power, and we are correct in thinking about it. Such sentences do what they need to do on a page like this. Less so sentences like "I am afraid" or "I love you." These work less well in print, simply because we have no way of judging their sincerity or veracity in print, and we have a huge stake in knowing whether they are true. Everything depends on the emotional horsepower behind such sentences, yet, in our intellectual tradition, worrying about emotional content is shunted off to the corner reserved for poets and misfits.

This seems a very odd bias when we chase these ideas into human evolution, to matters of survival. Where would we be as a species without emotion? This is not romanticism but a deadly practical matter. We may discount this in our present environment when messages scream at us from all sides, "Be afraid," this when we are probably safer than humans have ever been. Yet understand that we evolved as a species in an environment where comprehending such messages was vital to survival. We were prey.

I am a privileged person because I have some idea of what such a moment might look like. This is mostly a matter of luck, so overwhelming are the odds against such an encounter, even where I live in Montana, even though I spend far more time than most people do walking alone in wilderness. I have encountered several times now adult grizzly bears at relatively close range. A biologist I knew had schooled me that the important factor in such an encounter is communication: remain standing, but cast eyes down slightly, no eye contact, and begin speaking to the bear in straightforward sentences telling it as honestly as possible that you will do it no harm. Of course these words are meaningless to a bear, but it is important that you believe them yourself so that your body, the timbre, cadence, and lilt, communicate to the bear.

In her study of hunter-gatherer tribes of Africa, Elizabeth Marshall Thomas describes a similar scene between the Bushmen she knew well and lions, and it plays out almost exactly the same, as it no doubt has there for millennia. Communication without words has been key to our survival as a species.

The work has been done, experiments playing various harmonic combinations like minor and major scales and various rhythmic patterns to people of widely varying cultures, and the results are clear. These fundamental elements of music communicate to yield predictable and common emotional responses across cultures. You'd expect this by now, perhaps, but not so much something else, that the same sort of experimental set-up produces a similar response in—communicates to—starlings, birds. Animals share our response to the minor third. Yet a parallel discovery ramps this up to another important level. That same sort of experimental work has been done with infants, infants without any language whatever.

It is only in the last few years that this realization might have provoked more than a passing interest among those who think about human evolution. Because the discipline was and is a subset of the rationalist European intellectual tradition, it was blinkered, just as is any line of thought. More importantly, anthropology for a couple of centuries suffered some tunnel vision in that most anthropologists were men. This gave us ideas like the naked ape and selfish genes and social Darwinism, survival governed solely by relentless competition. It is so governed, but not solely.

The anthropologists best known for providing the corrective here is Sarah Hrdy. It is not wholly unfair to characterize all of anthropology before Hrdy as a series of thought experiments about men or, best case, fieldwork that followed men around. Explanations of human condition centered on manipulation of tools and weapons. It rested on some narrow assumptions about a guy with a spear provisioning his tribe by hunting. I don't mean to be dismissive; we did indeed evolve as hunters. This was our economy and what shaped us, but the emphasis slid the whole business rather far in the direction of laws of the club and the fang. And rather far in overemphasizing the plotting, scheming, talking human brain.

Hrdy and others greatly enriched our understanding by realizing that, yes, this brain of ours is indeed important but is not without its downsides, and those limitations also have a lot to say about who we are. Specifically, she zeroed in on what is undeniably a standout and unique feature of humans as a species, that we are extraordinarily altricial, a biologist's term that means offspring spend a long time dependent on adults because they are slow to mature. In our case, this burden is almost solely a result of our brains. In humans, the organ is so outsized in adults, so huge that were we born with fully developed brains, that is, brains proportionate to an infant's body size, our heads wouldn't fit through the birth canal. But infants' brains are not just smaller; they are incomplete. We are born with the primitive, reptilian nether part of our brain intact, but the higher regions that allow everything that define us as humans, the logic, the language, the reasoning and knowledge, form only slowly, a process like building a ship in a bottle, "slowly" meaning something like twenty years before the brain is fully formed and developed. Infants are not just slower to learn or stupid; they lack the very parts of the brain that make us who we are and confer fitness. Wholly dependent.

Hrdy points out that this trait dictates a social order. Because of it, humanity's largest task is raising these helpless infants, and, as any mother can tell us and could have told anthropology centuries ago, mothers cannot do this job alone. They need help, which means they must recruit that help by forming social networks. Helpless infants are not unique in the animal world, it's just that humans are the extreme example, but where altricial young show up in other species, those species tend to be social, depend on each other, on social networks.

Yet even at the level of individual mother, the topic at hand looms large. Back to those experiments with infants that showed an emotional response to musical scales. This immediately suggest a tool for mothers. Infants have no language, and they have brains that more resemble a lizard's in structure and function than they do a mammal, let alone the smartest mammal. They have no language, nothing for a mother to use to communicate to them the perilous nature of the world they have entered, and for all of hunter-gatherer time it was indeed perilous. Predators, for instance, focus on infants. Infant mortality was the limiting factor on rapid population growth. Elizabeth Marshall Thomas spends far more time describing the rearing of children among the hunter-gatherers she knew than she did guys talking to lions, because it was a lot more important to these people. These bush people of the Kalahari worried about real threats such as a toddler stumbling into a campfire at night. In the face of this, how useful then to have command of a tool that communicates emotional messages? Be afraid. You are safe. Run.

Yet the guy talking to lions is not at all irrelevant to this. Properly considered, these weird little beings, human infants, are like another species, so different are their brains from those of adults, and they remain so well into their teens. As is the case with the lions, humans have a means of communication with this other species, a language of sorts that science calls "motherese." This is the cooing and gurgling and singsong syllables common to all cultures, and singsong is the key. It is highly dependent on the pitch of the mom's voice, the lilt and the rhythm to communicate its message. It shares these aspects with music. The very same criteria we use to separate birdsong from birdcalls separate motherese from spoken adult language, or not really separate, but form two poles of opposition with all sorts of room for shading between, even among adults.

This mode of communication works with infants because their undeveloped brains, lousy at language, work to process music just fine, maybe even better than adults. Round up and begin questioning almost any collection you can imagine of famous and highly skilled musicians, make it as diverse as you can concerning culture and genre, and still you will find a common thread, that these people began this engagement and showed a facility with music as very young children, well before they could speak. We think of this as raw talent that emerges among a few while they are young, and this well may be a factor, but there is some evidence that all kids have these abilities, that music is something we unlearn as we age, just as we lose the ability to rapidly and effortlessly learn a new language as we age. We desperately need to understand the music of motherese as infants; less so later.

For instance, poll that same group we assembled in the last paragraph and you will find a large number of musicians trained as children have perfect pitch, that they can name a note on hearing it as if it were a printed word on a page. Perfect pitch is rare in the general population, but not among this group. Yet there are populations where it is far more common than others, and these give unique support to the idea that we unlearn music. One of the populations that is inordinately blessed with perfect pitch is Chinese, and the clue to why this might be true should be obvious to anyone who has tried to learn Mandarin as a second language. The problem here is distinguishing among different words that all sound the same to untrained ears. Mandarin is one of those languages that depends on pitch to distinguish between words. It is a musical language. There are others, and any speaker of one of those languages is far more likely to have perfect pitch, a phenomenon that holds up even among trained musicians. In the general population, about one in ten thousand adults have perfect or absolute pitch. One researcher compared two groups—one American and one Chinese—of musicians who began training between the ages of four and five. Among the Americans, 14 percent had perfect pitch, still far more than the general population, but 60 percent of the Chinese group had the trait.

###

The shaded distinction between music and language has a parallel within language itself in the distinction between prose and prosody, and a good way to think of this is the difference between the language of accountants and that of poets. Yet a better way is simply to understand that prose becomes prosody by borrowing from music, lilt, timbre, pitch, and rhythm, especially rhythm. There is no clear line between them, and even the most austere of accountants will edge toward a lilt now and again. Is this distinction or even this musical language at all important to us? Sure it is. We know full well that we reach to poetry when subjects are love, life and death, the ineffable. What could be more important? We do this instinctively when we wish to summon a depth and power unavailable in normal language. Be afraid, there are lions. Watch out, you may die. Be sad, for surely you will die.

Yet even in ordinary communication, in the simple act of speaking, all of this comes into play. The arguments about the power of our big brains have traditionally rested on matters like the ability to solve quadratic equations or design a 737 and make it fly, yet it turns out handling the logic that is the basis of this sort of thinking is relatively easy in terms of demands on our brain's computing power, precisely why we have had the most luck teaching computers to do these tasks and no luck whatever teaching one to write a passable poem. The neuroscience begins to tell us why, that any brain doing the grunt work of calculus is only lightly engaged, while the simple act of ordinary conversation lights up all the circuitry, demands the whole neural network because, as far as the brain is concerned, conversation is heavy lifting. Conversation engages the complex circuitry of the brain that we call "mirror neurons." When someone tells a story that involves, say, eating an apple, the circuits in that person's brain that would be involved in the motions of picking up the apple, moving it to the mouth, taking a bite, chewing, and then registering pleasure at its taste are all activated in the teller's mind, as if she were actually doing it. But so are the same circuits in the listener's brain, which is why these are called mirror neurons. But only in conversation, face-to-face communication with full range of lilt and rhythm and body cues.

The current thinking is that only about 10 percent of what is communicated in conversation is borne by the actual words. The rest of the message, the subtext, nuance, assembles itself from the music of language and communication, and the rest is lost in purely printed communication like letters, emails, and text messages, but it is not just random content lost; it is the stuff that allows us to climb inside another's skin, to connect, relate. It is empathy, the very glue of social species that we are. It is no small matter nor is it surprising that accepted tests for empathy in a generation of young people who rely heavily on email and text messages has shown a catastrophic decline in the trait, an empathy deficit. It is no small matter because it doesn't just mean we spend more time among more disagreeable people. (We do.) It is far more alarming in light of our evolution. Our ability to hang together, to function as a group, a tribe, a community assembled for the necessary business of raising our altricial young relies on our empathy. Our big brains' chief advantage is not so much making stone tools or solving Rubik's Cubes. They allow the devilishly complex task of simply being social.

The great late guitar player Bob Brozman, a lifelong student of the instrument and of the world's music, once said all songs are either about sex or dying except that in between you get "Happy Birthday." Maybe as distilled to commercial music, a subset of song that gives us every reason to side with the anthropologists who think music is all about sexual selection. But then there's "Dink's Song." Bedded in a gorgeous, simple melody it offers a plaintive lament of lost love that at first lulls us into believing we remain well within the territory Brozman has staked out for us. Modern players like Marcus Mumford can croon it with good results. Dylan recorded it on one bootleg and in fact claimed to have heard it from Dink herself, which was a lie, but still it remains a song that settles easily into the mainstream. Still, there are some curious references coded in the lyrics that offer a different story to the standard male display behavior and preening for mates that is the usual stuff of biology. Here's the setup:

> If I had wings
> Like Noah's dove
> I'd fly the river
> To the one I love
> Fare thee well, my honey
> Fare thee well

I had a man
Who was long and tall
Moved his body
Like a cannonball
Fare thee well, my honey
Fare thee well

Remember one evening
Was drizzling rain
And around my heart
I felt an aching pain
Fare thee well, my honey
Fare thee well

Once I wore
My apron low
Couldn't keep you
Away from my door
Fare thee well, my honey
Fare thee well

Now my apron
Is up to my chin
You pass my door
But you never come in
Fare thee well, my honey
Fare thee well

The giveaway is the apron, that and Dink's very real situation. The movement of her clothing up to her chin is caused by the swell of pregnancy. She is lamenting being pregnant and abandoned. Dylan didn't learn this song from Dink as he claimed because the folklorist John Lomax did sometime before 1910 on one of his earliest collection forays in his home state of Texas. He found Dink in a camp on the Brazos River among a clutch of black laborers living in tents and working on a levee project. The situation was not much different from slavery, especially for the women, only for them it was sex slavery. Lomax reported that the contractor for the job was having trouble handling his roughneck crew in their off hours, a bunch of single men, so he traveled to Memphis, recruited a number of women, brought them back to camp, and doled them out to the men, one to a tent. Dink was one of them.

How deeply such songs must run in the human line, a lone woman on a riverbank announcing her plight to her people, anyone who might help. Single pregnant women use song to recruit help. They have done so for all of human time.

###

Other animals can make music. But equally well-established is an indicator that our species alone relies on music more than any other. No other animal can dance. No other animal can sing in unison or chorus, because no other animal has rhythm the way we do. Yes, there is a sort of rhythm in birdsong, that the notes step along one after the other, even some coordination in the duets of some species, male trills a few bars, then female in with some licks of her own. But notice that these birds are working separately. Birds like sage grouse can perform elaborate courtship movements we call dance, but again, one at a time, solo act. A true sense of rhythm means a brain with an internal clock that can hear two beats and then predict exactly when the next regular beat will occur. We alone among animals can do this. It's why we can dance and play in orchestras. It's why we love both activities. It makes us move together.

Why would evolution go to the trouble of creating this? What good is it? Paleoanthropologists say it allows coordination, abilities as simple as: one, two, three, everybody push. Sure it does, as we shall see in more detail. But I can't help but think this conclusion only scrapes the surface. Dancing together, singing together are not only cultural universals, but also serve as the basis of ritual among all cultures we know of, present at times that seem to matter the most to us: weddings, funerals, rites of passage, going to war. We don't just go to war; we march. In rhythm.

The opposite of empathy is solipsism, a word we will need more and more as we confront the growing empathy deficit of our people. It is a philosophers' word and one completely necessary in the line of thought that results from: "I think, therefore I am." Any philosopher will tell you that logic cannot get you out of the prison that is your own head. The solipsistic brain has no empathy.

Why music evolved and continues to play such a prominent and underappreciated role in the human condition has lots of answers. Why do we persist? We've touched on a few answers here. Not complete, but a beginning: mating and selection, communication with animals and infants, fuller communication with others. Bonding and cohesion. All play some role, and there's plenty here to fuel the evolutionary engine with music. Much of the argument over which of these is governing or dominant or a full explanation misses the fact that they are not mutually exclusive, but rather are branches from a common stem. Nonetheless, the neurobiologist Walter Freeman, whom I quoted in entering this argument, also offers a conclusion, a sort of keystone idea that can take us forward to answer my question: Why do I persist in music? Freeman writes: "Here in its purest form is a human technology for crossing the solipsistic gulf. It is wordless, illogical, deeply emotional and self-less in its actualization of transient and then lasting harmony between individuals."

###

It took the musician in me a long time, decades, to be overtaken and obsessed with the lure of mountain music, many years after Delia headed me in this direction: the woody, confident ring of a vintage Martin guitar pushing the booms and chukkas and bass runs through simple three chord progressions, a fiddle and banjo up top and high vocal harmonies over. Hammers of nine pounds, pregnant dead girls washed away in rivers, and generations of unbroken circles. This all was there from the beginning because it lies at the beginning of all American music.

Yet as tastes and abilities matured, I found myself pulled to a pure distillation, a form of the music most people don't know exists. It's a vein of folk music that has exceptional fidelity to Appalachian string bands of the nineteenth century, that unique and musically powerful combination of fiddle and banjo, Celtic and African mostly, that lies at the headwaters of the American stream.

Almost everyone has heard banjo music, and there is a valid stereotype: the twanging metallic syncopated arpeggios of bluegrass. Earl Scruggs gets the credit for inventing this incarnation of the banjo as a subset of Bill Monroe's invention of bluegrass itself in the '40s, and the form thrives to this day in the hands of banjo virtuosos. Bluegrass came from Appalachian mountain music but sounds very different, an acorn that fell a bit away from the tree. I raise this idea not as a matter of musical taste or to quibble about authenticity or sound. Like a lot of players, I've played and enjoyed both Appalachian music and bluegrass. I bring this up to assert something more important to all of us. Both forms are celebrated by amateur musicians because both are accessible, participatory, and social—but social in different ways.

Bluegrass works much like jazz, is a form of hillbilly jazz, having a simple melody or refrain, what jazz players would call "the head," sung in those high lonesome harmonies distinctive to the genre, and between verses a break, short for breakdown. This is where the individual musicians each in turn riff on the melody: mandolin, banjo, and fiddle, separately, with the Martin D-18 providing the frame of rhythm and harmony.

Old-time music, how the original mountain music is usually known, works very differently. Often there are no lyrics. There are known, recognizable tunes, though, and one begins attempting to enter this world by learning a standard list of tunes, a canon, and then shyly, self-consciously, meekly asking to sit in with a group of players in a parking lot or at a campground somewhere where this sort of thing happens, hoping to sit down and catch on. And then comes around a simple tune that our novice happens to know, and he is ready, finally after all that practice, to perform. And his brain locks on to that series of notes so painstakingly memorized one after the other, and he begins with the others and quickly fails, crashes, burns, and deflates.

Old-time musicians play the same songs over and over, but they are never the same songs. There are variations in emphasis and melody, even single tunes with multiple tunes with the same name. No song is the same song twice. Practice, preparation, learning the canon is indeed important, a necessary but not a sufficient condition to playing this music. You can indeed go wrong, very wrong, but there are lots of ways to be right. More importantly, unlike bluegrass, there are no break-downs, separate solos. The assembled four or so musicians play together, in unison, the same tune, usually eight bars of an A part, repeat, then eight of a B part, repeat, then repeat this whole sequence, sometimes again and again and again. The fiddle is the guide in this, bowing out a melody line that is the fiddler's understanding of the tune, and it is everyone else's job to complement, meld, provide the several parts that produce a whole greater than the sum of the individual efforts.

If a player brings a rigid preconception of the song to this circle and plays it as it exists in his head, he will fail. The form demands a surrender of one's preconceptions. It is a form of meditation, of giving oneself to the moment done in a situation with deep and often realized possibilities of public embarrassment, a process addictive and sublime.

There are superstars of old-time music, teachers and performers widely recorded and highly regarded. Mainstream music has mostly never heard of them but they are deservedly famous in their own place. One of them is John Hermann, who often teaches banjo lessons as part of a Zen meditation practice. His goal is to prepare students to enter the larger circle of musicians and play, and he says this has a severe limit for any teacher. "I can only teach you what I know about playing the banjo, and everything beyond what I know is playing the banjo."

No one in his view is a player until they have sat in the circle and made music together unbound by ego. He says that playing together "is an act of compassion."

Then he says this, that within each of us, in each individual psyche, there is a series of characters we can label: an accountant, a teacher, a child, a cop, characters we know and summon variously depending our inclinations and the necessities of the situation. He says each of us also has within us a lunatic, and he believes it is necessary to enter music first and foremost as the lunatic. You have been warned.

3

UNDER MY THUMB

The great guitarist, philosopher, and teacher Ernie Hawkins was a student, a direct, literal student of the Reverend Gary Davis. Hawkins discovered political history on the neck of his guitar (like Davis's, a Gibson J-200) a simple little matter of six notes played in succession: tonic, flat third, third, sixth, resolve to the tonic again (variation: end on a flat seventh). Actually he didn't discover it. It's a famous riff that in one prominent circle has a name: the Lester Flatt G run. It's foundational to bluegrass. Sit in on any parking lot picking session and you'll hear it, a genetic marker as recognizable as a high, lonesome tenor.

Bluegrass was my gateway drug. My first whiffs came in the early '70s, when Flatt and his musical partner, Earl Scruggs, the founding father of bluegrass banjo, were riding high. It was Scruggs who drew us in then, not Flatt; that biting punch of a syncopated fingerpicked rolls barked by a hyper-tweaked resonator banjo could not be ignored. Scruggs also crossed a line that few hillbilly musicians did back then. Most were at least publicly deeply conservative; Scruggs broke with the party line to openly oppose the Vietnam War. He was musically innovative and a folkie at heart, and the sum of these made a lot of '70s hippies curious about his music.

Bluegrass then, though, turned out to be pretty tough going. I got to know some bluegrassers, went to some front porch picking sessions, and soon discovered that the music fronted for a subculture. I once listened drop-jawed when a musician I liked in northern Michigan, a guy who was becoming a friend, brandished a .357 Magnum revolver and announced he had acquired it in case the "niggers from Detroit" ever got out of hand. That sort of talk occurred in lilywhite bluegrass gatherings.

What Hawkins discovered—it's fairly obvious and others have realized this as well—is a bit of magic that occurs when you pitch the Lester Flatt G run an octave higher, or maybe in the key of E, maybe on an electric guitar and maybe torture a couple of the notes just a touch. Same notes played in just the same order. It then becomes a signature lick of Chicago blues, black blues, in particular the very riff that wrote a lot of the paychecks cashed by B.B. King. South Side of Chicago. Hillbilly heaven in West Virginia. Doesn't matter. Same notes.

I borrowed a banjo and took a couple of lessons in the '70s because of Earl Scruggs. Bluegrass was then and is now social music, and I wanted a part of it, but I had no experience playing stringed instruments. My musical resume to that point had just a couple of entries: accordion lessons forced on me as a kid and saxophone in high school marching band and jazz band. My first run at banjo failed when I couldn't rope up to climb the precipitous learning curve of intricate fingerpicked arpeggios that are the root of the style. A few years later, I bought my first guitar and slowly, stubbornly, ponderously learned through the years. By accident, I gravitated toward blues, fingerpicked, musty old country blues, an African form translated to acoustic guitar. One realizes in time that the banjo, a more primitive sort of banjo playing, is really the source of that style.

Now I own two banjos, both treasures. One is a Vega, an old Tubaphone model. The pot, the round part, is straight out of the 1920s. When I bought it in the early '90s it was in original condition, which means it was built for only four strings, a tenor banjo. My entire case that all American music is African revolves around this very issue, the four strings, a design that is a truncation of the banjo's original form. The circumcision of banjos was popular when mine was made in the flapper era. Makers simply removed the eccentric high-pitched drone string with its own tuning peg about a third of the way down the top of the neck. The modification made the instrument less eccentric so it could fit into the sort of bands that today only appear in straw boater hats to play "Dixieland" for tourists in New Orleans.

Almost no one wants such an instrument now, but a lot of us do have great regard for that round part of those old tenor banjos, the Vega Tubaphone pot, so named because a metal tube is bent to a perfect circle to rest just under the head and to give the instrument its signature metallic punch and ring. Vega and its predecessors like the A.C. Fairbanks Company and Bacon did continue to make five-stringed instruments then, and they are today regarded as the pinnacle, the holy grail, especially the handful of Fairbanks Whyte Laydies built between 1900 and 1906, but originals from that era fetch $4,000 and up, way up, if you can find one.

One can, however, buy a four-string tenor for a few hundred bucks. A competent luthier then makes a new, longer, wider neck to accommodate the fifth string, a "conversion" it is called, a term that appropriately captures the near religious significance of the transformation, an instrument cleansed of its crippling sins, freed and sanctified and reborn as the Good Lord intended. My banjo's conversion was effected by a friend, John Joyner, a luthier, a fiddler, a banjo and guitar player, the sort of character one can find in most any American town, a guy who strings together a modest living playing music. He is slight, curmudgeonly, well read, and hotly opinionated on music and politics. Leftist, defiant, and intense.

I had met Joyner in the mid-1980s when I was a newspaper reporter in same Montana town, Missoula, where both of us have lived most of our lives, although Joyner has roots in Appalachia and Iowa. Then I interviewed him for a story on Irish music, real Irish music, which he plays and which makes him viciously critical of Tin Pan Alley treacle like "Danny Boy," which is to actual Irish music what green-dyed Budweiser is to Guinness Stout. I remember very little of my years of newspaper reporting. Thirty years have passed. I have mostly forgotten what was said to me or the stories I wrote, but I remember this particular interview, and what Joyner told me then. He said simply and without preamble or prompting, "Music is tension and release." I have been trying to unpack the import of that statement ever since and will do so now at book length.

He made my banjo's neck by pulling a piece of straight-grained bird's-eye maple lumber from his cache laid by through the years, hand carving it complete with Victorian peghead, lacquering to a soft sheen, fitting an ebony fingerboard, slotting it precisely for frets, and inlaying it with mother-of-pearl designs just as Fairbanks would have done in his shop in Boston in 1903.

I have owned it for more than a decade, but only in the last couple of years have I negotiated a meaningful relationship with it. Partly this is a matter of skill, that the actual sound is complicated and highly dependent on technique: angle, of striking strings, rhythmic control, little whumps, taps, and clicks of hand on calfskin head. Over time, though, it teaches one how it wants to sound, pulls the dedicated student toward the one true direction and demands not so much a dedication as it does humility. One does not play the clawhammer banjo so much as one engages it.

My other banjo is brand-new. Kevin Enoch, a talented player and well-known builder, made it for me in his one-man shop in Beltsville, Maryland. I ordered it. Spoke to him about its final shape, composition (walnut and maple), head (calfskin), then waited four months until a FedEx truck brought it to my door. It is an Enoch Dobson, so named because it is a faithful, clean, and understated copy of the Silver Bell made by Henry C. Dobson and first patented in 1881 and not to be confused with banjos on offer from the other Dobson brothers, Charles E., George C., Frank P. and Edward C., banjo makers and players every one. These too were good banjos, but Henry's Silver Bells were and are great.

The Dobson brothers were then in both their performances and sales riding the crest of popularity of the instrument fostered by minstrel shows, formalized entertainments by urban white performers in burnt-cork blackface, offering zippy banjo music interspersed with crude, racist jokes. The form was wildly popular with white, urban working-class audiences, mostly immigrants, throughout the US, but also in England. The latter fact explains why one can today buy on eBay a high-quality nineteenth-century banjo manufactured in England. Minstrelsy rooted the banjo in traditional music in Ireland, where it remains, and in later English forms like skiffle, a genre that first brought John Lennon to the stage.

Minstrel shows arose in the late 1830s from a handful of circus performers, all white, all southerners or with southern roots or contacts, and all of whom learned banjo directly from slaves or freed slaves. Bill Whitlock, for instance, was not a southerner but was born in New York in 1813. He met Joel Sweeney, a white southerner, when both were performing in the circus, and he took banjo lessons from him but then periodically wandered away from the circus when it was touring the South, to learn from slaves. Dan Emmett, perhaps the most famous of the minstrels, whose compositions still figure in the canon of old-time music, followed a similar course. Both Emmett and Whitlock learned from Joel Sweeney, who had picked up banjo even earlier, learning from slaves on his family's plantation in Virginia.

The Dobson brothers, the family that eventually created the banjo I play, were New Yorkers, and their name would become synonymous with post–Civil War minstrelsy. They were infected with a passion for banjo when Henry learned a few licks from blacks who were his coworkers at the Astor House hotel in New York City.

Ego and commercial lures were then more or less what they are now, and accordingly some of the original minstrels claimed credit and were given credit in subsequent histories for inventing the form, writing individual songs, and even cutting the banjo itself from whole cloth. They were, however, in all of these matters, appropriating well-established rural folk tradition. Take "Zip Coon," for instance, a song that served as the basis for racist stereotypes, beginning with its title, and was one of the more famous minstrel tunes. It remains with us today under a sanitized title, "Arkansas Traveler," is one of the first four or five tunes traditional fiddlers and banjo players learn, and, during the string band era, was the widely used platform for endless jokes based on confrontations between city slickers and bumpkins. Before the minstrels appropriated it, though, it was called "Natchez" and was popular among frontier fiddlers and river boaters. Before that, British fiddlers knew it as "The Rose Tree."

"The Pateroller Song," standard in old-time repertoires today, gets its title from a corruption of the word "patroller," the name for white night riders who rounded up and sometimes lynched wandering slaves before the Civil War and traveling blacks during Reconstruction. These hooded vigilantes were the prototypes for the Ku Klux Klan. The song's earlier title was "Run, Nigger, Run." Dig a bit deeper, though, to find evidence it was composed by blacks and served not so much as a command from the riders as it was sound advice to fellow fugitives.

But the gold-plated and highly polished emblem of all of this is a tune that was seminal to minstrelsy, foundational: "Jim Crow." The title is the source of the still-current label for American apartheid. It emerged before the Civil War in performances by Thomas Rice, a white man born in New York City in 1808 and widely regarded as a founding father of minstrelsy. He built a career on the tune and took credit for composing it in original published sources, but "Jim Crow" was a work song widespread among plantation slaves before Rice came along.

The explosion of popularity of minstrel shows occurred in cities, especially in the Northeast, especially in New York, which helped publicize it and gave it an outsized role in popular history, an exaggeration that extended to the banjo itself. Some accounts claim the banjo was an invention of minstrels. Others deliver credit for adding that all-important and defining fifth string, the drone string, to Joel Sweeney. This may indeed be technically correct, but only narrowly, and, in terms of what matters to our train of thought here, it is wrong.

There are published descriptions and drawings of slaves playing banjos long before Sweeney came along, and some of those describe banjos with four strings. Sweeney played one with five, but there is far more than an ordinal number at stake here. One of the strings on those earlier banjos was indeed a drone string, shorter and higher-pitched, that fell under the thumb when the banjo was played. Sweeney's additional string was not what we call the fifth today but an additional ordinary string added between the drone string and the rest to give the banjo more range. The distinction is crucial. Everything rests on that shorter drone string.

The more telling detail is how the minstrels and the slaves who taught them used that fifth drone string, and the record on this is clear. They played it and the rest of the strings just as I play today, a style called clawhammer, a downstroke of the right hand across the strings. A single finger, for most players, the middle, is bent in a claw to present the end of the fingernail to the strings, striking notes on the beat. At the same time, the drive of the hand downward brings the thumb to rest on the drone string, then it arcs up to sound that quirky little string on the *offbeat*. A whole world hinges on this. Finger on the beat, thumb after, a technique that gives the offbeat a twang and twinge and that generates the herky-jerky rhythm of the music. This is syncopation, syncopation directly derived from the evolved structure of an eccentric instrument, a species naturally selected for this trait. One can find contemporary people (or on YouTube, videos of people), Africans, musicians in Senegambia, in the same region worked by slave traders, playing gourd-bodied banjos in just this way, exactly the same idiosyncratic, syncopated stroke that hillbillies call clawhammer. The banjo is African, and it came designed, ready-made, built and bred to play the most subversive of rhythms, syncopation.

This is more than a technical detail of banjo playing; a major schism of all of Western civilization and indeed of modern life hinges on this divide.

Once in the 1970s, during the run-up to the culture wars, a twenty-something, I gave in to a request from my humorless, Christian fundamentalist mother that I accompany her to church. Glad I went, although I did then and do now despise these people. The preacher, a stereotypical hellfire-and-brimstone bible-thumper, shouted jumped and wept as promised, but at the height of his frenzy inveighed, to my great delight, against rock and roll music. He called it "wild African jungle music," and in this matter, unlike most other matters, he was exactly, technically, factually correct. Syncopation makes it so, syncopation and the odd notes of the pentatonic scale that frame indigenous African music.

Aside from five strings, those early minstrels were playing banjos they copied from the slaves. The instruments were fretless. Frets—the thin metals strips embedded in fingerboards to sharply define the boundaries between tones—were only added later in the nineteenth century to make banjos easier to play for white people. (In fact, hardcore undomesticated hillbillies observed in their native habitat by field musicologists as late as the 1980s still played fretless.) Frets allow a clean break and definition between notes. It's a C or a C-sharp, not something between. The absence of frets allows ambiguous, weird tones in between. It makes it easier to play both the wrong notes and the "wrong" notes.

This is this where our train of thought bumps up against enemy territory, intellectual real estate heretofore held exclusively by the splitters. Biology's business of classifying species splits biologists into two camps: lumpers and splitters, depending on one's tendencies in classification. I tend to side with the lumpers. What various cultures define as right and wrong in music—the fact that various races and groups and peoples embrace wildly different and clearly identifiable styles of music—is considered proof positive of cultural relativism, a genetic marker of cultural taxonomy based on real differences in perception. Some traditions seem to enjoy music dominated by minor scales, modes, and clanging rhythms that other people find unpleasant. Some cultures build music of the "wrong" notes.

At bottom though, this is just like using skin color to mark our differences. There's plenty of shading at the edges that muddies the separation, a lumper's argument. At the same time this discussion offers a more revealing story.

As I reported in the last chapter, the neuroscience makes the case that there is an emotional response basic and common to all people regardless of culture to basic variations in pitch and rhythm. The core of this argument unfolds, as does much of music, on the third tone of the scale, where minors and majors are made. Flat the third to make a minor chord and everybody is put on edge, regardless of culture. Yet this is more than a purely emotional response, or, more accurately, more than a purely cerebral response. Entering that territory of edginess spreads the response through the literal central core of our being, through the vagus nerve that regulates emotional tension in our faces, heart and lungs and the rhythm of respiration, genitals and guts, a literal, readable, measurable, graphable, visceral response. The minor third is edgy because crossing the line from major to minor recruits the whole body, demands a whole-body response.

On this fundamental level, different cultures do not perceive music differently. The better explanation of why there are widespread and identifiable cultural preferences for this and other emotional prods and jolts of music is something like the masochist's explanation of his proclivities: it hurts so good. Humans also have a common, chemically based response to bitter compounds like tannin in tea or capsaicin in hot peppers. Neither is pleasant, yet some cultures overcome the pain as a matter of pride or even taste and actually relish the jolt. Further, my quote of a masochist is more appropriate than it might appear at first. Sexual tension mirrors all of this, travels along the same neural and visceral pathways as flatted thirds and hot peppers.

What's really going on in the musical version of this pathway is not simply discord and pain, wrong notes. And once you get the ear for it you can feel this idea at work in music long predating minstrelsy, certainly in the popular music that dominates the present. In American music, this idea crescendoed to a fever pitch when black musicians especially followed a nationwide fad for Hawaiian music in the early twentieth century. This was the source of slide guitar, the seminal sound of Delta blues that spread eventually to western swing, rockabilly, and rock 'n' roll. A slide (now a metal bar, but at first a hunk of beef bone or a neck knocked out of a whiskey bottle) allows the player to ignore the frets and play ambiguous, wrong notes that fall between, just as was possible on fretless banjos.

Only in both cases, the player does not simply play a wrong note. It sounds bad that way. Nobody likes it. Instead, the technique works the ground identified by the neuroscientists that wired multiethnic and multigenerational samples of subjects to listen to flatted thirds. The lick often begins with a flatted third, a minor, a wrong note, or more often still, a flatter flatted third, and then comes the slide, almost always up to a point between the two tones where it hangs just for tantalizing, exquisite microsecond of hurting so good and then a slippery quick liquid slide a microtone higher and higher to resolve on the major third. It takes a "wrong" note and makes it right. Tension and release. And does it again and again.

Syncopation is the rhythmic analogy of this melodic device, the slide. It works by emphasizing not all off beats, but some off beats, seeming at random and unexpected points, herky and jerky. Remember, humans are unique among all animals in having a hardwired sense of rhythm that tells them where the next beat should be. Syncopation works by subverting that expectation, the same way a good joke misdirects an expected conclusion to make us laugh. But with syncopation, the response is even more somatic, visceral requiring, commandeering, really, the listener's whole body, head, feet, heart, guts, and gonads.

The gourd-bodied drone-stringed banjo, as it evolved in Africa, came to us uniquely ready-made to deliver both of these effects, and this is likely no accident but guided by the human needs of the people who played it for far longer than we can imagine.

When I mentioned "Jim Crow" above, I deliberately glossed over a key fact by truncating the original title, as most now do. The longer original is "Jump Jim Crow." As a political matter, the longer title puts an extra twist on the knife in the mid-twentieth-century usage of the term: "Massa says jump, and Jim says how high?" But the song became the founding ditty of the minstrel canon because of the jump. It was a dance, a jigging infectious, syncopated dance. This fact gets almost wholly lost in everything we moderns say and think about music, simply because we are, in historical context, stuck with an impoverished idea of music. Remember, through most of human time and in most of human language, people used various words for music that signified something different than what our word means. In languages and cultures as varied as African, Native American, and ancient Greek, the words for and indeed the concept of music included dance. Dance and music were not separate categories, another way of saying the nature and status of music in earlier cultures—the very cultures that are the source of our most vital and creative musical traditions—demanded a wider commitment from the listener's body. Even the word "listener" is an obvious bias toward our present-day and impoverished notion of music, an act of specialization and isolation. Historically, there were no passive listeners. Everyone made the music regardless of one's role in the process. Music today inhabits smartphones and earbuds, creating the electronically enforced solipsism of our day. Through most of human time and most human cultures, even today in some cultures, no one was just a listener to the couple of guys with instruments. The room or fireside circle became wholly infected with all of it, and the extension of the instruments was dance.

Thomas Rice, the minstrel who found Jim Crow South, was first a dancer. That was his claim to fame, but press notices of the day also credit him as a gifted mimic. He first made his mark on American stages doing impersonations of other actors. One day he happened to watch a slave in a stable do an odd little dance while singing the refrain:

Wheel about, turn about, do just so,
And every time I wheel about, I jump Jim Crow.

Rice caught it, copied it, mimicked it. He took it to stage. By 1832, his performances of this specific song were hailed in the New York press, he was all the rage in Baltimore and Philadelphia and would go on to perform the slave dance in London, Dublin, and Cork. Other performers followed on, many of them dancers and some of them black. William Henry Lane, a black man, danced the same circuit, was known on stage as Master Juba and was once described by Charles Dickens as "the greatest dancer known." Dickens wrote of Lane: "In what walk of life, or dance of life, does man ever get such stimulating applause as thundered about him, when having danced his partner off her feet, and himself too, he finishes by leaping gloriously on the bar counter, and calling for something to drink, with the chuckle of a million counterfeit Jim Crows, in one inimitable sound!"

So what's really going on here, that the very tune title that would come to serve as an enduring metonymy for segregation and oppression arose in a form of theater we've come to regard as brutal hectoring by black-faced racists performing for unwashed groundling mobs of racist white immigrants could then, according to the record, according to what survives of the actual music played and actual and competent descriptions of the day, be then celebrated with such energy and joy?

Eric Lott's 1993 history of blackface minstrelsy is titled *Love and Theft*, because the two words so nicely summarize his argument, that minstrelsy was driven by a sincere fascination and appreciation for the talent of the slaves who the performers stole from. But Lott's title can also sound a bit familiar because it was picked up by Bob Dylan to title an album project in 2001. Sean Wilentz, a professor of history at Princeton, a mainstream scholar of American history and American democracy—and this would seem anomalous only to those who have not considered the significance of American music—writes often about Dylan, including in 2010 the book *Bob Dylan in America*. Therein, he picks up on Dylan's use of the title *Love and Theft* at a point where Dylan's mature work is revealing its deep understanding of the forces of American history, especially the mid-nineteenth century and the Civil War. Wilentz argues it was no accident Dylan chose then to present his music under a title rooted in minstrelsy. Dylan became but one more voice of appreciation. Wilentz writes:

> The minstrels stole from blacks and caricatured them, and often showed racist contempt—but their theft was also an act of envy and desire and love. Bluenoses condemned the shows as vulgar. Aficionados, from Walt Whitman to Abraham Lincoln to Mark Twain, adored the minstrels for their fun, and for much more than that. "'Nigger' singing with them," wrote Walt Whitman of one blackface troupe in 1846, "is a subject from obscure life in the hands of a divine painter." (264)

Wilentz also points out that a few years before his explicit acknowledgement of the minstrel influence, Dylan pulled off a curious stunt that folded irony back on itself. In 1975 he kicked off his Rolling Thunder tour, a sort of resurrection of minstrel/circus/traveling medicine shows of the nineteenth century, by performing with his face painted white, taken by most to be miming mimes. But it also could and probably should be read as a syncopated riff on blackface performers, a white guy performing in whiteface. I wonder if he knew then that the earliest days of film in the 1900s captured black actors performing then in blackface.

The blackface white banjo player Dan Emmett, a founding minstrel, did indeed write the tune "Dixie," but he was also upset when it was appropriated by the Confederacy as its anthem. He was a minstrel but also an abolitionist. He would likely be equally upset by the southern racists who preserve it today; they do not preserve its original meaning.

Cecelia Conway, a scholar, gets the credit for boiling all of this down to the banjo. Her 1995 book, *African Banjo Echoes in Appalachia*, did much of the spadework that undermined the then widely accepted claim that the banjo was an American invention. She firmly traces its roots to Africa but at the same time examines how it drove minstrelsy. She comes away from this agreeing with the love-and-theft hypothesis, citing especially the "apprenticeships" each of the known and famous white minstrels served with black musicians and dancers to learn their craft. The thing is, the skills they acquired—and they were skilled, thoroughly competent musicians and dancers—did not come easily. They learned them by studying long hours with blacks, with slaves. This too is a form of dedication and respect.

Conway, like Wilentz, come back to imitation and mimicry. Apprenticeship is itself a form of devotion, but mimicry is even more interesting. It is so simple and fundamental to the human experience that we have come to take it for granted, and we shouldn't. This is an idea that music will develop for us, especially through neuroscience and evolutionary biology as this book unwraps itself, but for now I need to flag mimicry as vitally important to our line of thought. The problem is, we have become almost wholly dependent on a truncated, westernized, and impoverished form of learning, by rote, logic, abstraction, analysis, education, and repetition of facts. One can, in fact, learn music just this way, learn to read music notation, break it down to time signatures, keys, notes and note values, then put this finger there then, step by painstaking step, learn. Many of us learn exactly this way, but to truly make music one must move beyond the cerebral to the whole body learning. One learns to make music a lot faster and better by mimicry, by playing what one hears, not what one sees written on a page. This is the way almost everyone learns to sing. No one really learns to sing by following the directions: make a C-sharp for two beats here. One simply hears and does. Most people singing that C-sharp can't even name the note.

Mimicry does not break an activity to its component parts in order to execute the parts. Rather, it relies on comprehension of the whole, the totality, all perceived in a rush and reproducing that whole without thinking it through. This is not a small distinction. It hinges on the great divide of our brains and being.

Mimicry is how traditional musicians tend to learn to play the banjo, usually as children, before anyone tells them they can't do it or tells them it is hard. This was what was going on with those apprenticeships Conway was writing about.

Mimicry is even more important in learning dance, in making the whole-body commitment dance requires. The motions and carriage and attitude are far too complex to be reducible to basic steps: put this foot there then. Anyone who has tried to learn to dance as a mature adult can appreciate this. You may learn to put this foot there then, but you look ridiculous in doing it. Dance is the purview of young people because they are at a point in their brain development when they are particularly gifted at mimicry, which is exactly why a fad spreads among them immediately.

The demands of dance, however, get more than doubled, more like squared, when syncopation get tossed into the mix. Anyone can learn to march, a sort of hyper-Caucasian and hyper-Western form of dance. Every step is on the beat, so military marching can be reduced and counted and reproduced as faultless as an assembly line. That is more or less the point, regimentation, into, well, regiments. But throw in syncopation, and all bets are off.

Mimicry is like intelligence in that it is highly refined in humans. We are the species that relies on cultural evolution arguably even more so than we rely on genetic evolution. Cultural innovations spread among us as learned information, true enough, but even more so, even more rapidly, effectively, and effortlessly through mimicry. This monkey sees it, and that monkey does it.

Mimicry is rooted in a subset of our brains usually labeled as mirror neurons. That is, in this mode of learning, we do not break down and analyze, or we are not even conscious of duplicating a movement. Rather, our brains take us to a place where we are not so much witnessing another persons' dance or action; we are experiencing it in our brains as if we ourselves were doing it. The experiments in this regard have been done with monkeys and peanuts, and when a monkey watches another eat a peanut, all its brain circuitry—pleasure points, satisfaction, basic motion—light up as if it were itself eating the peanut. It participates in the other monkey's experience.

One cannot ponder this long with invoking words like "empathy." The simple act of learning to play "Jim Crow" on the banjo and dance its jig step takes us there. If you're going to do it well.

Conway thinks the role of minstrelsy in infecting the whole of American music with the African genius and germ is overrated. So do I. There is reason to believe minstrelsy was at least a factor. The minstrel shows were wildly popular and toured throughout the country, even to remote areas of Appalachia and the Mississippi River valley. Much of the commercial drive behind the music was aimed at publication, both of sheet music and of banjo primers, and those too made it into Appalachia. The minstrels, in fact, often hawked sheet music. This alone can explain why tunes like "Jim Crow" certainly, "Arkansas Traveler," and Dan Emmett's "Boatman's Dance" survive more or less intact in the repertoires of hillbilly fiddlers in isolated hollers of North Carolina and Virginia.

Yet the influence of minstrelsy on American music has gotten overrated as a result of some of the same biases at work then, as they are today. It arose in the Northeast in cities, particularly New York, the center of publication and celebrity. It engaged prominent intellectuals of the day and so left a paper trail. There's more to this story, details we miss, distracted as we are then and now by celebrity.

Eavesdrop in the lobby of the Astor House and in an upstairs room on Fulton Street in New York City, where the Dobson brothers took their first banjo lesson from black workers from the hotel well before the Civil War, and then watch minstrelsy spring up all around in the Bowery. This can look like ground zero, but scenes like this repeat throughout the history of our music. Henry Dobson reported that after those first lessons he "went to bed nights, and found it impossible to sleep, for the mellow notes of the banjo were continually ringing. . . . All his thoughts and his impulse were tinged with rich music."

Likely Bob Dylan likewise had some tinged thoughts one late night after a particular conversation with the great black blues and jazz guitarist

Lonnie Johnson in the mid-1960s. Dylan reports that Johnson, then an old man—he'd been recording since the '20s—took him aside one night and explained a near-mystical mathematical system of understanding music. In his autobiography *Chronicles: Volume One*, Dylan reports that he failed to grasp the significance at the time, but only decades later did the conversation come back to him at a low point in his career. He describes the system in detail in *Chronicles*. I have a reasonably good grasp of musical theory, but not enough to allow me to understand what he is saying. From what I can tell, it reforms all music to a framework dependent on triplets, syncopation, and the pentatonic scale. I have a fantasy that one day I will interview Bob Dylan but will only be allowed one question. I'll ask him to explain to me what Lonnie Johnson told him, which I take to be the secret sign, his moment of enlightenment.

The African echoes in Dylan's work are by no means limited to Johnson's influence. If you do not hear the distinctive roll and drive of the Reverend Gary Davis in Dylan's solo guitar, you are not listening.

The long landscape of American music between the Dobsons and Dylan has been marked every step of the way by parallel conversations and collaborations. Bluegrass? The Lester Flatt G run? Bill Monroe is not simply regarded as the father of bluegrass; he *is* the father of bluegrass, and he fronted the band from which both Flatt and Scruggs matriculated. Monroe's first gig was with an innovative thumb-style guitar player named Arnold Schultz, a black man. The Carter Family is widely regarded as the first family of country music. A.P. Carter, the musical force of the family, had a longtime friend, Leslie Riddle, a black songster and guitar player, who tried to teach him guitar (a hopeless task) and helped him collect and rework hillbilly songs but also was Carter's link to other black players, including the great Brownie McGhee. Bob Wills, the father of western swing, worked in the cotton fields with black people and cited that experience as formative for his music. Similarly with the Mississippian Jimmie Rodgers, who mirrored the Carters' role in country music: Rodgers eventually recorded (secretly) with Louis Armstrong, just as Lonnie Johnson recorded in the '20s with the white jazz guitarist Eddie Lang, who was identified on the record label in virtual blackface as Blind Willie Dunn.

Hobart Smith, a well-known figure in Appalachian string band music, lit up his style after hearing a performance by Blind Lemon Jefferson. (There is some dispute as to whether this was indeed the famous Texas bluesman, who did in tour Appalachia, though it may have been another black bluesman using Jefferson's name.)

Dock Boggs, another hillbilly banjo player who became an important influence in the '60s folk revival, consciously rejected the clawhammer banjo style common among his fellow white musicians in West Virginia in the '20s. Instead, he deliberately sought out black blues guitar players to learn what would become his haunting modal fingerpicked style. There are layers of irony in this. The style he rejected was in fact the same original frailing brought by African slaves. The style he learned was based on the delicate fingerpicking of classical guitar, European, but by then adopted by black players, syncopated and rendered cool as blues. It is the same style that Nashville would come to denigrate as "nigger picking."

This sort of tension was well established in American music. For instance, Samuel Swaim Stewart was an early and hugely successful maker of great banjos after the Civil War and based in Boston, which eventually became the center of the banjo during the minstrel heyday and on into the '20s and was then the chief competitor of the Dobsons. Together, they were the Microsoft and Apple of the popular musical world. Stewart was an early advocate of eradicating the African frailing style and of replacing it with the European style of guitar picking modified for the banjo, just as Dock Boggs did. At the same time, he insisted in his widely circulated newsletter and instructional manuals that banjo players stop learning by ear and instead rely on Western music notation. In all this, there is a pinch-faced regard of those primitive (African) forms as barbaric. Stewart clearly believed his mission was to civilize the instrument and make it fit for white people. He writes in the same spirit that propelled that sermon from my mother's Baptist preacher a century later, that frailing and syncopation would lead to wild African jungle music and all manner of licentiousness, and of course it would. It led to rock 'n' roll.

Yet even focusing on a handful of conversations, lessons, contacts, and influences in the recorded history, and this list of examples can stretch to both horizon lines, misses a crucial point by biasing the conversation toward celebrity, as we invariably do in thinking about music and history in general. No doubt these contacts were crucial in considering the question before us, how African music was transmitted to every single corner of American music. This played a role, but there was at the same time an even greater number of everyday, common, and unrecorded contacts. Cecilia Conway develops this line thoroughly in her investigations, especially as she did in the 1970s and '80s by searching out African American banjo players then still playing in Appalachia and learning of their lives.

Notice now that this discussion seems to be settling on Appalachia, even though the topic is the broad sweep of American music, a fact made odder still in that we are tracking a thread of African influence on music, and Appalachia is not now and never really was regarded as a center of African culture.

Biologists have a concept that makes a good analogy here, the idea of a refugium, a biological refuge. In times of climatic or geologic upheaval, in times of great catastrophe, species that can move do and often wind up concentrated in a refugium, a place safe from the storm. More often than not, refugia are in mountainous terrain, simply because the landscape is marginal and out of reach of destructive forces plaguing the mainstream of life. And just as often, refugia gather diverse species that do not share habitat under normal circumstances. And just as often this diversity mixes it up and hybridizes, in a vortex of biological creativity that then sweeps out of the mountains to flourish in the mainstream.

In the period before the Civil War, the population of Appalachia was about 13 percent African. Further, the rugged terrain made it inhospitable to the catastrophe that was plaguing the mainstream just down slope on the flatlands surrounding, where fertile land allowed plantation agriculture and slavery. Many of the blacks in Appalachia then were not slaves. And the whites were not slaveholders but instead Celtic recalcitrants who had fled English domination and persecution in the British Isles. They had their own musical traditions, modal, primitive, and vibrant, a fact that I've glossed over so far but looms very large.

All of these people, black and white, needed music and they found and created it in each other. The histories often mention a particular generic scene, actual, no doubt, but that recalled in imagination serves to stand for the whole history of American music. There was segregation in pre–Civil War Appalachia, but imagine this, a big house with big rooms and in one whites are dancing and in another blacks are, and in a room between the two a string band, fiddles and banjos, maybe even mixed in race, playing for both.

###

For years, I knew only a few tunes on my banjo, and one was a simple little ditty I had first heard sung by Ramblin' Jack Elliott—his real name is Elliot Charles Adnopoz—the Brooklyn Jew turned cowboy who tagged along with and modeled himself on Woody Guthrie and became great in his own right, a proto Dylan and a direct influence on the slightly younger Jewish kid from Minnesota. One summer day in the 1980s, I walked into a dim little bar in a small town in Montana, just at the opening bell of the cocktail hour, as was my habit then. The place was mostly empty except for one guy sitting at a corner booth. I recognized him and was stunned, but gutsy enough to walk on over and say, "Hey, you're Ramblin' Jack Elliott." And he said, "Yes, I am. Sit down." And I did and stayed for a couple of hours. I drank a lot of beer and now cannot remember what we talked about.

I remember the tune—not Elliott's, but I first heard him do it—as "I Wish I Was a Mole in the Ground," but it is usually titled "Tempy" (or "Timpe," among other variations), the name of the song's female lead. Second verse: "My Tempy wants a nine-dollar shawl." This small detail sets the story on ground common to all, but the rest of the song is a cipher; the singer speaks of wishing to be "a mole in the ground," "a lizard in the spring," of being isolated in "the bend," which we can infer is the place he goes to earn the nine dollars to buy the shawl for Tempy. The singer also expresses some serious antipathy toward "the railroad men." Part of the reason it took so long to understand all of this is that I failed to take into account the nature of the guy usually cited as the source for this tune, Bascom Lamar Lunsford. He was a banjo player from Asheville, North Carolina, but also something of dandy, a practicing lawyer, and a fruit tree salesman. The last role is crucial, but also probably more excuse than vocation. It allowed him to travel Appalachia visiting farm after farm, which in the early part of the twentieth century, when he plied this trade, meant he could collect songs as well as fruit tree orders. "Tempy" is one of these collected songs, not his, but something that was common currency of the hills.

Lunsford was also, at least by some accounts, a racist. Not so by others, who point out he collected and respected music by blacks living in Appalachia, but during the '60s folk revival Dave Van Ronk called him "a racist anti-semite White supremacist." Elliott called him "Bastard Lampoon Lunchfart." Still, Elliott recorded "Tempy," and I am glad, because that's how I first heard it and learned it.

In it, Tempy asks the singer where he has been so long, and more to the point, why he has been so long. He answers: "I have been in the bend with the rough and rowdy men."

In 1870 the Chesapeake and Ohio Railroad began work on the Big Bend Tunnel near Talcott, West Virginia, a project that drew itinerant construction workers from throughout Appalachia, itinerants earning wages brought home for nine-dollar shawls. Tunneling through a mountain was enough of a daunting and specific task to make a man wish to be a mole in the ground with the ability "to root that mountain down." The project also, coming as it did less than decade after the Civil War, drew an influx of freed slaves to drive the steel that poked the hole through the mountain. Literally drive the steel, and the Big Bend itself is also considered the likely workplace of John Henry, the steel-driving man, likely black, who spawned a whole series of mountain songs. Two seminal folk songs still recorded today, by contemporary and hip young artists, from a single construction project?

But in "Tempy," the singer reports:

I never liked those railroad men.
Railroad men, will kill you if they can,
Drink up your blood like wine.

Similar sentiment comes in a snippet of song that is a floater. It shows up in an Appalachian standard called "Roustabout," which is a term for a roughneck construction worker:

Where did you get those high-top shoes
Dress that you wear so fine
Got my shoes from a railroad man
Dress from a driver in the mine

A refrain then suggests how the ladies might earn this: "Hop high, ladies, hop high."

And, from another tune that shows up, what appears to be a kids' ditty but in its original seems to have a bit too much anger and veiled references to be, as its title says, about chickens:

My ole hen is a good ole hen,
She lays eggs for the railroad men
Sometimes one, sometimes two,
Sometimes enough for the whole damn crew

Antipathy, toward the railroad men, yes indeed. The railroad men were black, strong, viral, vital, muscular, musical. But at the same time the hillbilly who worked these projects with the railroad men came back home singing new songs, more than likely a whole series of new songs he learned from Africans. It couldn't have been any other way, nor was it otherwise in a flurry of construction activity just after the Civil War that allowed the industrialization of the country's midsection, but at the same time became the infrastructure of American music. Roots music, American music, is dynamic and arose from the admixture of disparate cultures, especially African with rural people, but dynamic in ways that also played out as motion, as movement of people and songs and slaves that tracked transportation. The motion placed disparate cultures together but also depended on armies of laborers.

The railroads' punching through the Appalachian Mountains certainly snuffed out the isolation, that and the upheaval of the Civil War that drew so many men from the hollers and ridges to flatland battles. But more than railroads, well before and well after, rivers moved the people and songs. The hillbilly repertoire is founded on tunes like "Sandy Boys" and "Sandy River Belle." The Sandy River is the line between Kentucky and West Virginia, and an important vein of transportation in riverboat days. "Big Scioty" is a placid fiddle tune still played today, even by people who do not know it refers to Ohio's Scioto River, a major tributary of the Ohio River and a nineteenth-century throughway.

These smaller streams are simply Appalachian headwaters of the Ohio and the upper Mississippi. Rivers string it all together and begin in mountains. Every mountain man knows the act of coming down out of the mountains necessarily involves following a river. This is axiomatic.

At one end of the Mississippi River system looms the musical vortex of Appalachia and a pool of cheap labor. At the other, a musical vortex of New Orleans, also with a longstanding tradition of slave music and banjos, but there linked up with Creole culture and Arcadian fiddling, the term truncated in its transplanted home in the former French colony as Cajun, the same musical tradition that French trappers spread to Native Americans to create the fiddling culture of the Métis people of southern Canada and the northern Great Plains.

Between, Appalachia and New Orleans, linked by current, Memphis, St. Louis and Kansas City, every one a river town, a riverboat town, and every one pivotal in the flow of American music, jazz in New Orleans, ragtime and blues in St. Louis and Kansas City, rock 'n' roll in Memphis, blues on a riverine route from Memphis to New Orleans, the Mississippi Delta, string bands, gospel, bluegrass on the tributaries of the upper Ohio, and creative tension and connection at every point between.

In the twentieth century, some of rivers' role would migrate to railroads then to storied highways, both of which allowed epic migra-tions of both whites and blacks to hubs in the north: Chicago, the blues town; and Detroit, Motown. Highway 61, the blues highway that winds through the Delta then north through Memphis and St. Louis on north to St. Paul and the headwaters of the Mississippi where Dylan came of age. US 23, the Hillbilly Highway from Appalachia north to Detroit.

The whole of this is a vast pulsing network rooted in slavery, motion sure enough, but a particular sort of motion. All of this got built, the levies humped up with mules and slush scrapers, muleskinners singing, the steel driven with nine-pound hammers, tracks laid, rocks broke, river-boat twains marked and boilers fired. Roustabouts and rough and rowdy men. Legions of slaves, former slaves and people who worked like slaves.

Alan Lomax, the famous folklorist, made a film in the late '70s set along Highway 61, which parallels the Mississippi. It all comes together here, the swirl of forces, but especially the motion and the work. The river was funneled into its role there as a slave of transportation by a massive series of levies, the construction of which rivaled the Great Wall of China, and in its use of forced labor, probably didn't look all that different. Then on top of the levies, railroads and then the Blues Highway, 61, get layered on.

Titled *The Land Where the Blues Began*, the film follows poor black farmers and stoop laborers of its time, but also kids with cheap snare drums and homemade cane fifes, a vestige of fife and drum marches left over from the time of Andrew Jackson. This is the newer material. One guy filmed shows how to make a diddley bow, a single metal wire nailed to a front porch post to make a single-string proto-guitar with a tin can resonator, played with a water glass slide. Then we see footage of Bushmen in Africa playing a bowed stringed instrument that looks just the same.

Yet the scene most relevant to our train of thought here, my invocation of evolutionary biology to trace the music back to the African bushman we have just seen, shows a gang, a group of men laying railroad track. One of them, Wilbur Puckett, sets the scene:

> When you come to work on Monday morning at seven o'clock and get out there on the job working, singing comes according to what job you're doing. Now you take lining track. That singing was just a rhythm that the labor used in keeping the time and getting the track lined like the boss man wanted. But now, singing—wasn't no joy in it whatsoever. I mean, that was just a part of the way we men set up to work. To get the job done.

They begin their work setting it to a classic call-and-response field holler, a captain calling and a crew responding and heaving real steel:

Captain:
What the old lady say when she come to die
She put a hand on her hip and one on her thigh

Crew:
Good Lord, have mercy
Good Lord, have mercy
Good Lord, have mercy
All right, quarter back
All right, all right
Just a little bit just a hair
Just a little bit right there
Just a little bit just a hair
Just a little bit right there
Alrighty
Jack the Rabbit, Jack the Bear,
Just a little bit right there

The filmed action is a dance around levers and rails, a performance choreographed by centuries of work. Embedded in this song are instructions and more importantly a rhythm that keeps the men shifting and rocking in unison, the only way sheer muscle power moves a long steel rail. Music gets the job done. Confers fitness. Enables survival. It allows us to work together.

"Jump Jim Crow" was first a work song, more accurately, in our terms, a work dance. It coordinated and coded the instructions for hoeing corn.

Some serious evolutionary biologists seriously argue that music is a knickknack, a frill, an accident of brain development. Clearly, they have not seen these guys lay track. If music is the purview of privilege and leisure, then why do we track the creative center of American music by following slaves and railroads? It began right here and propagated along these rail lines and up and down this system. Leisure? Privilege? Too many slaves and dirt farmers here to let that case stand.

As I write this, two stories appear in the nation's newspaper of record. One tells of a gentle act of subversion, that Americans are finding a softening of relations with people in Iran as a result of a series of concerts performed by American jazz musicians there. Syncopated subversion, and there is nothing unique or singular about this story.

There are hundreds of comparable examples stretching back to Charles Dickens's crowing about minstrels.

The second *New York Times* story is a profile of a favorite performer of mine, a new face in the pantheon, Rhiannon Giddens. She first appeared on my radar in a remarkable documentary that was really a filmed concert performance produced by Dylan's old sidekick, T Bone Burnett, in conjunction with the Coen brothers' film *Inside Llewyn Davis*. The documentary *Another Day Another Time* features a number of roots music stalwarts like Joan Baez, Dirk Powell, the mandolin virtuoso and MacArthur genius Chris Thile, the great Gillian Welch, David Rawlings, and Willie Watson. But Giddens at one point soared above the crowd with her preternatural gift of pipes that rival Baez's, and she has been since awarded a MacArthur grant.

Giddens has developed her art performing with a band called the Carolina Chocolate Drops, a group of African American musicians who perform minstrel music and come by it honestly. Giddens plays banjo and fiddle. The band's rhythm section is driven by bones, just as was the case in minstrel music. Slaves played bones because the masters banned drums, believing they would incite insurrection.

Giddens is native to Appalachia. She and a couple of fellow band members studied directly with Joe Thompson, one of the rural black men from Appalachia who were the sources of Cecilia Conway's work in tracing the African roots of banjo. My own banjo repertoire includes Giddens's version of "Colored Aristocracy," a cakewalk tune.

Following the first documentary in 2014, Giddens quickly emerged from the pack and has become a popular solo act. She, Elvis Costello, and Marcus Mumford were featured in a second Burnett documentary, this one revolving around a reworking of Dylan lyrics that were more or less outtakes from the "Basement Tapes" made in the 1960s. In my mind, and this is in many ways wrong, but still how I like to think about it, the Basement Tapes were the distillation of all of American music to one white-hot moment of essence. I am not alone in this. Greil Marcus argued this case at book length. Everything I have been talking about in this strain of music funneled down through Harry Smith and Greenwich Village to that house near Woodstock, New York, that produced the

Basement Tapes, and then it exploded back outward again. Giddens belongs in that sweep now, especially as an African American woman unabashedly performing minstrel music.

When Jon Pareles profiled Giddens for the *Times*, a detail in his lead paragraph said what needed to be said. Setting scene in a studio where Giddens was recording, he noted the presence of a reproduction of an "1858 fretless minstrel banjo." Well, he should note the presence of this instrument. It is never absent in American music.

4

JUST A WANDERING WORKER

I entered this story at an oblique angle, by accident really, but also through fraud and deception, just as most do. I needed a personal facade, a mask, and the one I had been given would not do. I was a bumpkin, a hick, an imposter, a kid not yet twenty flung by good luck into a hip town—Ann Arbor. The deception required not a black face but could then be accomplished—and this is nearly impossible to imagine today—by affecting a blue collar. The term "working class" still had some resonance and honor then. The masquerade as wandering worker, however, would also set me on a course that would eventually put a guitar in my hands, and I am glad that happened, no matter the route.

Then, the music was still ascendant. The Great Folk Music Scare of the '60s, so named by Dave Van Ronk, the self-proclaimed mayor of Greenwich Village's MacDougal Street, had not subsided, providing me with fellow travelers every bit as eager to accept working-class nobility as I was to claim it, but I still did not realize I was joining a long line of hucksters and poseurs, all smeared up in burnt cork, the better to sell snake oil at medicine shows, good friends all.

Working-class nobility wasn't all that big of stretch for me. Most of the people I was trying to impress were gullible, like most then and more now at universities, children of privilege, suburban, open to the con. I had no money, nor did I have any idea what it meant to have money. Rube manners, the cheap J.C. Penney suitcase that carried my clothes into the dorm, my dimestore record player and the hairnet I had to wear when I bussed the dishes of my peers in the cafeteria, scraped their leavings and cigarette butts, told who I was. Nor was it a big stretch to dress the part, a black cotton T-shirt, Camel straights in the single front pocket, jeans, lace-up leather work boots. Except for the cigarettes, this had been my uniform every day since I was eight years old. In Ann Arbor, radical chic.

Leftist politics were then still Marxist, and there were still labor unions and people who built things with machines in factories. Even the suburban kids were adjacent to the then-functioning city of Detroit and had some sense that manufacture buttered their bread and bought their Corvettes.

My claim to a proletarian pedigree, however, was fraudulent. True enough, my old man was a construction worker at the time, a power lineman and dues-paying member of the International Brotherhood of Electrical Workers, but he hated unions, stole from the companies that employed him, was an active John Bircher, a drifter, a dreamer, and mostly just a failure. He was an itinerant construction worker, "tramp lineman" was the term, not to be a worker, but to be itinerant, wandering. Working-class nobility? Not in my house. But close enough for a story. Close enough to let me pass. So I got on just as most of us do, by happenstance, by forgetting, ignoring, inventing, and by falling in with good friends. Some of them played guitars, and they sang the songs. Something in those songs seemed true.

These were, of course, also the golden years of rock 'n' roll. Woodstock had roared into American consciousness that summer on a stack of Marshall amps. The masses were begging Dylan to lead the revolution. A rumor that Paul McCartney was dead could sweep campus in minutes, and we spent our nights playing Beatles albums backward hoping a close hearing fine-tuned by marijuana might allow us to crack the code and reveal how Nixon had killed him.

But my friends with guitars drew me into a little back-stream eddy and undercurrent to the main, away from rock. The Band, surely, and Dylan along with, but we favored the music that traced the thread backward: Koerner, Ray & Glover, the white bluesmen from Minneapolis who Dylan first linked up with in his brief stay there between Hibbing and Greenwich Village. Rosalie Sorrels and U. Utah Phillips. David

Bromberg. Doc Watson and his taciturn son, Merle. Flatt and Scruggs. Maybelle Carter's scratch strum on of her Gibson L-5 archtop. New Lost City Ramblers, Tom Paxton, Steve Goodman, Gordon Lightfoot, and Phil Ochs. Bonnie Raitt.

This was folk music, and my friends were folkies, and the founding myth of folk music is that it is authentic, a music cut, hewn, and worn round at its edges by good country people, by workers and yeomen.

It would take some years, but eventually this story would envelop me. Then, I didn't even own or know how to play a guitar. I admitted to no one my childhood of accordion lessons, polkas, and high school marching band, or that I could read music. Eventually, I left Ann Arbor, my friends, and music. I became a newspaper reporter, an alternate form of subversion, and I liked it well enough. I wouldn't be the first inchoate lefty to believe it was my destiny to enlighten the yearning masses by smearing barrels of ink on newsprint. And I began to settle in: marriage, a child, a couple of newspapers, and promotions on a path that began to look like a career. I moved to the Rocky Mountain West, to rivers and mountains.

There are even actual mountains and a picturesque babbling brook in a pivotal scene of my life, a storied trout stream, a little tributary of the Henry's Fork of the Snake River that tumbles down in a series of falls from Yellowstone National Park to the lava-strewn plains below. I was there as a fly fisher and family man, not yet thirty, a weekend outing like everyone else in the campground, assigned to our numbered campsite, each on retreat from the several jobs that claimed us and assigned us to cubicles. Only I wasn't fishing, but instead watching, as the Winnebagos and pickup campers parked and leveled on graveled pads, paid the two bucks, cranked out awnings and fired up generators for lights and television. And I was among them taking my place in a line, backing into my own assigned and numbered space. Then one day, late, as the sun was setting, I stood at the end of that campground, took in the scene, and decided then and there I wanted nothing to do with it. It was too revoltingly normal.

Shortly thereafter I walked into a music store on the main street of Idaho Falls, Idaho, my town then, and picked out a cheap acoustic guitar from the rack on the wall, a Japanese knockoff of a Martin dread-naught, what I could then afford, and with it a flat pick and instruction book that would guide me through the intricacies of the chord shapes necessary for Michael's rowing his boat ashore. And shortly after that I would begin an extramarital affair that if nothing else fully explains why the phrase "wild and tempestuous" has survived as the cliché of record in these matters. Other than the wholly explosive and consuming sex, this liaison came fully equipped with built-in advantages. It would of course eventually wreck my marriage and any pretense of a settled existence, but she also happened to be a reporter under my supervision, so it would set my career on a bit of a wobble as well, a twofer. It was the right thing to do. I was grasping at any straw that may have prevented me from being ordinary.

This is Alan Lomax speaking in the late 1970s:

> Generations of steel muscled black axemen hacked away at the endless forests of the Delta bringing daylight into the river bottoms and opening up the richest land in the world for cultivation. Land suitable for vast cotton plantations where agriculture became a big, impersonal business that grew richer and richer at the expense of hired black labor.

Even then, this bleeding prose had an antique ring to it, a relic that would seem more at home in the *Daily Worker*, the official Communist Party house organ of the 1930s. But this aired on PBS as a discourse on the blues, that is, on entertainment. Yet much of what we know about and believe about American music traces this very thread of working-class heroes, in fact to this very man, to Alan Lomax and his father and a tiny group of influential experts whose truncated and doctrinaire version of the reality held direct and personal sway over the Great Folk Scare in the '60s. More bluntly stated, these guys were Communists, card-carrying, big-C. This sort of thing did indeed make it into the *Daily Worker*, was in fact a key element of Communist strategy in the United States in the first half of the twentieth century.

This chain of influence is pretty easy to track, because both performance and publication records are outsized for a very few people, to the point that hindsight is easily blinkered to believe that Alan Lomax and his father, John, were the only musicologists and folk collectors of the twentieth century and their friend Pete Seeger was the only radical with a banjo. It gets tighter still. Track it to Pete's father Charles, a Harvard-trained composer (just as John Lomax was a Harvard-trained musicologist), professor, and also a musicologist. The elder Seeger also wrote for the *Daily Worker* under the pen name Carl Sands, and he proved his ability to toe the party line by executing a crisp about-face in his beliefs precisely as the party dictated, a pivot that left him facing in exactly the opposite direction of folk music. Sean Wilentz, in *Bob Dylan in America*, reports:

> At this point [1934, Charles] Seeger, a musical modernist, had little
> use for traditional folk music as a model for revolutionary culture.
> "Many folksongs are complacent, melancholy, defeatist," he wrote,
> "intended to make the slaves endure their lot—pretty, but not the
> stuff for a militant proletariat to feed on." (19)

This was a direct parroting of the party line that at that point completely denigrated folk music, which shortly after 1934 reversed itself—a full 180—with the creation of the Popular Front. The party's new brand specifically favored folk music as the authentic voice of good country people. Seeger "took the shift in stride" reports Wilentz, and he moved his young family to Washington, DC, took a New Deal job, and began collecting folk songs for the Library of Congress along with his friend John Lomax and Lomax's son Alan. Seeger's son Pete got involved in the family business, started traveling to collect folk music, was energized by meeting Bascom Lamar Lunsford, the same guy who gave us "Tempy." Pete then formed a band that included a songwriter Lomax had discovered, Woody Guthrie, and the Almanac Singers would then make a name for themselves, all the time wound up in Communist politics, union organizing, and the developing cause of racial justice. All of this would flower directly into popular culture up until the red-baiting days of the fifties, when Seeger was blacklisted as a Communist. Pete Seeger and Guthrie took on apostles, personal acolytes like Jack Elliott,

Dave Van Ronk (a dyed-in-the-wool leftist in his own right), and Dylan himself. Mike Seeger, Pete's half brother, founded the widely influential string band, the New Lost City Ramblers, became a respected musicologist too, and by Dylan's own account was a great influence on his music.

Yet what wears so thin in all of this is not so much the leftist politics. As I have said, I tended in that direction myself and still do. A lot of people were Communists then. Lampooning the language and the tactics of the day is a bit like, as someone once said, criticizing Christ for not flossing. That's how they did it then. The problem is our account of American music largely rests on this handful of people, and it is without a doubt a limited account, narrowed not so much by the Popular Front and the party as it was by the even more pinched vision of academia. All of these guys were intellectuals and warped the picture to serve the intellectual constructs of the day. Plenty of people say folk music is of the people, and it is, but much of what we know and believe about folk music is of the professors.

One need not lean solely on the Lomaxes and Seegers to develop this idea. There is, for instance, the singular case of Cecil Sharp, a batty British intellectual with deep expertise in collecting folk tales among people in the English countryside (he called them "peasants") at the turn of the twentieth century. Sharp happened to be doing a lecture tour in the United States and teaching actors folk dances for Shakespearean theatre when someone told him there were indeed folk songs to be collected in the United States, a possibility he had earlier considered and ruled out. He got in touch with Olive Dame Campbell in Asheville, North Carolina, Bascom Lunsford's hometown, who had already collected a number of songs in Appalachia, many of them songs Sharp already knew well as the very tunes sung and played by the English "peasants." He would go on to spend years collecting thousands of songs from a handful of Appalachian towns, often hearing far more complete and well-preserved versions than anything remaining in Britain, the source of the songs.

There is some sense in this history, then, that Sharp is an original, predating even the Lomaxes in this endeavor. (He in fact knew of the Lomaxes' work and was sharply critical of it.) Yet he was not. When he began his collections in what he regarded as virgin territory in 1916, there were already established, state-sponsored folklore societies as formal institutions in Kentucky, North Carolina, Virginia, and West Virginia and a string of collectors like Campbell already working the ground.

Yet, curiously, Sharp developed a unique composite picture of Appalachian folklore, that it was dominated by English tunes, the songs he already happened to know. This is the same place where today (and this phenomenon continues despite Sharp's belief that he was seeing the very last of folk music preserved by isolation and about to die as it was dying among the English "peasants") traditional Irish musicians join jam sessions and discover they already know many Appalachian tunes but by Irish names. Sharp does note the existence of the odd Irish immigrant in his travels and generally heads in the opposite direction when he does. To this Englishman, the music of Appalachia was English and noble, not Irish and low.

He also, though, notes that some of the English tunes were coming back to him a bit weirdly rendered with some flatted thirds, sevenths, and fifths, the mark of the pentatonic scale, the African scale. There was plenty of evidence all around him to explain how this might have happened. He reports that the isolated reaches of rural Appalachia were then dotted with segregated communities of blacks. He even wandered, by accident into a few of them: He wrote: "We tramped—mainly uphill. When we reached the cove we found it peopled by niggers . . . . All our troubles and spent energy for nought."

No music to be had there. Sharp's sidekick in his travels, his "secretary" Maud Karpeles also wrote of the same encounter: "We arrived at a cove and got sight of log cabins that seemed just what we wanted. Called at one. A musical 'Good Morning,' turned round and behold he was a negro. We had struck a negro settlement. Nothing for it but to toil back again."

###

The Lomaxes' most successful introduction in the folk music scene of the midcentury was probably Huddie Ledbetter, better known as Leadbelly, a murderer and a black man who they helped free from his sentence at the notorious Angola prison in Louisiana. Leadbelly was is widely believed to be the source of the folk song "Goodnight Irene," which was a popular, runaway, lucrative hit for Pete Seeger's and Woody Guthrie's band but eventually recorded by literally hundreds of performers from Frank Sinatra and Judy Garland to Eric Clapton, Jerry Garcia, and Jimi Hendrix. The tune is not Ledbetter's; it was in fact a minstrel show staple during the 1880s and written by a man named Gussie Davis.

The Lomaxes, though, presented Leadbelly as the genuine article, and there is no doubt he was, a gifted performer and a musician with a past set in the real-world conditions of the Delta blues and some pretty credible claims to legitimacy in the tradition. He had been a lead boy and student of the great Blind Lemon Jefferson. And as a respectable bluesman, he had his preferences and dignity. Especially after spending time in prison, he favored wearing decent suits when he was performing, only the Lomaxes insisted on dressing him in prison garb—dungarees and work shirts—like a trained monkey, the Popular Front version of blackface.

John Lomax also cut a deal with Leadbelly, a management contract under which the two of them would split Leadbelly's earnings down the middle. This was about the time, though, when son Alan was coming into the family business, so John renegotiated with his client. Henceforth, the split would be into three equal parts, and Leadbelly would settle for a third to allow for Alan's share.

Woody Guthrie liked to perform in dungarees and such, and made much of his Oklahoma roots during the Dust Bowl, but he was not a tractored-out farmer or a wandering worker. He was the son of a failed businessman, a dreamer, who more or less abandoned his family after real estate deals went sour, disappearing to Texas. Woody did later join the migration of Okies west to California when he was still a teenager, but it was a brief spot in his life at an age when a lot of young men wander. He learned much of what he knew about the Dust Bowl from reading Steinbeck, like the rest of us. And when he left Oklahoma, he was already a musician and songwriter. He quickly signed on for a radio show in California, started recording, and wound up—like many who succeeded in music—in New York City, where he would live most of his adult life as a thoroughly urban intellectual, performer, and Communist. His lasting and pivotal relationships were with the nation's big city and a small knot of Harvard-trained radical professors who were busily erecting a facade for folk music.

In all this, his life history was not all that different from the entire pantheon of early-day recording stars ranging from the Carter Family and Jimmie Rodgers in country music to blues giants like Robert Johnson, Blind Willie McTell, Lonnie Johnson, and Muddy Waters and the country boys who would drive traditional music into rock 'n' roll in the '50s—people like Johnny Cash and even Elvis Presley. All could claim roots in rural poverty and traditional simple music, and all used music in some way to establish for themselves a bit of fame, a bit of income (in some cases, more than a bit) that bought new cars, nice suits, and (most notably in Robert Johnson's case) nice shoes. In this matter they had a great deal more sense than the Popular Front radicals and more than I do in idealizing the life of the noble worker. There was nothing particularly ennobling about the conditions of the rural South or the Dust Bowl in the Dirty Thirties. The poverty was grinding and brutalizing, and every one of these performers knew people and came from people who had been ground up and brutalized as a result. They did the sensible thing and took the leg up that the fame and income offered them. They made records and sold songs and used what story they had or needed to adopt to drive the process. Who wouldn't?

More than selling their story, though, they were selling music, much of it passed off as the pure and distilled manifestation of good country people, the pure proletariat, and noble savages. This was the version of folk music that the Lomaxes and Pete Seeger would so jealously guard and protect from electric guitars and commercialism. In fact, the music had lost its virginity and turned to whorin' long before.

Follow A.P. Carter in his travels in Appalachia, and his peregrinations were legendary. He was constantly on the move, to the point of abandoning his family, actual neglect that no doubt played into the development of his wife's affair that wrecked their marriage. Nonetheless, Carter had good reason for traveling, the need for grist in the mill. The Carter Family—A.P., wife Sara, and Maybelle, who was sister-in-law to A.P. and cousin to Sara—were hugely popular then at the beginning of the Great Depression. With Jimmie Rodgers, they were the leading country acts and cash cows for the New York–based Victor Records and then RCA Victor. Then as now, the recording industry was driven by a bottomless pit of an appetite for novelty that required artists to record about thirty new sides a year. (These were 78 rpm records, not vinyl but shellac, each with a song on each side, "sides".) Carter wandered Appalachia to gather those songs, and some of them were indeed traditional, but many came from piano benches and pantry shelves as forgotten sheet music. Before recording came along with Edison and became commercialized early in the twentieth century, music made money as sheet music. That's how the minstrel music propagated but also how Tin Pan Alley came to be, a mill for grinding out ditties. Likewise, hymnals were lucrative, and producing them was a business every bit as cutthroat and competitive as recording a half century later.

Carter couldn't read music, but sometimes he'd stay at a family's house, maybe have them sing the song as they knew it, maybe even take the sheet music, and he and Leslie Riddle, his friend, the African American guitar picker and Carter's companion in these trips, would figure it out, assemble a tune, tweak some lyrics, record and copyright the tune.

The process was not at all unique to the Carters. The rise of the recording industry brought the demand to copyright. That's where the big money was made. The Carters made money on recording, but the truth is it wasn't much, enough for a decent house and a new car, a notch above their Appalachian neighbors, but not great wealth. Ralph Peer, however, was the record company executive that would more or less make the mold for what the industry came to call A&R men, artist and repertoire. He signed new talent, and with it management contracts and deals that gave him the copyrights, not just of the Carters but also Jimmie Rodgers, a whole skein of bluesmen and women, jazz players like Louis Armstrong, and even Mexican and Brazilian performers. On one trip, the Carters went to New Jersey by train to record but, once there, didn't have enough money to afford food, so they went hungry. But they rode around town in Peer's limousine.

The better frame, though, for consideration of authenticity for performers like the Carters is the character of John Romulus Brinkley, who preferred being known as "Doctor," no article preceding. The title he earned by virtue of six weeks' worth of intensive medical training at Eclectic School of Medicine in Kansas City at a cost of $150. In practice, Doctor perfected a technique of sexual rejuvenation for lagging middle-aged men, which involved an incision in the scrotum to implant a smidgen of goat testicle. (Patients could supply their own goat if they knew of a particularly promising donor.) Doctor touted these services on his very own radio station in Kansas and made a fortune but then ran afoul of the authorities in 1930 and was hauled into court on a pile of evidence that included forty-two death certificates. Guilty was the verdict.

Carter biographers Mark Zwonitzer and Charles Hirschberg pick up the story at this turn: "A man of less sturdy constitution might have folded up his tents and left the state altogether. Brinkley decided to run for governor." As a write-in, and he got more votes than either of the legitimate candidates, but his constituency was somewhat lacking in literacy, and misspellings of his name spoiled enough ballots to cause him to lose. Nonetheless, he put together a de facto majority by blasting his message on radio, thereby using broadcasting to spin stupidity and fraud into political power. He probably should get some credit for working out the business model for Fox News and for framing the modern political question: What's the matter with Kansas?

Doctor was not done, though. He moved to Mexico and started a pirate station, a clear channel screamer that sent his signal all across the United States and well into Canada, and then he hired the Carters. Their regular gig as resident in-house performers was to provide the music that sold goat testicle transplants and patent medicines.

Nothing unusual in all of this. Much of what we regard as folk music today germinated in traveling medicine shows and in places that are, if not as colorful, at least as commercial. The pure strain of collected folk music fed on this commercial stream. Woody Guthrie actively and openly recycled hymns and Carter Family tunes to serve as melodies for his songs. Even the Lomaxes' work was not immune to this sort of taint. When I was growing up, every schoolkid knew "Home on the Range," and we didn't know, but it was nonetheless true, that the song made it to the schoolhouse by way of the Lomax collections of great American cowboy folks song published in 1909. Only it wasn't. It had been written by Brewster Higley, another Kansas doctor, and published as a poem in a local newspaper in 1876.

The Lomaxes also included a deep and dark cowboy tune in their published collections of folk music called "Spanish Johnny," which was resurrected, retooled a bit, and recorded by, among others, David Bromberg and Paul Seibel. Often as not, Seibel gets credit for writing it. The song was collected by the Lomaxes not through spadework in the field but by digging it out of the published works of Willa Cather, then an established, well-known writer and magazine editor living in New York City.

The most prominent practitioner of this sort of theft was and is, of course, Bob Dylan, and the advent of powerful search engines and the digitization of almost everything have allowed even lowly bloggers to identify his borrowings from sources far and wide: from obscure Civil War–era poets to Japanese pulp novels. Dylan stole liberally throughout his career, and if you want to play an endless game of "gotcha" designed to sully folk music, there is no better place to start. But the deal is, Dylan knows this, and so should we. Alleging plagiarism misses the point.

So too does entombing music as a museum piece of working-class or rural nobility, and oddly enough this other approach also erupted most prominently in a famous confrontation with Dylan, the 1965 Newport Folk Festival, when he dared to stand before that audience with an electric guitar. This event has been recounted endlessly precisely because one could not imagine a better cast of characters for the apotheosis of the Great Folk Music Scare. The outrage that day was headed by both Pete Seeger and Alan Lomax, then the high priests of the Popular Front flame. Dylan was not free to use the music to advance his story; they were using it to advance theirs. Yet the very stream they so unctuously guarded from pollution had been sullied long before Dylan came along, by recycled poems, Tin Pan Alley treacle, potboiler hymnals, snake oil, anonymous masquerades, blackface, RCA Victor, con men, hustlers, pimps, and prop dungarees.

###

Taking to the stage that pleasant fall evening on an island at a repurposed World War II Army base in the Puget Sound, I was terrified of being exposed as a fraud. I was about to play a banjo and was not very good at it, just learning. Worse, my audience was not the usual clutch of friends, fellow travelers, or a few unsuspecting locals who had wandered into a coffeehouse open mic. Every single one of the hundred or so sets of ears and eyes lined before me belonged to a banjo player. Some in the audience were famous, the elite of the sport—Adam Hurt, Paul Brown, Riley Baugus, Terri McMurray—assembled there for a weeklong banjo camp, a retreat for instruction that was kicked off with an open mic offering students opportunities to make fools of themselves.

I was most nervous about Alan Jabbour; I knew he was there. He is a looming figure, even physically, a tall gray eminence with erect and proper bearing, the manners of an East Coast blue blood patrician professor, an impression that dissolves quickly when he sits to drive his fiddle in keening Appalachian rhythms. He's mostly known, though, as a folklorist. In the 1970s he was a graduate student and found himself working the Appalachian vein, then dominated by studying Tommy Jarrell and Fred Cockerham, two hillbilly musicians who became prominent during the folk scare and still loom as the giants of mountain music, though both are dead now. Both were being overexposed in the '70s, so Jabbour decided to work new territory, hillbillies of his own discovery. He recorded and interviewed the members of the Hammons family. Then there was Henry Reed, a fiddler from Glen Lyn, Virginia.

In 1969, Jabbour joined the Library of Congress as a folklorist, the same shop run by Charles Seeger and the Lomaxes. He served a stint with the National Endowment for the Arts. He retired in 1999 after twenty-three years as the founding director of the American Folklife Center of the Library of Congress. All to say, he picked up where the Lomaxes left off. He died in 2017, not long after I met him.

I mostly think of Jabbour now, though, when I play an impish sprite of a tune called "Quince Dillon's High D," which Jabbour learned from

Henry Reed when Reed was a very old man. Reed himself had learned it from his mentor, Quince Dillon, when Dillon was an old man. The latter gets the credit for writing it, but there's no way to fact check that now. Dillon is long dead, born in 1813, a musician, a fifer during the Civil War. Reed learned the tune from Dillon and Jabbour learned it from Reed, so these two jumps cover a whole lot of ground. Jabbour likes to believe—and there is no way he can be wrong about this—that when he plays it, there is something of the sound that is Quince Dillon and Jacksonian America hanging in the air. Until Jabbour got hold of it, the tune had never been scored or written down. The old men learned it by hearing it, so something of what they heard lives on.

And against all of this, I had little to offer when I took to that stage, so I decided to do a tune of Woody Guthrie's, or more accurately, lyrics of his, or at least credited to him. The melody was, like most of his, stolen, this one from an old hymn that worked the founding fraud of Christianity, counting on the next world and streets of gold to compensate for the suffering in this world. Elsewhere in folk music, this tenet of Christianity is summarized as "Pie in the Sky."

The refrain of Guthrie's song is a direct paraphrase of the hymn: "I ain't got no home in your world anymore." It was a set piece of Popular Front propaganda, not a real folk song at all. It begins: "I ain't got no home, I'm just a-wandering round. I'm just a wandering worker, that goes from town to town." He never was.

But the thing is, then, just a couple of years ago, 2014, during that period when I took to the stage, I couldn't make that tune go away. Every time I picked up a guitar and opened my mouth, it came out. Something about "bankers took my home and drove me from my door" pulled it out of the dust and stood it on its feet in the real and the present financial crisis brought on by bankers. It came alive again because we seem to need it.

Further, I had known the hymn even before I knew the Guthrie version, but even that gave the song some stature and breath, the deeper, less time-bound message of alienation and weariness with this world, that some of us, no matter who and where and when we are, shall never feel part of this one.

Propaganda it may be, but there are substrates. Parts of Guthrie, of who he really was: son of a bum father, failed dreamer, drifter, never home. Something of all of us in here.

I stood on stage, head back, and sang it, plunked my banjo along. My lungs filled and sent it sailing in the air. I could see the force and power of it reflected in the faces of the people in the audience, power. After, we all filed out, and Jabbour sought me out from the crowd. We had not yet met, but he wanted to introduce himself. He found me and thanked me for singing the song, said it needed to be sung.

We exploit, steal, mimic, commercialize, analyze, trivialize, all for our own puny purposes, all to assemble a story that helps step us forward through the day. This is what we do, and singling out a thread or strain of this process as illegitimate or fraudulent misses the point. In singing a song, none of us captures more than a child's stick-figure drawing of the reality of song. The point we miss in our incessant bickering and criticism is the reality that lies beneath.

None of us is really wrong in this, not the minstrels or the Seegers or Lomaxes or Dylan or A.P. Carter. It's easy enough to impugn their crude stick drawings and forget that the music lives on because of what they did, no matter their intentions or abilities. Pete Seeger may have been a hidebound pain in the ass or a fraud, but he stared down the House Un-American Activities Committee and the forces of McCarthyism. He gave Martin Luther King directly and personally his first hearing of "We Shall Overcome." Dylan spent much of his career getting booed off stage.

The ancient Chinese gave us the concept the Tao, the way, the great and immutable force and path that unseen directs and organizes all life. Even then, 2,500 years ago, those philosophers wrote that the Tao is unnamable, that we may approach it through music or right living or meditation but never comprehend it sufficiently to give it a name. They said quite explicitly that if you name the Tao, it is not the Tao.

My mother's bible-thumping Baptist preacher, after inveighing against the terrors of African jungle music, would also remind us that "all have sinned and fallen short of the glory of God."

###

The game of folklorically correct musical gotcha often is played on racial grounds. American music is African, and the history of its commercialization is riddled from beginning to end with appropriation of black music by white people. True enough, but there's something to be gained by poking holes in that case. In the end it will stand in some way, but the contradictions now can help strip off a surface layer that covers a deeper purpose.

Often and justly this issue of theft of African music in general rests on individual cases of theft and exploitation. In the noxious language of our present, music is an "industry," so it should surprise no one that a subset of capitalism exploits black people. American capitalism, after all, was erected on a foundation of slavery. Yet these issues channel the broad sweep of social justice into a narrow little canal of intellectual property law, and for better or worse we have more or less maneuvered our way as a society into a place where courts and lawyers and letters of laws decide who owns what and who is exploited. None of this is very satisfying or in the end very relevant to where we are headed. Ultimately there is only one song, and each of us steals it again and again to sing in our own way, a position that has no standing in the courts.

Even in a less-than-legalistic sense, a narrow individual read on the justice in this matter is difficult to assess. It depends on individual cases but also context, especially the social context of a time that is lost to us. We cannot, for instance, fully reconstruct the circumstance of the exploitation of Blind Willie McTell, one of the famous examples. There's a strong case to be made supporting a charge of exploitation. Dozens of times, I have fingerpicked the deft little dropped D riff that McTell used to frame "Statesboro Blues," and the circle of listeners will be at first puzzled at the apparent novelty of the music, but then the lyrics come around as McTell wrote them, "Wake up Mama, turn your lamp down low." "Oh yeah, Allman Brothers," say the listeners. People invariably think the song comes from the white rockers, who made a name for themselves on McTell's song, and got stupidly rich in the bargain. McTell had died penniless and drunk on the streets of Atlanta in the 1950s.

Yes, he did, but he did not live a life of desperation that this ending might imply. He spent most of it in nicely furnished and comfortable apartments in Atlanta. He made good money, had a successful career, and recorded widely. He did not become a blind, black beggar in the streets for most of his life because a benefactor, a white man, encountered the twelve-year-old, orphaned, and blind McTell and paid to send him to a special school for the blind where music was taught, a fortuitous fit with McTell's underlying genius and drive. McTell was a savvy professional and adopted a series of stage names so he could record under contract to competing record labels, and in these incarnations commanded $100 a side for his recordings, top dollar then in the '30s, which netted him earnings about eight times those of the average black workingman of Atlanta. He claimed authorship of many of the tunes he recorded, but they were in fact lifted, stolen, borrowed, from sources both black and white.

John Lomax found McTell in Atlanta and arranged to record him talking and playing. The musicologist dominated those session with a series of ham-handedly leading questions trying to lure McTell to complain about his lot and the treatment of blacks in the South in general. McTell deflected, wouldn't do it. He may have been afraid to do so, not wishing to rock his boat on the public record. Maybe. But he may have also been aware that he hadn't gotten such a bad deal out of life, all considered.

The Lomaxes may also have exploited Huddie Ledbetter, but we need to remember Leadbelly was in the Angola Prison Farm when they found him and out when they cut their lopsided deal with him. The musicologists indeed used the Library of Congress recordings to lobby for Leadbelly's release, though there is some reason to believe their efforts were unnecessary; he was getting out anyway. But this misses the point of what happened to black ex-con murderers left to their own devices in Louisiana in the first half of the twentieth century or what happens to them in the first half of the twenty-first for that matter. When not dolled up in dungarees, Leadbelly got to wear nice suits, lived in New York City, and had a solid career. He was famous. Bad deal? No way we can know. Ask Leadbelly.

The more relevant line of thought here, though, moves away from these individual cases that are matters for lawyers or more likely unknowable, to the whole, that great amorphous stream of American music that I have already argued is African, and the case here is prima facie, the pentatonic scale, those weird jungle notes clearly traceable to African scales and clearly forming the foundation of the various strains of American music today, that and the rhythmic companion of blue notes, syncopation, and the instrument that is uniquely suited as habitat for both of these musical devices, the African banjo.

But what this misses is the traceable history of all of this, traceable in one important seminal vein to the Ohio River tributary of the Mississippi River basin in Appalachia. And if you are only hearing banjos there and throughout the Mississippi basin before the Civil War, you are not listening. The real power of Appalachian music was a spark struck in the interplay between two instruments, the banjo and the fiddle, the source of the flame that still burns. Further, the oversimplification of pinpointing this to Appalachia can be quickly overcome by having a listen in the other hotbeds of creativity for American music down the Mississippi, in New Orleans, but also throughout Ohio, Missouri, Kansas, on east out on to the Piedmont, areas that all had fiddling traditions.

The fiddle is not African; it is as white-bread and European as any instrument can be, the carrier of those very British folk tunes Cecil Sharp and his intellectual descendants recorded throughout Appalachia more than a hundred years ago. But more to the point (Sharp mostly ignored this, being British; others do not), there was a little melodic hitch in those tunes that serves as a marker of their DNA. The rural fiddle tunes were mostly modal, meaning they work a scale unlike conventional Western music. The marker says they are ancient and primitive and Celtic. Further, and Sharp himself noted this, but it remains true of the parking lot pickers and Brooklyn hipsters who favor this traditional music today: the fiddles themselves often ignored conventional, civilized concert violin tuning. It made it lots easier to hit and sustain those weird drone notes and modal scales that drive Celtic music, the practice that makes the instrument sound more like a bagpipe than a violin. Our use of a separate name for them, call them fiddles, not violins, is in some way technically justified, the Irish and Scots fiddlers, but also the

Continental Celtic groups that factored into French Canadian, Métis Indian and Cajun fiddling, had something else in mind.

The explosively creative period of American music came in the last half of the nineteenth century, and it coincided with an explosion in immigration. During that period, immigrants from Ireland dominated the flow, the largest group. For instance, just before the Civil War, almost half of all immigrants were Irish. About 4.5 million Irish immigrated between 1820 and 1930. Most were desperately poor and went to work on the toughest, dirtiest, most oppressive jobs. So did former slaves, so African musicians found an instant and natural alliance here. Well before the nineteenth century, fiddles were already in the hands of slaves, partly because masters had banned African instruments like drums, partly because of isolation, that the whites needed somebody to play dances, and partly because there was a more or less easy fit with their own traditions. It is that correspondence between these two lines that exploded into American music.

Skimming the commercialized surface of what this music has become in the hands of celebrities and industry and tracking copyrights can undermine the argument that folk music is a pure stream sprung from pristine mountain sources, but that too is a distortion twisted by the fact that this analysis follows celebrity and commerce, just as I have been doing here. It tracks a few hundred songs, and even Cecil Sharp, working in a handful of mountain counties among a few thousand poor and mostly illiterate people collected close to two thousand distinct tunes in a single summer in 1916. Where in our country could one do this today, collect thousands of unique tunes being actively performed and appreciated by the poor rural people inhabiting a small patch of ground? And would one be able to collect a unique style of music powerful enough to serve as the foundation for all of the several American forms that have spread throughout the world in a continuous and vital beat?

At the very least, we have a pretty clear case that those who consider music a luxury, a creature of conservatories and concert halls supported by the affluent and leisure time are just plain wrong. As was the case with the slaves, the hillbillies were working stiffs, miners, laborers, and dirt farmers, probably the poorest among all farmers in the nation. These are the people that carried, maintained, enlivened, and created with homemade fiddles and banjos.

The very odd thing is that this combination, so fundamental, elemental, and universal in American music, is almost never really heard today, not the way ecstatic dancers white and black heard it in the nineteenth century. We all think we have heard it but have in mind a caricatured version of "Turkey in the Straw" and a floppy-hatted ersatz hillbilly in rolled-up overalls, red flannel, wheat stem in mouth, mascara freckles painted on as the whiteface version of blackface, sitting on a hay bale in a broad satire of the form. But it's not much better to go to the original to hear the recordings of the masters of this form. Thanks to people like the Lomaxes and Alan Jabbour, such recordings are readily available. They nonetheless have all the shortcomings of recordings: music in a bottle, no context.

Nor does it help much to listen to modern recordings of genuine contemporary masters of the form, and they too exist. Those of us who play the music do listen to all of these sources but suffer no illusions that we are hearing the music. We mostly do it to steal licks, to learn. To really appreciate the power, you must enter room where it is, live, real, with real wood, hide, and steel under the hands of people who love it, let it consume you, and be among people who are so consumed. The essence of this music cannot be captured in recording. Its essence is motion, and unmistakable drive and step that immediately captures your entire body. It is not whole without dance, without your full participation, and then you know the value of the fiddle's long bow pushing a syncopation and the Zen temple drone of the banjo just under the surface.

All of this is not about blackness or Celticness or banjo or fiddle. It is about the primitive, a word I hold in great regard, not a pejorative. I am firmly in the "noble savage" camp. Romanticism? Guilty. No apologies here. We are, after all, talking about music. Romanticism might cause an error here and there but ultimately and historically is far less threat to the music than the alternative. Where would we be without romance in our lives? What will our music be like when it is written by algorithms?

Our music is African because ultimately each of us is African at our source. Humanity began in Africa. This is not about who wrote what. Rather, we need a sense—real and touchable sense—that everything we know about and think about, steal, sing, copyright, record, and cherish as music is derivative and a poor copy at that. Caricature is all we can do, and it does have value in its own right, or we wouldn't do it. But we are trying to tap into a deeper and ineffable stream. Something lies beneath.

5

GUITAR GEEK

Neuroscience tells us that one of the more rigid cranial categorizations appears to be the divide between animate and inanimate, that the human brain handles information about sentient beings in a specific region and reserves another wholly separate set of neurons for inanimate objects. People and dogs here, chairs and rocks there. There are two prominent exceptions: We process information about two other categories—clearly inanimate objects—in the same region we reserve for the animate: food and musical instruments.

###

One of the more unsettling aspects of becoming a musician is hearing differently, in new dimensions, deeper, a process that seems to offer a glimpse of a parallel universe, a ghost world before hidden in ordinary sound. The result is moving and beautiful when listening to music itself but can be irritating and painful in confronting the cacophony of everyday life. Elevated hearing offers far too much sonic insight into what we humans have become, but these downsides seem more than offset by the ability to hear the world anew. I understood one day that this was happening to me when I heard a concrete delivery truck release its airbrakes in two consecutive, piercing, flatulent moans and without thinking about it realized the two aligned perfectly as a major third. Music emerges.

This ability seems to awaken in fits and starts, and during one such rising wave of comprehension in the summer of 2015 I was putting this newfound power to good musical purpose, listening intently to a variety of high-quality vinyl recordings of acoustic music, delving ever deeper in for new clues and direction about music itself, a gourmand at a series of sumptuous meals. It suddenly struck me that I was hearing in certain guitar parts something new and exciting, not nuance and notes, but a clear voice, a timbre not at all ostentatious or even remarkable, simply confident, worn, and wise. It persisted across a variety of artists, genres, and periods of recording but throughout seemed to speak like a single character's voice, a sound not so much thought-out, designed, and manufactured, but something that had always been there, borne on a wind and revealed periodically to my hearing. I looked for a common thread among the diverse recordings and found one unmistakable. In almost all cases the guitar in play was an early-'50s Gibson slope shouldered jumbo, a J-45. This new information expressed itself as a clear spoken command loud and clear in my tinfoil hat.

This was deeply unsettling. I was then and had forever been a Martin guy, had never owned a Gibson. As is so often the case in these passionate preferences, I had no reason for it. Just never had been. Further, I was a small-body player, and a J-45 is a big beast of a guitar, Gibson's answer to Martin's dreadnought. But then there was this voice in my head.

Within a matter of seconds after putting all of this together, I Googled and was fully informed that there were at that very moment a number of early-'50s J-45s on offer at reputable dealers with websites and a handful of iffy propositions on eBay. Ballpark, $5,000, and that to tread a slippery slope. Gibsons are inconsistent in their construction, especially those from the postwar boom. The war itself had winnowed the company's luthiers to a handful of old men, and their ranks had thinned even more by the late '40s. Postwar demand was putting chisels and planes into the hands of a lot of inexperienced makers, and it showed, but tantalizingly, sometimes in serendipitous error. Sometimes braces got thinned too much or not anchored properly, making an even more delicate top. Given the right life history, such a guitar could become an accidental masterpiece because of its extraordinary unplanned delicacy. Or sometimes it was made perfectly and sounded it, but such guitars had long before been discovered and secreted away well out of the reaches of eBay and such. Chances of finding a good one were close to nothing, and even if one such guitar existed in cyberspace, no way to confirm it by playing it. And then there was the matter of $5,000. Beyond me, really. I make my living as a writer. I already had one perfectly good guitar, a masterpiece in its own right that had cost me exactly that amount. Bought it when times were better.

Still there was that voice in my head, and so I began asking around. Maybe I could at least locate one languishing within my circle of musical acquaintances, maybe just to borrow and play to shatter the illusion and deflate my infatuation. Initial inquiries came up empty, even a dealer friend I knew. He'd handled plenty, but, no, nothing at the moment, nothing coming in. Collings makes a nice reproduction. Wouldn't I like to try that one? No. The tinfoil voices had been very specific. Must be original. Must be vintage.

The intricate and venerable story of the guitar—and the steel-strung instrument the world knows as acoustic guitar today is deeply and undeniably American—winds around two names: Gibson and Martin. The first name identifies a company pretty much like any other, the second, a company that is also a remarkable story of tradition, artistry, craft, and characters, beginning with Christian Frederick Martin. Born in 1796, he had grown up among cabinetmakers in the town of Neukirchen (now Markneukirchen) in Saxony and had apprenticed to the great German guitar maker Johann Georg Stauffer in Vienna. The European guitar was much smaller, stringed with gut strings, not steel, and wholly fit for polite company and rigid, obsessive German manufacture.

Guitars were something of a fad in early nineteenth-century northern Europe but had only recently shown up there, migrating from Italy and Spain. The new instruments, though, met with a longstanding and highly evolved craftsmanship honed in Germany on violins and cellos.

Martin emigrated to New York City in 1833, arriving in what one writer (Philip Gura, noted Martin historian, also the same guy encountered earlier as a historian of the banjo and of American transcendentalism) called "guitarmania." It was not Gura's term but was taken from a French writer who applied it to the instrument's wildfire spread in Europe almost two hundred years ago. The guitar's status in the US then, however, took a back seat to the status of amateur music in general. Music was a fundamental fact of life in most households, no matter economic status. Americans made music. Gura writes: "With the spread of labor-saving technology, for example, and the concomitant extension of leisure even in rural communities, Americans not only flocked to concerts and musical theater, but to minstrel shows and burlesque opera. What most marked the culture, however, was amateur music making in the home."

C.F. Martin first set up shop in Manhattan in 1833 and began building a few guitars but mostly retailing supplies like violin strings and musical instruments of all sorts. Within six years Martin was in the midst of moving his operations to a small settlement of Moravians (a German religious sect) in Nazareth, Pennsylvania, where the company remains today headed by Chris Martin, C.F. Martin IV, great-great-great grandson of C.F. Pre–Civil War guitars from the hands of C.F. are still obtainable, playable, and sublime, as are examples from nearly every period since.

The hallmark through most of this, the saving grace of Martin, was a near-pathological conservatism. From 1833 until about 1850, C.F. Martin turned out one-off guitars of a dizzying variety, but then all of a sudden just before the Civil War he standardized to a plain, clean design and a short list of models. They haven't changed all that much since and still follow a system of nomenclature he established then.

There's a famous story that illustrates the source and pace of change. Martins are known for an exceedingly clean, straightforward squared-up countenance, few frills and fads, and there is no better place to display this attitude than on the headstock, the trapezoid top of the neck that holds the tuners and often, especially among other makers, a dollop of ornament, a mother of pearl inlay of a frog, a Harley-Davidson, or an earth mother. Martin would not go so far even as to display the company logo there until early in the twentieth century, and then only in simple gold script the iconic "Martin and Co. EST. 1833."

Almost always the Martin headstock had been defined by two corners, crisp, clean, and knife-edged square, but then in the mid-twentieth century someone noticed a subtle bit of evolution in the Martin design. The headstock corners changed to be slightly rounded, softening the sharp jutting chin of the old design. The obsessive attention to seemingly minor cosmetic details such as this is not unique to guitars. Industry analysts trace the success of Apple Computer, for instance, to just this sort of detail, and Steve Jobs devoted much of his life to hand-wringing over single millimeter changes in a corner radius. Jobs would never have rounded a corner on one of his gadget's boxes without months of analysis, market studies, prototypes, and soul searching.

So somebody checked with Martin about the corners. Nope. No such decision, they said. See here, this is the template that guides the tools that shape the headstocks, and it's the same one we've been using for a while. It was indeed. A template that could be whittled up in a half hour from scrap wood had never been replaced. And over the decades, repeated use had rounded its corners.

Throughout the second half of the nineteenth century, Martin occupied precisely the same position in the guitar world as it does today, the recognized standard. The era's celebrity performers and teachers played Martins. Mark Twain played one, an 1835 model he bought used in 1861. It survives and still makes music. Just after the Civil War, some unscrupulous wholesalers began importing cheap knockoffs from Germany and selling them as genuine Martins, counterfeiting being the surest measure of a brand's status. Martin's dominance, however, was of a particular niche aimed especially at amateurs and at women. The guitar in general was at the time considered a woman's instrument, in keeping with the era's social prejudices about gender: slight, delicate, polite, and refined.

Before electronic amplification, the best instruments for social music were the loudest ones, which is why banjos, fiddles, and mandolins came to dominate dance music, and the emerging music of the masses was indeed dance music by the late nineteenth century. C.F.'s sweet little guitars were fine for polite parlor plucking but couldn't hold their own at a cakewalk. Still, people liked guitars and so set about figuring out ways to make them louder, which was a matter of building them with bigger bodies, then beefing them up a bit so they could handle the tension of steel strings instead of the gut strings of European classical guitars. This was the American guitar in the making, the bite and boom that drives everything we hear today. Guitars became what they are because people wanted to dance.

Martin was dragged by market forces kicking and screaming into this but also had long before adopted an innovative new bracing pattern for the delicate tops that allowed those very changes demanded by the market. Called "x-bracing," it is the dominant system of today's guitars. C.F. Martin began using the novel bracing system in the 1850s, probably even invented it. While player demand pushed guitars to bigger bodies in imperceptibly slow increments through the nineteenth century, the whole process accelerated early in the twentieth. Both recorded music and radio channeled music through microphones, and steel strings spoke more clearly to this new technology.

Martin also was being pushed along in this evolution by commercial pressures, especially the dominance of department stores, mail-order catalogs, and a rapidly rising standard of living that allowed mass consumer culture. Sale of mail-order instruments became a mainstay of firms such as Sears and Montgomery Ward plus a single company dedicated solely to mail-order musical instruments, Lyon and Healy. Martin wanted in on the action, but selling to the masses meant giving the masses what they wanted and cutting prices, and Gibson was quicker to learn that lesson than Martin.

Still, Gibson came to the game from a different angle, which proved to be an advantage. Founded by Orville Gibson in 1902 in Kalamazoo, Michigan, the firm was an upstart; Martin had already weathered nearly seventy years of an intensely competitive business, evolved its methods, and learned to deal with the demands of distributing, mail-order houses, and cut-rate competition. Meanwhile, Orville Gibson was a mandolin maker first and started his firm as the Gibson Mandolin-Guitar Company. His early guitars were built like giant mandolins, archtop guitars with heavy carved tops and, from the beginning, steel strings. Thus Gibson was positioned in products readily adapted to the demands that quickly emerged as a result of new recording technology and radio.

At this point, Martin was headed by Frank Henry Martin, grandson of C.F., the third in the strictly patrilineal succession, but Gibson would establish no such hidebound tradition. Orville Gibson died in 1918, leaving no heirs in charge, but the company was already behaving like a more modern and anonymous corporation. The following year, it hired Lloyd Loar, a mandolin designer whose name commands almost as much reverence today as that of C.F. Martin. He would stay with Gibson only six years but in that time developed the legendary F-5 mandolin. Surviving examples are known simply as "Lloyd Loars," command now $100,000 or more and are not museum pieces but wind up in the hands of the world's finest players, on stage and working. Today's acknowledged wunderkind of the mandolin, Chris Thile, the only mandolin player to win a MacArthur genius grant, has two Loars with, no less, consecutive serial numbers. Loar, in almost the same stroke, also designed Gibson's L-5 archtop guitar, which became the standard for carved top guitars. These were the guitar of choice for jazz players until electric guitars came along and even for Mother Maybelle Carter, the matriarch of country music.

Despite the differences, though, these developments in the teens and '20s set Martin and Gibson on converging courses that would produce in the '30s what players revere as the "Golden Era" of the American guitar. The beast that heralded this was the dreadnought, named for a class of battleships because it was huge by the standards of the day. Martin made it for a mail-order house, Ditson, and at first refused to market this faddish freak under its own name, but players loved it, and so in 1931 the legendary Martin D-28 entered the world. This is the quintessential American guitar. It was then; it is today.

The dreadnought was not, however, a wholesale departure. It was indeed bigger with a different shape but, under the hood, bore seminal elements of Martin's methods. Key was x-bracing, which supported the tension of steel strings over the span of a larger top and while maintaining sensitivity to vibrations subtle and not. Less obviously, but probably more importantly, Martin's build standards translated to tighter, stronger joinery that held up under the strain. Tighter joints also serve as acoustic coupling, better transmitting sound's vibrations through the instrument and beyond. Meantime, Gibson responded by building a dreadnought of its own, the J-35, so named because it cost $35. It had earlier developed a slightly smaller model, the L-1 that evolved to L-0 and L-00, favorites especially of blues players. The best-known photo of blues legend Robert Johnson shows him playing an L-1 from the '20s.

Given the proliferation of models and names, this can also sound like an eruption of diversity, but what was really happening here was just the opposite. An array of diverse designs and brands that had been churning about for nearly a century all of a sudden converged to a single American guitar. As often happens with newly evolved creatures, this new species swamped its predecessors. Both Martin's and Gibson's own lines had been far more diverse before the Golden Era, as had those of a whole series of competitors. Yet all this diversity converged on a handful of models, foundational shapes, sizes, and designs. Gibson's offerings in flattop acoustic guitars would boil down to three basic guitars. Martin's line boils to two. That's it. And this core ignited to a wildfire spread that became the standard of country music, cowboy crooners, bluegrass, rockabilly, folk—especially folk—folk rock, Beatlemania, and the British invasion on up to and including the present-day pestilence of singer-songwriters.

Yet to see this as a result of actions by two companies is to miss a larger point. Martin was through this period headed by probably the most Martinesque of all its patriarchs, Frank Henry Martin. Under his command, the company adopted a new tool that became standard issue on every worker's bench: a short length of copper tubing sized so that a standard pencil fit nicely inside. Workers were expected to wear a pencil down to the nub, then put the nub in the tubing and thereby gain a couple of extra days wear out of it. He routinely patrolled the shop floor each night, going through trash bins assigned to each workbench looking for sheets of sandpaper with grit left on them, then would confront the offending worker the next day with a lecture on how those bits of grit might be productively employed.

Frank Henry was rigidly conservative because there was much to conserve in the Martin name but was still an unlikely choice to preside over a creative flourish. Meantime, pushing against this immovable object was the irresistible force of the players, a boisterous bunch of illiterate hillbillies, narcissistic matinee idols, and drugstore cowboys. It's difficult to pinpoint the source of a spark of creative genius in any of this. Worse, the demands for bigger guitars were pushed as much by the drive toward bigger sound as they were performers' urges to preen in public with bigger, flashier instruments. Both Gibson and Martin caved in to this commercial pressure, and were this the end of the story, we wouldn't be talking about it today because it would have given us nothing but big, flashy, lousy guitars.

Bluegrass is the outstanding example of the more subtle forces in play. Bill Monroe gets the credit for inventing bluegrass, driven along by his dizzying double-timed arpeggios, a pyrotechnic style aided by the Lloyd Loar mandolin he played. But he also needed a foundation, a driving bass line and a thumping rhythm. Most bluegrass string band players and proto-bluegrassers could not afford a standup bass and hated drums. The Grand Old Opry enforced a blanket ban on drums. So both functions had to be served by the authoritative thrum of a Martin dreadnought. The Martin D-28, that exact model, remains the standard in that role to this day. For most of the history of bluegrass, one was considered iconoclast or rebel or innovator if he played instead a Martin D-18, identical in every way except the body is mahogany, not rosewood.

Frank Henry Martin gave Bill Monroe the guitar he demanded, a lunker, but rendered with the refinements Martin had developed and conserved through a hundred years. As a result, this big guitar was equally capable of nuance, detail, and pathos. Those qualities infected the musicians who played those guitars and soon enough would begin to define the music itself. The music made on these Golden Era guitars is foundational to all American roots music. Lloyd Loar and Frank Henry Martin had an enormous role in defining it, every bit as great a role as the musicians'.

What's more, the explosion of creativity has been oddly frozen in place by commercial pressures. Guitarists intone the term "Golden Era" with nostalgia and awe because it ended. Mass marketing, greed, personal quirks, and players themselves killed it. Both Martin and Gibson were wounded by their own successes in the 1970s, and the numbers alone tell a big part of that story. All through the nineteenth century when Martin had already established itself as the leading maker of guitars in a booming nation populated coast to coast with amateur musicians, Martin's sales averaged about 250 guitars a year. During the postwar period, sales began climbing driven by the Golden Era designs, hitting about 7,000 guitars in 1955. The company would more than double that total in 1970, only fifteen years later. That sort of growth caught the attention of the sort of people for whom the guitar business was just another business, and both Martin and Gibson began to cut corners, electrify, automate, standardize, and cheapen their guitars. New shapes, sizes, and glitzier designs came on the market, then withered and died. Both began marketing cheap Asian knockoffs of their own venerated models. Both Martin and Gibson shot, plucked, and ate the golden-egg-laying goose.

At Martin, the descent was a soap opera starring Frank Henry's grandson, Frank, as head of the company. His father, C.F. Martin III, still chaired the board but gave the younger Martin a lot more latitude than he deserved. Frank was a drunk, womanizer, and playboy. He started selling drums.

But beneath these commercial machinations of the sort that has all too often plagued any American business was a tension, a literal creative tension that was oddly the very soul of the music. An acoustic guitar is a grand compromise with tension, the force of the strings tugging incessantly on the thin wood top. Tuned to standard pitch, a steel string exerts about 160 pounds of tension on the center of a piece of soft spruce wood the thickness of a quarter. The wood itself would split under such tension and so is reinforced with spruce braces arrayed in a delicate substructure of pencil-thin girders beneath the top. Braces have an enormous effect on the instrument's tone. The thinner the top and braces, the better the tone and projection, but also the weaker the top. Players' push for ever-louder guitars led them to install ever-heavier strings for greater mass and therefore greater volume, but also more tension—elementary physics.

In 1944, Martin finally tired of repairing free (all Martins then, now, and almost without interruption since the beginning have lifetime warranties) tops and bridges bulged and split as a result of heavier strings, so Martin thickened the braces. Gibson eventually followed suit, although not so cleanly, but in fits and starts. Guitar players mark this as the end of the Golden Era, although this is arguable. There were still great-sounding examples of both brands into the '50s and '60s, but the slide had been triggered. By the '70s, both companies were warding off warranty work by stiffening their guitars in all sorts of ways. Hard to blame them. The players brought this on themselves.

In 1974, Gibson began shifting its production to a new automated factory in Nashville, Tennessee, both to cut corners and as a marketing ploy. A decade later, Gibson was within three months of going broke. By 1984, Martin was also nearly broke, facing liquidation and only staved it off because the board chairman, C.F. Martin III, allowed his stock to devalue to zero. The elder Martin and his grandson, Chris, the current head of the company, joined forces to fire Frank. But a series of bone-headed business decisions lay behind this swath of ruin in both cases. The Golden Era was clearly over.

Yet the salvation from this disaster was right there in blueprints in both companies' file cabinets. Plenty of dedicated guitar players knew this, and it's not all that hard to buy wood, glue, chisels and planes. A number of names track this new thread of the story, but probably none as well as Eric Schoenberg, a virtuoso fingerstyle guitar player from the '60s with a strong preference for an extinct Martin design, the Orchestra Model, thought by many to be the company's first truly modern guitar. Known as the OM, it morphed early on into the 000, technically the triple zero but always referred to as the "Triple Oh." The latter is a great guitar. Eric Clapton played one when he went "unplugged." Bob Dylan did in two seminal albums of blues in the late '90s. Paul Simon does. They are still being made and nearly identical to the OM, but Schoenberg was more interested in the extremely light bracing of the original OM that gave it an exquisite voice. Surviving examples of the original now command in the neighborhood of $100,000 on the vintage market.

Schoenberg's idea was to begin building a reproduction of the 1930 OM. Weirdly, he even contracted with Martin to do the actual building beginning in 1987. He still does, and Schoenberg guitars still command premium prices, a story one can gather in person from Schoenberg himself at the boutique of a shop he personally staffs in Tiburon, California.

In the early days, Schoenberg teamed with Dana Bourgeois, who now builds several hundred guitars a year in a small factory in Lewiston, Maine. He built my guitar, one I have played for fifteen years. That's how I thought I had settled the whole issue, by buying a new guitar, but of vintage design executed with old school methods and materials. On the subsequent years, I have played literally hundreds of guitars at shows and dealers throughout the US. I have never found one I like better and only a couple I have liked as well.

Bourgeois has branched out to a full line of a half dozen models, and every single one is a reproduction with minor modifications of Golden Era Martin and Gibson models. Same with Bill Collings, the most well-known of the new generation of makers and probably the one with the biggest operation. His factory is in Austin, Texas, though he died in 2017. He was known for being a near-psychotic perfectionist and for turning out guitars commensurate. Similar with Santa Cruz guitars, reproductions of vintage models. In all cases there are some minor variations and innovations. The new makers have figured out ways of making the guitars more consistent and reliable over time and under a range of conditions. Still, the bulk of this new wave of business rests on the handful of models, reproductions of Golden Era Gibsons and Martins. The guitar world, though, is now fully recovered from the dismal days of the early '80s and is enjoying what most players now regard as the new Golden Era.

Completing that trend are two relatively new entries among the resurrectionists. Both Martin and Gibson figured out there was money to be made in making guitars the way they did eighty years ago. So they do. It has left acoustic musicians in a curious world. Imagine taking to the present-day highway and seeing that 95 percent of the cars are either 1938 Chevy coupes, Hudson Phaetons, Nash Ramblers, or faithful reproductions thereof. That's where we are.

This is where the present-day player enters the story, with a choice of buying vintage, the original, a surviving example of a Golden Era, or a reproduction. There are reasons for going vintage beyond their unsurpassed time-tested designs and impeccable construction (at least for Martins). Wood dries with age, thereby gaining a more mature voice. Many of the old guitars are heartbreakingly weathered, patinaed, and checked, simply beautiful in the promise of the stories they hold. Life history of a guitar is a part of its sound. If they have been played hard and in a certain way, the wood learns to roll with the vibrations, a process that players call "opening up." Vintage guitars can speak to their history in complex and unpredictable ways.

Yet the new ones are dead-nuts accurately made, impeccable in operation, survive much better changes in weather and location, and some of them promise to sound even better than vintage in a matter of a few years. Can't go wrong, really. In any event one is tapping into a remarkable evolution. Pop a mirror into a brand-new, off-the-rack Santa Cruz or Collings and look at the under structure of the top, the delicate web of the bracing, looking for all the world as if C.F. Martin himself had hand-carved it in 1854. No one has figured out a better way of doing this since, other than doing it well.

Given all this, one of course does the rational thing. Vintage is for collectors, and they're rich and have bid up the prices beyond all reason. Opt for reliability and performance. Buy the new Bourgeois. This settles the matter. Play it. Love it. It's the rational thing to do. Rational? Silly fellow. What's rationality got to do with it?

###

There was no reason to think Mike Williams would know anything about locating a vintage Gibson J-45, the object of my search. Mike is not a guitar guy; he's a fiddler mostly, and, even more than most fiddlers, he has an advanced case of disregard for guitar players' obsession with collection. Fiddlers as a species are not fickle and tend to be perversely loyal to a single instrument, monogamous, married for life. Mike also plays guitar and banjo but prides himself on getting by with nothing more than a minimalist arsenal of dilapidated, cheap mail-order instruments from the '50s that he has rescued like stray dogs. A single no-name guitar and no-name banjo both worn to a frazzle. Ten bucks apiece new, since depreciated.

Mike is a new friend of mine but an old one and well-known to the network of players in the northern Rockies. He's in his late seventies, elfin, sagging and round, a Jabba the Hutt of string band music. During the Great Folk Music Scare, when he was in college and not yet a musician, someone put a mandolin in his hands and told him to play it, which he did at a paid gig that same week and has been playing ever since, gravitating soon enough to fiddle. He teaches a bit, plays out with several bands, and makes a living of sorts the way he always has, by playing music. I got to know him in the process of my learning banjo and for a time visited him once a week for practice playing with a fiddler. He was my teacher. His mental collection of tunes is encyclopedic, eclectic: Texas, Missouri riverboat, Ozarks, Mississippi Sheiks, Appalachia, north and south. Nothing he plays is the same as he heard it first played, but one listens and learns what endures.

He lives in Helena, Montana, at the frayed edge of town, a tiny wood-frame house on a big lot he has filled with an organic garden and fruit trees to feed himself. He lives alone, and on decent summer days I would find him tending his garden, usually in a pair of baggy, plaid, oversized Bermuda shorts, a stained frazzled T-shirt lettered and logoed for some forgotten festival or fiddle camp and flaccid aqua shower flip-flops that exposed the twisted toes of a gnome.

We played in his shack, a two-room outbuilding at the back of his lot divided in half to form a couple of rooms, each the size of a standard-issue office cubicle, but a lot more interesting. The back room is a shop with a woodstove for heat in winter. Its walls are hung with tools and aging broken fiddles and banjos. Drawers are stuffed with bridge pins, bone saddles and nut blanks, tuners, tools, all ancient, collected over the course of fifty years. In the front room, a couple of chairs, a desk with a corded telephone and answering machine (his business's IT center), shelves of vinyl records, cases of cracked yellowed cassette tapes, a boom box, and a library stuffed on sagging shelves with hand-drawn sheet music for fiddle and banjo. Here we play some, but mostly I listen to his stream of stories about hillbillies, hippies, pickers, misfits, and cranks. One day I found him there sitting upright in a wooden chair, intent, in a near trance, and for a moment feared he was dead, but he was only listening to a Thelonious Monk recording, trying to comprehend and compress the whole tangle into a composition for fiddle.

"Mike," I said. "I been looking around for somebody with a '50s J-45 for sale. Happen to know of one, do you?"

Mike's facial expressions often seem more ruled by the effects of gravity on flesh than by any underlying sentiment, leaving one to guess as to what the underlying sentiment might be, but after maybe fifteen seconds of inscrutable, there was a glimmer of recognition. He arose from his chair, walked the few steps into his shop, and opened a closet door that appeared to have never before been opened, sealed centuries ago as some sort of crypt. Dust and years' worth of soot from the woodstove billowed and winnowed in a slant of sunlight. He entered the crypt and emerged bearing a tan, battered guitar case, opened it.

"I think that's what this is," he says.

It was not. It was in fact a Southern Jumbo, which was in shape, size, and bone exactly the guitar I was looking for, but in 1942, Gibson had dolled up the J-45 with fancier trim and premium woods and construction and called it the Southern Jumbo or Southerner Jumbo to appeal to southern pride, which at the time happened to be defiantly Jim Crow. Were Gibson to try a parallel marketing ploy today, they would likely inlay a mother of pearl confederate battle flag in the headstock. Hank Williams, the quintessential cracker crooner, played this exact model, but then so did Woody Guthrie, the communist.

I lifted it out of its case, horrified to realize I was lifting a lifeless, limp carcass. The soul had departed, I could tell, from the lack of resonance when my finger tapped its face. It sounded like it had been eviscerated because it had been. Its back was off, and the guitar's box peeled open like a spent can of sardines. Bits of plastic trim clung to the bottom of the case along with the battered detached back, split end to end by a series of four or five long cracks. Somewhere along the way, the body had taken a sharp, blunt blow to the bottom edge of its lower bout and the side had caved in. Forensic pathology might speculate as to what sort of instrument dealt the lethal blow, whether it came in a barroom brawl, a lover's quarrel, or from being slammed beneath the lid of a car trunk, all common assaults. The crime itself probably unknowable, but still not the full extent of its injuries. Someone had started to repair it, badly, even my amateur eye could tell. This guitar was a mess, a basket case, beyond redemption. Only one sensible course of action for me.

"How much you want for it, Mike?"

"I don't know. How's a hundred sound?"

Five twenties flew from my hands like a flock of flushed birds. Almost as fast, the case was in my Jeep, and I was headed off to cross the Great Divide, literally, to make the two-hour drive through the Rockies from Helena to Missoula. If I had lights and siren, I would have used them. In Missoula, I knock on John Joyner's door. He's a luthier, a fiddler too, a banjo player and like Mike makes his living at music. He fixes these things, redeems the irredeemable. He says he's not really a luthier; he's a conservator. It is not a hollow claim.

"I brought you something interesting."

"I can see that," he said. I had not yet opened the case, but there was really no need to, just as there is no need to tell your dog there is a freshly roasted chicken hidden in your shopping bag. The battered tan case was original and recognizable. We sat on straight-backed wooden chairs in John's oak-floored craftsman-style living room and opened the lid, staring down in silence for full minutes like stunned tourists gaping at the Grand Canyon. John began palpating the patient.

"It's kind of a mess." He of course saw first what I had seen, that somebody had attempted a repair, surely decades ago, with the dreaded Bondo, a plastic resin filler paste meant for patching dented automobile bodies. This is more or less like a physician discovering a new patient had been previously treated by being bled with leeches.

"That will have to come off."

"I know." But had no idea how. Bondo hardens like steel bars and sticks like a felony.

Then he spotted the bridge, the patch of dark wood where strings attach to the body, which was not broken and appeared completely serviceable. "That will have to come off too. Not original. Should be Brazilian."

Brazilian? He meant Brazilian rosewood, by which he meant expensive. Very. If he could get it. It's mostly extinct and forbidden in international trade just as elephant ivory is. Indian rosewood or mahogany could serve as well. No effect on the sound. No one would notice. John could see these objections forming on my face.

"It will have to come off. I'll make a new one. I've got a stash of Brazilian."

It was clear to me that the task ahead transcended issues of sound and playability. The new and period-correct bridge was a moral imperative. At stake were imponderables at the center of the instrument's being, the point of tension, between strings and wood. Luthiers have a near-mystical reverence for what goes on here, a deep regard justified by the physical facts of the matter and by experience. But even the uninformed can see we have entered hallowed ground. The bridge and bridge plate are the seats of its soul.

The evolution of guitar shapes during the Golden Era was ever more anthropomorphic, culminating in the narrow waist and voluptuous hips. If the sound hole is the navel in this array, then the bridge rides on the radiation of wood nerves just below, the solar plexus, so named in humans because the array of nerves looks like rays of the sun shooting off from the energetic center. "Plexus" shares a common root with "complex." Mystics make a big deal out of this. So do makers of guitars. Gibson in the '20s developed a distinctive, complicated finish called a sunburst, with a solar glow centered on the bridge shading outward to a deep tobacco brown at the instrument's edges. This is the point from which the complex of vibrations radiates. My guitar indeed has a sunburst finish.

"But what do we do about the finish?" I asked John.

The side where the cracks and Bondo were had been scraped to raw, wounded wood. The sunburst top had a big dent and scrapes and bruises leaving the instrument with the face of a veteran, old-school hockey player. What do we do about this?

John looked at me as if I had tweeted him the question using emoticons.

"Nothing. We leave it like it is." Also, apparently, a moral imperative.

One restores a guitar to playability; one definitely does not counterfeit its story. There were hints its story was indeed relevant and, despite the obvious battering, fortuitous. Both of us could see the back of the neck worn clear through its finish, but only up high, only one spot, what guitar players call "first position." Both of us could see heavy-duty, widespread pick wear on the guitar's face. These two bits of evidence suggested a life history of cowboy chords, big, simple primary tones rendered with a heavy hand, not great as music if you happen to be around when it's happening, but over the years, this style that can open up an instrument like this wide and full. Could be. No way to know until the very last day of John's work on it.

I had in my pocket a bullet point list of notes made, problems spotted, and for each a corresponding question about the remedy. I had carefully prepared it, meaning to go over it point by point with John. I felt for the list in my pocket, found it, but left it there. "Okay. Do what needs to be done. Do what you'd do if it was going to be your guitar." Smartest thing I ever said.

"Okay. $1,500. Six months."

I of course was dispatching John on a descent straight into the chaos and treachery of Bondo, cracks and crevices in woodwork older than both of us. A year or so older, but still. An outsider hearing this transaction would have every reason to suspect the quote of a price was as meaningful as that of a Yellow Pages building contractor's beginning a kitchen remodel on a Victorian. Every reason, but I didn't. I've known John for a while, and I left it in his hands, got up to leave.

"Where'd you get it?"

"Mike Williams."

This set him back a bit. He and Mike were longtime friends, and my information told John he had been caught napping, that there was a guitar like this shut up for decades in closet in Montana, a friend's closet, and he had not gotten his hands on it.

"Where'd Mike get it?"

"He said some guy named Sonnenberg."

Now John was even more taken aback, suddenly recoiling from the guitar case as if it were a coffin of a vampire.

"Who is Sonnenberg?" I asked, realizing I should have asked this of Mike.

"Who *was* Sonnenberg. He's dead. He was Darryl Sonnenberg. He was a drunk."

###

Then months passed into the long Montana winter. Slowly. Every now and again I called John to attempt to make arrangements. He had granted me visitation rights during the process, and I kept trying to schedule a viewing, but he put me off. "Nothing much happening. Nothing to see here. Move along. Need to really think about it for a few months before I start." He was in fact not thinking but working with tweezers and magnifier, chip by weathered battered chip, patiently steaming the glue out of every crack, chipping off every bit of Bondo. Each crack's repair absorbed a full day of benchwork, and there were dozens. The guitar had really suffered two assaults, the first a collision of some sorts and the second with the ham-handed drunk who had botched repairs and then abandoned it, the equivalent of a priceless Renaissance painting being given to a schoolkid with a box of crayons for restoration.

Then I noticed that during every one of our telephone conversations on these matters, John repeated a couple of lines that had first come up when I took him the guitar.

"The case. I can't believe you got the case too."

Vintage cases add value to a surviving instrument, and this particular model, just the case, sells for at least $500.

And then he'd say of the guitar itself. "You know everybody's going to want it."

This second statement is far more significant. By everyone, he meant the larger community of musicians spread around the northern Rockies, most of whom know each other. He meant my guitar was going to become something of a legend. And it finally occurred to me, he meant something more, that that vintage case held what would become a burden I would bear.

All this gave me some time to piece together what I could of the guitar's story, and I did, but not much, but some, and certainly not from Mike Williams. It was clear from the beginning he had already said what he wanted to say about this matter. Darryl Sonnenberg had indeed been a drunk and a musician. (The categories, you may have noticed, align with some frequency.) He had owned a small music shop in Helena. Toward the end, he would often be passed-out drunk in the shop by late morning, and kids who knew this would come into the shop and, depending on the state of his inebriation, either swap a cheap guitar's price tag onto an expensive one and pay for it, or, if he was further gone, simply take a guitar and walk out.

About this time, Sonnenberg had a wife, also a musician, but she became Mike Williams's wife, then later divorced Mike and married another guy. The transition from Sonnenberg to Mike was not altogether smooth, and there some accounts that include details of a drunken Sonnenberg raging. About this time, Mike got the guitar. Then Sonnenberg died.

Six months to the day, now April 2016, I'm on the phone to John.

"I was afraid it was you. Has it been six months already? It's not done yet. Maybe by Weiser."

Weiser is a fiddle festival held in Idaho every year in mid-June and had no relevance to my guitar whatsoever. John had just used it as a universally recognized marker of the passing of time, the way one would say "by the New Year."

Two days before Weiser, on a Friday afternoon at four, I answered a phone call from Missoula. "It's done." Friday afternoon. No notice. No warning. Dinner in the making. Plans for the night. I was in my Jeep and driving pell-mell for the Great Divide in fewer than three minutes.

###

It was there from the very first pluck of a string, but I know enough about guitars now to expect to learn very little from the very first pluck of a string, especially this one. The buildup had been epic, but even in less loaded circumstances, acoustic instruments only reveal themselves to the player over time, especially because over time the instrument teaches the player to reveal himself.

But it was there. Unmistakably, undeniably what I had first heard in the series of recordings, a calm, confident American voice. True to his word, John had done nothing to hide the wear and abuse, but everything to restore the integrity of the wood beneath. The spot where the Bondo had been, about the size and shape of a child's thumb, was a bit rough and fissured from the chemical abuse, but the Bondo was gone and the original wood gently coaxed back to its original position, not a blemish but a stigmata. Sliver by shard, all of the original wood had been restored, all except for one patch of new wood, in size and shape a fat toothpick. It's original sunburst face, now crazed and battered, seemed to glow again at its center. So I played it more then and more every day ever since.

"You know everyone's going to want it," John reminded me. And finally, having heard the guitar beneath by inadequate fingers, the depth of his meaning began to dawn on me. More so still as I was getting used to this guitar and showing it to a few friends. Conversations like this would pop up: "Have you shown it to Mike yet? Don't. I wouldn't." Each person who had offered this advice supported it with a different reason, but they seemed to converge on a single rationale. The guitar had come from a tough patch in Mike's life, and he wouldn't want to be reminded of it. That he'd let it go because he was old. That he would be jealous because John Joyner had effected its resurrection, and he had not. That he had been cheated, selling it for less than it was worth.

It slowly dawned that what they were telling me was that I had no right to this instrument, a conclusion supported by what I was hearing in the guitar, depth, wisdom, nuance, power, articulation. In every way it was better than I was. I was beginning to feel a bit like Tom Cruise's character in Stanley Kubrick's last film, *Eyes Wide Shut*, that I had somehow stumbled onto a secret password that gave me undeserved entree to a mansion load of statuesque naked women with prominent cheekbones joyously copulating with masked strangers. I was an imposter and would be soon enough be unmasked and ejected.

The guitar, it slowly occurred to me, was a living breathing example of what among cognoscenti is called a "player's guitar." This term is thrown about on eBay, usually meaning a basket case or a mess that collectors don't want but players can afford. There's some truth to this, especially that collectors don't want it, thereby suppressing the price, but the real player guitars are treasured not so much in spite of collectors' lack of interest but because of it. A reverse snobbery is in play, and it extends beyond the basket cases.

Real players' guitars never see eBay or a dealer's website or even a display case. They get traded in the underground, quietly, unseen, never so much as a hint they exist to anyone who has not been told the password to the mansion. There is a cabal that ensures that some guitars wind up in gifted, practiced hands and not hanging on the wall of a Silicon Valley office. I have been around guitars and known guitar people a long time yet for decades never realized this underworld existed, but I began to suspect so by what was missing, what I was not seeing. And then one day at a show I watched it happen, a case off in the corner of a trader's booth, and I knew his inventory and that it was definitely not therein listed. The case sat unopened, hidden and unmentioned until the dealer picked it up, slipped into the adjacent dark hallway without a word, out of sight and in the shadows. Then a guy showed up to meet him—T-shirt, jeans, running shoes, bad haircut like the rest of us—opened the case, looked, grinned broadly, counted off a stack of hundred-dollar bills, then walked away with a Gibson much like mine.

That dealer could have gotten well more than $10,000 for that guitar; I know what it was. He didn't. Sold it for less to get it into the hands of a gifted player. This is another aspect of the same ethic that drove John Joyner to remake my guitar the way he did, all battered and beautiful, but there is a flip side to this ethic. Players are resentful, often openly, bluntly and vocally of imposters, anyone who gets one of these guitars but doesn't play well enough to deserve it. Taking to the stage with a beat-up guitar simply for effect is regarded much like painting someone else's wrinkles on your face so you'll be taken for wise. Of course, it's true that anyone who plays a vintage instrument is masquerading in wrinkles that are not one's own, but at some point one earns them. Some players are donning a mask not to hide but to venerate all that has come before. Anthropologists tell us carved wooden masks appeared together with bone flutes at the very beginning, at the convergence of music, dance, ceremony, and veneration. Masks, music, and veneration of tradition have run together ever since.

People who are judged as poseurs or imposters by the inner circle usually don't have to surmise. Some of the chosen and anointed are sufficiently and willingly vicious enough to level the charge straight to the imposter's face. A favored tactic is humiliation in public performance, during a jam session or class. The inquisitor will simply set off on a tune or progression that leads the imposter to a musical cliff then pushes him off, searing humiliation one might recover from but never will forget.

I'd had the guitar for a few weeks and decided—or maybe not decided but had let negligence plot a safe course—that I could indeed avoid showing that guitar to Mike, that my friends had given me sound advice. I could in fact hide it away in my house, play alone for hours, which is mostly what I do anyway. Often I tell myself that this music, my music, is a meditation, and need not ever be heard. And so it sits in safe solitude a few feet away. It has already passed the crucial test. I can find myself lost and listless on an empty afternoon wondering if I have lived long enough. Always dangerous to pick up a guitar at a moment like this; depression can horribly warp anything you might play to noise, can weigh on your fingers like your mind already is and sink you deeper into the gloom. Especially this guitar almost killed by a drunk. My own regrets and recrimination for the years I have lost travel in this same territory. Yet on these days I find something in this guitar that lifts the weight. Always. Can't tell you what this is worth on the vintage market. Nor will I ever know.

I ran into Mike on line at the grocery store. "I hear you got that guitar back from Joyner," he says.

Musicians inhabit a tight little world, and nothing remains secret for long.

"I did. He did a good job. Wanna see it?"

"Sure. Bring it by."

So I did a couple of days later, a June afternoon, and he was in his garden. We adjourned to the shack and opened the case.

Mike took it and gave it a once over.

"That Joyner's some kind of a magician. Good job."

"Yeah. Really good."

"He must think I am crazy for selling it to you for $100."

"Yeah. He thinks you're crazy."

Mike laughed. Went on playing some chords. Then I knew: It wasn't about money. Mike sold me the guitar because he wanted me to have it. He was my teacher.

"You know now I am forever in your debt."

A grin and more chords.

"This is really good," he says.

"Yeah. Really good."

Then we spoke of the weather and its salubrious effect on his strawberries.

6

IN YOUR EAR

For many years it was my habit to begin my public performances with "Cocaine Blues." I like the song, always have. It has grit, history, relevance and humor. It uses a fallible narrator, as any drug tale should ("Cocaine's for horses, it's not for men, they say it's gonna kill me, they don't say when"), and a storyline that manages to reveal the contagion of the narrator's troubles. The opening verse I learned:

> Yonder come my baby, she is dressed in red,
> Got a big shotgun, gonna kill me dead.

He doesn't say why she is so murderous, but probably doesn't have to. Then a closing verse that circles back just as these matters usually do in the narrator's time and in ours:

> Yonder comes my baby she is dressed in black
> I believe in my soul she's gonna take me back

And you know she will. It's an old story, but then it's an old song.

"Cocaine Blues" is largely associated with the druggy days of the '60s when there was a bloom of commercial recordings of it: Dylan, Dave Van Ronk, Jackson Browne, David Bromberg, Ramblin' Jack Elliott, the Byrds, and Johnny Cash. All these guys probably picked it up in one way or another from the Reverend Gary Davis. One need not know this source to catch a whiff of it in those derivative versions, the eccentric little raggy lope.

Davis didn't write the song. We know this because he said so, and we know this because good songs are not really written; they evolve. Davis said he learned it in 1904. There are separate threads and strands of it that don't go through Davis, different titles even. John Lomax, the musicologist, collected it in the early twentieth century in both New York City and Texas as "Honey, Take a Whiff on Me." Then there are "Coco Blues," "Tell It to Me," and "Take a Drink on Me." None of these is wholly separate. Same genetics.

Nonetheless, the lineage makes it clear that the song's heyday in those addled mid-twentieth-century drug years wasn't much more than a blip in a more significant etymology. As long as I thought it was set in the '60s, it was just another song, but what so thoroughly embedded it my memory was finally understanding that it arose in the sharecropper South late in the nineteenth century when bosses pushed cocaine on fieldworkers to keep them working faster. Its popularity grew after World War I when soldiers returned to the fields having acquired drug habits.

Nothing new about this. To this day, one of the first fiddle tunes a student learns is "Soldier's Joy," which probably predates the Civil War, but probably under a different name. "Soldiers' joy" was then the slang term for morphine, a popular addiction after the Civil War.

I can't sing "Cocaine Blues" without descending into this string of associations, but it's not why I open with it. My habit has a lot more to do with the basic mechanics of memory. I do so because I am terrified whenever I start singing and playing in public. I do not mean nervous or anxious; I mean terrified to the point of dissociation, the technical term for a symptom of pathological performance anxiety. It can crop up for other people in demanding moments like public speaking, taking a test, delivering lines in a play, or having sex. (My case could be worse.) The indicator that the problem has moved beyond simple anxiety is dissociation, a set of perceptions I know well, that my fingers are not my own, someone else's, made of rubber, incapable of fretting guitar strings. I can't breathe, let alone sing, and, if I do manage a verse, I hear a stranger's voice, distant, winding down a long and lonely steel tunnel from miles away. The lyrics are gibberish. There is the perceptible sense that I have left my body.

I open with "Cocaine Blues" for the simple and practical reason that one day I learned I could. I had crashed and burned with this tune before, but eventually I discovered I could perform this song and this song alone without falling to pieces. I came to believe there was something about "Cocaine Blues" that allowed me to throttle the terrorist in my brain, something in the way I had learned it.

There are disadvantages to having a famous musician as a teacher, especially if the student has performance anxiety. The set-up is that periodically the student gets to sit down one-on-one, instrument in hand and stumble through a piece he has learned, the whole point being to demonstrate to a highly skilled and highly regarded performer the student's shaky mastery of elementary material. New to the banjo, I was learning simple pieces, tunes I could easily master in private, yet when it came time to deliver, to sit and play for Adam Hurt, everything fell apart.

Even more than a normal audience, Adam is massively intimidating, and not because of his behavior in our lessons. Generally speaking, one of the more common disadvantages of having a famous musician as a teacher is that often they are not very good teachers and often not particularly easy to get along with: arrogant pricks. Not Adam. He's a nice guy, engaged, polite nearly to a fault, and considerate, but beyond the personal traits, he is the rare breed: a gifted musician who also happens to be an extraordinarily competent teacher.

He is naturally analytical, grasps the deep logic of music, and is able to pull students into better playing by applying that analysis case by case. Many musicians know music so well they forget how they learned it, but Adam knows both music and the pathway to it. He doesn't prescribe an outline of steps on that path so much as he sets students up for their own meanders, exploration, and discovery. I had been lucky enough to sign up for a class or two of his in banjo camps where a student typically is exposed to a half dozen or so teachers in the course of a week. All of these people were good at what they did, but Adam had another level of command. He mentioned in one of these camp classes that he taught students individually by Skype, so I applied, and we began to work together.

Hurt is an enigmatic figure in the tight little world of traditional old-time music. He is not a hillbilly but grew up in Minneapolis, a genuine child prodigy who started by playing piano. His parents are classical musicians, but when his fourth-grade teacher brought a banjo and a mandolin to class, Adam got hooked on banjo, first bluegrass, but then he was drawn to the ancient eccentric style of playing brought to this continent from Africa by slaves. He was a virtuoso by the time he was a teenager. Now in his forties, he lives in Appalachia but still a less-than-traditional figure, tall, gangly, with spiked hair, bejeweled purple shoes, often a fat silver ring clamped to the backside of one ear's auricle, well-spoken, polite, and precise.

His music is no less enigmatic. Hurt's resume seems a set-up for innovator, and he is, but not in the way the term is usually used. There are performers who deploy traditional instruments like clawhammer banjo in new directions, from adaptations of Bach partitas to Dylan covers. This is not Hurt. The first impression on listening to one of his recordings is indeed of innovation, but he is instead delving deeply into traditional songs and sources. One of his best CDs (*Earth Tones*) is performed solely on a fretless banjo made with a gourd and tacked-on skin head, a copy of slave instruments of centuries ago. All of his recordings are elegant, ethereal, and rhythmic, nearly mystical. He has a reputation for precise execution of melody, and it is deserved, but he frames his music in a solid harmonic and rhythmic superstructure that is at once subtle and potent.

He's not a maverick but is engaged with and respects the larger cohort of old-time music players. I've watched him in jam sessions with some of the greats and the famous, and he settles in among them, just another one of the parts producing the whole greater than their sum. Yet he is unique, like John Hartford, Norman Blake, or Doc Watson, a player that comes along rarely but leaves a mark on everything that follows. Yes, it is indeed intimidating to sit before him, banjo in hand.

Through maybe six or so monthly lessons, my problem persisted. I would work a piece to death in practice, having it down cold, then would fall apart in the lesson, playing it then with my rubber fingers that belonged to someone else at maybe 40 percent of my ability. Adam and I talked about this, took it on directly. It was not a unique problem. He had other students who had performance anxiety much worse than mine, unable to play at all in lessons and would instead submit recordings to him. Would I like to try this? No, I would not. What was the point? Music is not to be emailed to people as recordings; it is to be performed, delivered in performance, and if I could not clear this hurdle, then how could I begin to call myself a musician? No, we'd tough this out, punch through, and for months I did, maybe even got a bit better, from, say, 60 to 65 percent of my ability. I was flailing.

Nonetheless, a separate idea already had me headed in the right direction, and it was not my doing but Adam's. From the beginning, Adam sets a course with his students not only designed to teach them more music but also to change the way in which they learn music. He had done so with me. This approach is not his alone but axiomatic among traditional musicians. The rule is—and it is a rule that almost all students and some teachers honor mostly in the breach—one learns this music by ear. This idea defines a longstanding divide in traditional music and not just traditional music, not just music, but in civilization itself and increasingly everything civilization regards as proper knowledge. In traditional banjo music the conflict dates to the Civil War and the subtext was decidedly racist and elitist.

This book has already delved into the importance of the Dobson family in the history of the banjo, and in fact the lineage has already slipped unmentioned into this conversation. Adam Hurt's recording banjo is an original, vintage Henry Dobson Silver Bell from the 1880s, the pinnacle of the company's manufacture. George Dobson, Henry's brother, also sold banjos branded with his name, but he was primarily a teacher, and in the 1870s he began marketing a "Simplified Method" of banjo instruction he claimed to have invented in a flash of inspiration. He may have believed this, because it's an obvious trick. Dobson's marketing aside, the system is generally known as tablature, or tab for short, and forms of it were originally developed for lute players in Europe hundreds of years before the Dobson family came along. Instead of standard music notation, the system encodes music by writing it on staff lines that correspond to the five strings of the banjo. Instead of standard notes, the staff is occupied by open circles or numbers indicating strings that should be struck and where they should be fretted.

Dobson's impetus was not so much musical as it was commercial and social. His method was simple and allowed the printed page to substitute for hiring a music teacher, learning a song by ear from a person. Dobson touted it as a way one might learn music by mail, which was in keeping with the popularity of amateur musicians throughout the nineteenth century. He was democratizing music in democratic America. Before recordings, sales of sheet music, folios, and instruction books were a major cash cow of the business, creating a clamor for ever-simpler tunes accessible to unsophisticated players, and in no way was this limited to the banjo. About the same time, shape note singing, a simplified form of notation for choral music, arose. The method swept the nation's rural, fundamentalist churches and is still practiced in the South. All of this was populism, and the political implications were made explicit in the banjo world.

Samuel Swain Stewart, Dobson's main competitor in the banjo business, immediately saw the simplified method as seditious, launching a decades-long series of published diatribes against it. Stewart was a believer instead in standard music notation, lines notes and staffs, the system we're referring today when we say someone "reads music." Forms of music notation date back thousands of years to the beginning of writing itself, some as old as four thousand years in Mesopotamia, Greece and the Byzantine Empire. The system we know today, however, really became standardized in Europe in the Middle Ages. A major force for its propagation then parallels nicely Stewart's advocacy for it in nineteenth-century America. The Catholic Church adopted notation as a way of standardizing liturgical chanting, to ensure that everyone under the Church's thumb chanted the same chant, that everyone was literally on the same page. Conformity is civilization's first imperative.

This sort of Catholicism was not far from what was on Stewart's mind when his turn came. He attacked Dobson's method by summoning Edgar Allan Poe's raven as analogy, saying this method announces: I will "haunt you until I blacken your very existence." For good measure, he threw in a comparison to opium addiction in its deleterious effects. In a later publication he suggested Dobson's democratic banjo tablature was the product of a "set of unscrupulous individuals, possessing a very limited knowledge of music and very little love for science and the art—and therefore being ignorant and also disinclined to labor and effort." Lazy, unschooled, drug-addicted, and black. Nineteenth-century dog whistles didn't need to be subtle.

As odd as it sounds considering that the topic here was the banjo, Stewart was an elitist. Despite their differences, however, both Stewart and Dobson were meaning to civilize the banjo, and their immediate task in this was to rescue it from its primitive roots. The proximate threat to the instrument's civility then were the minstrels in blackface, the people who had learned the banjo by ear, by listening to slaves. The ultimate threat was Africa itself, the primitive. Both Stewart and Dobson specifically urged students to adopt a method of playing we refer to today as "up-picking" derived from European techniques for playing classical guitar. Both refused to teach the original African method that survives today as clawhammer banjo, the style that Adam Hurt plays, and in his hands modern-day reviewers called it "elegant."

Both Dobson and Stewart favored different forms of the same thing, of literary, printed music. Dobson was just a bit more downmarket. Nonetheless, he turned out to be on the winning side of the battle. Almost all guitar players except for classical players and certainly all banjo players today do not use standard music notation, Stewart's warnings notwithstanding. Those who rely on printed music as opposed to learning strictly by ear use tablature. The system is especially appropriate for stringed instruments, because unlike the case with say a piano or saxophone, the same note can exist on several different strings at different positions along the neck. Standard musical notation only specifies the pitch to be played but doesn't say which of the several options works best. Tablature does. Tablature also survives for some of the same reasons Dobson favored. Today's amateur musicians rely on a number of publishers of printed tablature and on swapping tabs on the internet.

Still, the subtext of especially S.S. Stewart's fulminations remain relevant. This is not just about music. Indeed one of the markers for the advent of civilization itself was the beginning of writing, the ability to represent language with symbols. The basis of the process is abstraction, a mental bait and switch that suggests that the word "chair" can stand in for the real thing. This trick, of course, gave humanity all sorts of new abilities: to record, account, to communicate across time, to communicate beyond an immediate audience, to regiment, and to write and sell books, but there's a cost. Ultimately, abstraction has stripped our world of its essence and has redrawn and re-presented it to us as crayoned stick figures. Virtual reality is not a modern disease; we were infected with it when writing began. The epidemic took some time to incubate properly.

A letter, no matter how moving or well-written, is not the equal of conversation, with its ability to communicate tone, tenor, and nuance through subtle and complex cues: rise and fall of the voice, eye movement, a twitch in the corner of the eye and a glance to the distance. And a text message? Forget about it.

The industrialization of education, of learning, in many ways best summarizes this trend, that the process is no longer learning or education but distillation of knowledge to bullet points, boxes to be checked, data delivered. Lives and wisdom stand reduced to checklists, and performance means a successful regurgitation of the list. This is how we are taught, and the real value of music is that it refuses to tolerate this trivialization, at least for long.

The problem with modern education and our idea of learning is that it almost completely discounts and ignores our most powerful mode of learning. We think of learning as mastering facts and information and using those in abstract reasoning to effect solutions and create ideas. Nothing wrong with this. This indeed is learning and always will be important to our navigation of the world, especially this world, but it ignores that some of the more difficult and complex tasks we must master don't come to our command this way.

The evidence for this is obviously at play in a miracle that we have all seen, the ability of an infant to return a smile in the first two months of living. Smiles are not hardwired, not inherent in an infant's brain. Mimicry is. The human infant—not just human for that matter—comes ready-made to mimic facial expressions, vocal noises, motions, all of them complex, without anyone walking her through the step-by-step instructions necessary to manipulate facial muscles and form that smile. Of course not. No language yet. No way for anyone to walk her through the steps. No brain really; the prefrontal cortex, the part of the brain we address when we believe we are teaching, is not even yet formed in this infant, but the smile nonetheless appears, and it is learned. This same infant will use mimicry to acquire a daunting list of complex skills, including language, all before the brain develops its reasoning capacity, effortlessly, without drills, textbooks, or tests, and then she will be sent to a university where mimicry is devalued and the inherent skill to learn will atrophy.

One can see this great power at work in a delightful display common among adolescent girls, that a new dance craze, often something they have seen on television, elaborately choreographed, staged, and rehearsed, will infect a group, and they teach themselves a convincing version of it without choreographer, rehearsal or staging. They just do it. This is mimicry. If adults were told to accomplish this same thing, especially male adults, they'd want the whole business broken down and abstracted, this step then that, turn here, hop after four beats. They might even manage to memorize these instructions, the map of the dance. Might even learn the routine, but they will never look as engaged or as charming and as natural in the flow as did these adolescent girls who just saw it done, then did it.

Mimicry works by allowing our brains to become someone else, by crossing the solipsistic divide. The drivers of mimicry in our brains are exceedingly complex and in fact demand a great deal of neural power, just power we are not really aware of, unconscious. Many of the useful things our brains do—as much as 90 percent—are unconscious, not dependent at all on the prefrontal cortex, that bit of forebrain that is the target of all education.

Mimicry runs on a set of neurons highly developed in the human brain, mirror neurons. The term stems from a unique phenomenon present in other animals as well, that when a monkey eats a peanut, its brain activates a series of neurons associated with its body going through those motions, moving arms and hands to pick up peanut, to mouth, chew, swallow, feel pleasure. If another monkey watches its colleague in this process, its brain lights up in exactly the same way and same places as the monkey doing the actual eating, as if it were going through the same experience, a reflection, a mirror. This is the neural infrastructure of empathy, the process of putting ourselves in the experience of someone else, the force that allows humanity to exist. This is the force that atrophies when we live in a world abstracted to text messages and virtual relationships. The very odd thing about our discounting and degrading empathy is it drives an effortless and powerful mode of learning.

Every musician knows this, especially those of us who learn as adults. We have all encountered the brilliant parking lot picker or virtuoso—and this is true across forms of music, from country to classical. The common story of each of these virtuosos is they began playing as children, but the more common story is that much of their learning was informal. A guitar wound up in her hands when she was twelve and then hours sequestered away in the basement, simply finding notes, hear a melody line, find the same notes on the neck of that guitar, now an octave higher, now in a different key, now some chords that seem to fit. Listen then play. Monkey see, monkey do. Why not? Nobody told her she couldn't.

Yet it seems very odd that most of us find this odd, given that most of us can and do learn exactly this way with the oldest and most common way of making music. We can hear a simple melody and sing it, even in the key we hear. Nobody told us what the notes were, or how to make the complex vocal cord manipulations that allow us to hit those notes of the melody. We just do it. Virtually all great musicians have precisely this facility with their instruments. They get it in exactly the same way they learned to speak their native language. They just did it.

###

Adam was adamant from day one, our first lesson. We would, he said, be learning by ear, from now on and forever more, a mode I had avoided for years, although I knew better. I knew all the great musicians I admired and emulated learned by ear. I play blues. Many of my guitar heroes were illiterate or blind. Like most players who learn as adults, however, we can't shake the deep prejudice of civilization pounded into us by formal education. Information is gleaned from the printed page, good hard dependable information, I thought. I had always been reluctant to feel my way in the squishy world of my own unreliable perceptions. What if I heard it wrong and played it wrong? I knew what: ridicule and embarrassment. So for thirty years I had learned almost every song I know, both guitar and banjo from tablature. I knew full well those lines and dots could not capture the spirit of a song, but I had the outlines, and in time, with practice, a song might form, emerge magically.

Adam's method was analogous to learning to ride a bike with training wheels. He would play a song at tempo and email me a recording of this so I could repeat the listening process, but then he would repeat the song very slowly, phrase by phrase, then deliver spoken instructions about what my fingers should be doing. He recorded this also. This step was the training wheels. What he was really doing was giving me straightforward directions that amounted to verbal tablature. As with tablature, I could be confident in each step along the way and could memorize the steps then link them into a song. I took no notes. Nothing was written down. Complete oral transmission. We were working this through on Skype, email, and iTunes, but the content was preliterate.

Understand that what is being communicated between student and teacher is enormously complicated. A typical traditional banjo tune is thirty-two measures long, but there is repetition, so there are really sixteen or fewer measures of unique content. Still, a moderate pace for a traditional tune is about 140 beats per minute, so each beat covers less than a half second. In that space of time there is usually at least one note, but more often as many as three to be executed on separate strings with separate fingers, fretted or not fretted. That is, in the space of less than a minute that it takes to play through a typical tune once, the player will need to execute maybe three hundred separate steps. If this was really about memorization, then it would be analogous to memorizing a sequence of three hundred digits, then reciting the sequence again and again for fun and entertainment, rapidly and without mistakes. Do it all again next lesson. Keep a hundred (knowing a hundred tunes is a modest goal for a traditional picker) or so of these sequences in your head under separate and vague titles ready to recall on demand.

More vexingly still, the notes are not always the result of the right hand sounding a string and the left fretting. Both banjo and guitar rely on a series of moves called pull-offs and hammer-ons, where the left hand is often striking or changing the note on the offbeat. Pull-offs are especially demanding. To sound make them sound right, the left-hand finger must execute with just the right force, touch and angle to produce a clean note. What sounds like a simple tune is really the result of a series of instructions that would tax the memory of a computer. Just the straightforward instructions, as in dance, put this foot there then. And as with dance, simply following these instructions, even correctly, as a computer no doubt could, still fails to produce music. Otherwise, computers would make music. The instructions must be woven together with flow, form, and finesse.

Adam's method worked. Sort of. I was learning songs from him every bit as well as I could from tablature, could memorize the instructions in the matter of an hour's practice (much faster than using printed tablature) then set about trying to pound the result into something resembling music. Usually we scheduled lessons about once a month, so this gave me plenty of time for pounding, and for six months or so, the process was the same, that the deadline of lesson time would approach, and I would begin to feel good about my command of the piece, that this time I would clear the hurdle, that this time I would sit before my computer screen in virtual contact with Adam, sit and deliver, perform, play to demonstrate my swelling abilities, and they were swelling. In private. I knew that, reveled. Then the lesson would come. I would stare straight at Adam staring at me and then would crash and burn, stumble, founder, and mutilate material I knew I could play, had played perfectly, five minutes before. As I said, there is a downside to having a famous musician for a teacher. I could not overcome my intimidation. Performance anxiety emerged stubbornly, maddeningly, embarrassingly, month on month. So I couldn't get my gold star from teacher and move on. We talked about it, acknowledged it, and I settled in, hoping it would evaporate in time. It didn't, but then "Shady Grove" came along.

One of the problems was that Adam is an especially nice guy, so I was always entertaining thoughts that he was telling me I was doing okay just to be polite, that he really believed me an unteachable dolt and was stringing me along until I figured this out for myself. His suggestion that I learn the tune "Shady Grove" was confirmation of my fears. "Shady Grove" is a simple, basic piece, a kids' tune really, so Adam's assignment was a bit like enrolling in a graduate seminar on James Joyce's work and being taken aside by the instructor and separately handed a couple of Harry Potter books.

The tune was a seminal part of the folk canon in the '60s, popularized by the recording made by Clarence Ashley and Doc Watson. Those of us who first heard it then cannot hear it today without hearing somewhere in the back of the brain Doc's warm baritone:

Wish I had a big white horse
and corn to feed him on
and Shady Grove to stay at home
and feed him when I'm gone.

This is not quite the version that figures now in the old-time music. In traditional mountain music, "Shady Grove" is a fiddle tune, almost never sung, but the connection is there. The melody Doc sang sits at the center of the banjo version Adam wanted me to learn. Easy enough. I already knew the melody, but when I hear "Shady Grove" I don't think so much of Doc as I do Tenley Stephens, the married name she had when I first met her.

In the early '80s, when I decided to learn guitar, I was more or less sentenced to live in a drab ag town in southern Idaho, Twin Falls, as a result of a day job as city editor of the newspaper there. Someone had told me about some local counterculture types, rare in this town, who had bought an old church and were turning it into a space for teaching and performing acoustic music, so I investigated and in the church found a woman a few years younger than I was: flashing golden eyes, warm, lovely, angular features, ready laugh, the singing voice and beaming smile of the queen of the rodeo. She taught guitar. Sure, I signed up, and she taught me "Shady Grove," first lesson, guitar 101. The melody lays out in a simple pattern over two chords, so it's as good a place as any to begin, and then we moved on. Tenley and I got to be friends, but I moved on from that too, a couple of years later, to a new job in Montana, a six-hour drive and a century or so distant from conservative, Mormon southern Idaho. We lost touch, but I did not forget her, prodded to warm memories every time someone played "Shady Grove."

A few years on, and I was attending a big, outdoor house party in Montana where there happened to be a band including a fiddler I knew, Ellie Nuno, a great talent, warm woman and valued member of the community of musicians in the Rockies. Standing next to Ellie, Martin guitar deployed, bird-toned vocals soaring, was Tenley. She had moved to Montana, my town, and we'd run into each other from time to time, here and there, nothing regular, and then one day I got a telephone call from her, cold, straight, and unsolicited.

"How come we're not better friends?" she challenged.

Not because I didn't want to be. Because I am socially inept, but in her case I vowed right there in that call to do whatever I could to overcome that deficiency, that we would become closer. Then time passed as it does, and I forgot about Tenley's overture. A couple of years later I was at Greg Boyd's guitar shop one day trying out a powerful new Collings guitar, and it seemed to fall naturally to the opening sequence of "Deep River Blues," another benchmark tune Doc Watson recorded. I was in fact playing Doc's version. Greg noted this and complimented me.

"Thanks. I learned it from Tenley a long time ago. Speaking of which, how is Tenley? Haven't seen her in a bit." One reason for stopping by Greg's shop was it was an efficient way to gather news on the network of friends. They all stopped by too.

"She's dead. Brain tumor."

Her diagnosis of terminal cancer roughly matched the timing of the out-of-the-blue call to me. How had I become so deeply encased in solipsism that my ears could not hear a dying woman's plea for friendship?

###

I decided a fresh approach was required for Adam Hurt's assignment of "Shady Grove." I began by realizing there is no such thing as an elementary song. How it could it be trivial? It endures.

My usual pattern was to struggle to memorize a string of notes I had read from a page. Adam had moved me beyond, but in reality I was simply memorizing a string of verbal instructions he had given me then struggling to string them together flawlessly in the hopes that music might eventually emerge. It occurred to me that I might reverse the process, to demand of each note, one by one, each in its initial rendering, a tone pure and simple that each on its own hung in the air as music. What this meant practically was demanding from each phrase, each very short collection of tones, some sort of emotional content. Music was not the end; it became the beginning.

The great guitarist Leo Kottke is fond of telling a story about his attempts to learn music, that he would approach a song and play its first note and would hear in that single note something unbearably lovely, and so he would not go on to learn the next note. He'd go back and play that single same note again and again. This fault of his is probably how he became a great musician. I started to play this way, listening to each phrase develop, and if it did not deliver immediate emotional content, then I stopped and played again, ever more slowly, governing myself with a metronome to play slowly and listen.

Then I began to hear distinct notes exert their unique organizing roles within phrases. The simple tonic note became my favorite, generally an open string, not hard to play and so never gets the attention it deserves when you are struggling with the notes that are difficult to execute. The tonic note is the root, the C note when playing in the key of C, for instance. It is home, resolution, the anchor, the relief that comes in music's recursive pattern of tension and release. I learned a way of striking it to make it ring like a temple bell and found this was a sonic reward, a bit of clarity and peace that would issue forth every few seconds, then a new phrase loaded with tension, a five chord, a flatted third, then ring the bell of calm.

Our culture has a truly vicious and destructive habit, that when people, young people try to make music by singing, the ridicule is directed at mistakes in pitch. We then begin to think that music is about pitch, as in perfect pitch, and so learning to sing and play music is a matter of reproducing pitch. Pitch in turn has a numerical value and so is quantifiable (and therefore printable), a matter of a little more or a little less. You try to hear the pitch, but this is not how musicians hear notes. I was struggling with this and trying to hear pitch for many years, failing, and came to regard it as a matter of inherent talent, a magic that was and would forever be beyond me. I would always need the instruction of the printed page. Try as I might, I could not reproduce notes, or so I thought.

But then one day I noticed something when I was restringing one of my guitars. My usual practice was to install new strings and crank them up to tension, then use an electronic tuner to bring them to pitch, but when I turned on the tuner, I found each string already in perfect tune, that unconsciously I had automatically hit each string's pitch, without thinking about it. Then did it again and again. When I consciously tried to repeat this trick, I failed. My conscious, logical brain sent me back to listening for pitch. Much of learning is packing things into your brain and much of learning is discovering how to make your brain get out of the way.

What a musician hears is not a numerical value of pitch but a unique character and color that each note has and that causes it to stand out. Descriptions of these musical perceptions are invariably synesthetic. These perceptions reveal the unquantifiable, ineffable nature of music that effects our unconscious knowledge of it.

In fact, I had been told exactly this idea many times through the years of learning music, or at least people had tried to teach me. I even believed I was learning by going through the motions, but it's like telling the guy learning to dance with those printed foot patterns on the floor to put some feeling into it. He'll go through the motions of not going through the motions but is still a klutz. Nonetheless, I eventually learned. Some things cannot be taught, but they can be learned.

Learning music as a memorized string of notes draws one's attention to the technically difficult passages, the cataracts embedded throughout that will require deft acrobatic fingering if one is to not crash on the rocks. I often think that the people who understand chaos best are rafters and kayakers who run white-water rapids. I am one of these people. The trick is to not wrap your raft on the rocks in rapids, and so beginners pay great attention to the rocks, and as a result founder. Successfully navigating the chaos requires a complicated series of definite, deft, and complicated paddle strokes properly executed in micro time under enormous pressure. If you panic here, you are no longer a boater; you are a swimmer in a fierce maelstrom. On the surface, it would seem the first order of business is to keep your head, but in reality, the requirement is that you lose it. You must function here without thinking, unconsciously. There is no time to think.

There is a mental trick for accomplishing this explicitly taught by white-water instructors. The trick is to not focus your attention on the rocks. Don't look at them. If you do, you will turn your body toward them and consequently turn your boat toward them. You will founder. Focus instead on the clean, clear line of water that is the course of the river. Don't focus on what you mean to avoid, but on where you want to go. This is not a squishy mystic's aphorism; it is a hard lesson taught by the basic mechanics of our bodies and brains.

Neuroscientists have long recognized that our brains process music in a completely separate way from how we process other information, at least eventually. There is, for instance, the recognized phenomenon of general memory loss of all information except music. That is—and the cases are well documented—many victims of Alzheimer's disease who are musicians can still recall their music, note for note, even lyrics. People who can no longer speak a coherent sentence can still sing long strings of lyrics. The phenomenon and other findings have led to a conclusion that the brain has a separate melody memory, a separate location where it stores music.

When we first learn a song, especially if we do so from an abstraction, from notation or tablature, then we gather it as a series of commands memorized like all other abstractions in the prefrontal cortex of the brain. Over time, though, as the song begins to form as a song and not a collection of commands, those memories physically migrate to the more primitive section of our brain.

The prefrontal cortex is shaky ground, notoriously subject to breaking down under attack, shutting down in times of panic. Memories there are fragile and fly apart, not only with Alzheimer's but also shattered by white-water rapids, audiences, and famous teachers. Memories stored in our primitive brains are less fragile. Learning songs as an abstraction strips them of their emotional content, and this is the content that speaks to the primitive brain. Learning by ear is a way of transcending abstraction and letting the emotional content begin to speak and to settle quickly to its cranial sanctuary.

I was always able to play "Cocaine Blues" despite performance anxiety, because I had played it for a very long time, and so over that time it gradually emerged from the notes on the printed page as I had racked them up in my logical memory and made the move to my reptilian brain. Learning by ear is not magic, but it makes the process a lot faster.

It finally occurred to me that my struggle with performance anxiety was not about eliminating anxiety. Anxiety ebbs and flows in lives, part of what keeps us alive. It was about eliminating the concept of performance. Believing that music exists for performance to bolster and embellish our egos with gold stars from teachers misses the point. A song is not a box to be checked, a sequence of notes to be memorized and regurgitated. It is to be lived and relived.

I have come to best understand my profound compatibility with my wife through the experience of wilderness. Throughout our marriage, wild places have been our most reliable touchstone, so we go there often as we can, weeks-long walks in un-roaded mountains. All we need are backpacks and boots and each other. Oddly, though, this is where one of our biggest disagreements comes into play, so much so that we no longer disagree. Instead, she does it her way, and I do it mine. The bone of contention is the reliance on maps. When there is a question about being lost, a moment of anxiety, she pulls out a map. My inclination then is to put it away. We go our separate ways on this because we are both right.

I know full well this tiff of ours is a variation on the clichéd inter-spousal agon over his refusal to ask directions, but there is rather more at stake in this situation than in finding the nearest Starbucks or antique mall. One can get lost in wilderness, and doing so has consequences beyond being a few minutes late for the restaurant reservation: a night sleeping on a rock face stuck atop a cliff, no water for an afternoon, an extra day's hike when the food has run out. To prevent against such consequences, she uses a map. To prevent against these consequences, I do exactly the opposite. She's right as often as I am, but if the subject comes up (it almost never does anymore, we just do what we do) I remind her of when we first met. Early on in our relationship, all those years ago, we took a trip so I could meet her family on the East Coast. We landed at a big airport and on the ride to her house, a cloudy day, I asked her: Which way is east? We were in her neighborhood, her childhood home, just outside of Washington DC, yet she did not know. Couldn't tell me. She was raised in the suburbs, and I was not.

I put the maps away to orient (literally the word means to find the east) myself, because after years of mountain life, one learns to read the terrain, understand that the run of a ridge defines a water course, and lays out on the skyline a parallel restatement of the unseen land and river below. How the trees bend, which species, sound of water, the smell of afternoon thermals, all serve in orientation and provide a more complete picture than the stick drawings, the abstractions of a map. You don't need a map if you have a body and a full set of senses to enliven it with perception.

Yet the use of the map, I have recently learned, is a rather nice diagnostic. In recent years, as she has become more successful at what she does, my wife has been pulled into increasingly demanding jobs, long hours, high stakes, managing an ever-wider array of people and problems. She's good at it, and I am proud of her, but it takes its toll. She constantly carries two phones and is often simultaneously talking on one and texting on another. It's not behavior she would choose, but her work demands it. Over time she has become the sort who checks the weather by reaching for her phone instead of looking at the sky. This is the disease of our time, epidemic and viciously contagious.

On our backpacking trips, I can tell when her week before has been demanding and anxiety high: she pulls the map out of her pack about twice as often as usual. Mostly she's right, though; this prevents us from getting lost, but lately I find I don't mind getting lost, because it's how I find my place in the world. Information is rightly viewed as the path to knowledge, but I am beginning to understand that information is also a barrier to knowledge.

7

PRACTICE

My high school band teacher (saxophone, marching band, concert band, I was merely adequate) was an affable guy, Archie Best, bald with Bozo-the-Clown frizz, favored tweed jackets, smoked a pipe, and liked old, bad jokes. He needed his sense humor to herd a few dozen adolescent cats, not just in a general direction, but in formation, in step, in tune and on time. One joke he liked a lot—it was old even then—he told often but nonetheless would collapse into rubber-faced laughter every time he did. It was my first hint that enduring jokes are the equivalent of Buddhist koans. You've heard it. A lost tourist stops a cop on the streets of Manhattan to ask, "How do I get to Carnegie Hall?" Says the cop, "Practice, man, practice."

Old joke. Really older than you think. Properly considered, its thesis was central to Chinese Taoist thought as it evolved there in the Warring States period in China 2,500 years ago. Taoism, not really a religion but a loose set of writers who shared some ideas, offers directions for finding the way, the heavenly way, and toward that end gave us the butcher Ding, cleaver in hand, ready to slay an ox. Ding was not just any hacker, but the butcher summoned periodically to dismember sacrificial oxen during full-dress communal ceremonies. Ding was the go-to guy because he was good at it. He not only could kill an ox, he could dismember it with grace and poise:

> At every touch of his hand every bending of his shoulder, every step
> of his feet, every thrust of his knee—swish, swoosh! He guided

his blade along with a whoosh, and all was in perfect tune: one moment as if he were joining in the Dance of the Mulberry Grove, another as if he were performing in the Jingshou Symphony (quoted in Slingerland 2014, 19).

The tipoff to a subtext here is the comparison to dance and music. For the ancient Chinese philosophers, these elegant and refined activities served as a benchmark for butchering, a practical, mundane, manual skill, but not wholly manual. The task of disassembling a huge ox is complicated and depends on a thorough knowledge of the structure of the beast, and Ding appears to perform the task without effort. In the ancient texts, Ding himself is called upon to explain his performance:

> When I first began cutting up oxen, all I could see was the ox itself. After three years, I no longer saw the ox as a whole. And now—now I meet it with my spirit and don't look with my eyes. My senses and conscious awareness have shut down and my spiritual desires take me away. I follow the Heavenly pattern of the ox, thrusting into the big hollows, guiding the knife through the big openings, and adapting my motions to the fixed structure of the ox. In this way, I never touch the smallest ligament or tendon, much less a main joint. . . . A skilled butcher has to change his cleaver once a year, because he cuts; an ordinary butcher has to change his cleaver once a month, because he hacks. As for me, I have been using this particular cleaver for nineteen years now, and have cut up thousands of oxen with it, and yet its edge is still as sharp as when it first came off the whetstone (ibid., 20).

Yes, the way to learn to cut up an ox is precisely the same as the pathway to Carnegie Hall. Ding is clear on this, but he's telling us a great deal more.

This account comes from a present-day book by Edward Slingerland, who has retranslated some of the ancient Chinese texts. Slingerland studies Chinese thought, comparative religion and cognitive science, brain science, how we learn. In his book *Trying Not to Try: The Art and Science of Spontaneity*, he explains that he arrived at his unusual combination of disciplines as a result of understanding recent advances in cognitive science. Neuroscientists are beginning to piece together a working outline of our brains to better understand the processes by which we learn, and many of these new findings contradict or undermine Western philosophy's basic assumptions. Eastern philosophy, however, especially Chinese traditions, seemed much closer to the mark, better at grasping the actual workings of our brains as modern science understands them. Slingerland writes:

> A small but growing number of psychologically attuned philosophers now recognize that the early Chinese tradition, with its embodied model of the self, offers an important corrective to the tendency of modern Western philosophy to focus on conscious thought, rationality, and willpower. For instance, whole recent Western thought has emphasized the importance of abstract, representational knowledge—that is information about the world like the fact that Rome is the capital of Italy or that $E = mc^2$—early Chinese thought emphasized what we call *know-how*: the practical, tacit, and often unformulizable ability to *do* something well (ibid., 13, emphasis in the original)

Our brains do most of what they do, most of what gets us through our lives, without our conscious participation. This goes well beyond involuntary controls like pulse rate and breathing. The exceedingly complicated tasks of locomotion—walking, running—on through emotion and further on through to major leaps of logic we call inspiration or intuition or epiphany. All these happen without much conscious oversight. Further, much of our ability to perform well in these matters requires that we get our consciousness out of the way. If we think about it, we fail.

This idea was explicit in Taoist and Confucian religious practice and captured in a central tenet of Taoism with the term *wu-wei*, which translates as "no trying" or "no doing." "In fact, it refers to the dynamic, effortless, and unselfconscious state of mind of a person who is optimally active and effective," Slingerland writes. "Evolution has offloaded the vast bulk of our everyday decision-making and judgment formation onto our automatic hot unconscious system because in most situations it is fast, computationally frugal and reliable."

The word "Tao," the root of Taoism, is generally understood and translated as "the way," but already we have lost our way in stating it so directly as a word. Taoism is explicit about this, that there is no word for the Tao, and if someone offers a word for the Tao then the Tao would not be the Tao. It is ineffable, not capable of being captured in abstraction, so it cannot be taught; it must be learned. The founding Taoist philosopher is usually identified as Laozi, who may not have existed, may simply be legend. Still, he is credited with this: "The Way that can be spoken of is not the enduring Way. The name that can be named is not the enduring name."

Those of us with Western-trained minds easily consign ideas like this to the mist of mysticism, but recall that Ding was dismembering an actual boned and blooded ox, and he was doing so by grasping the Tao, the point of the story. He had found the way and by flowing with it was rendering a difficult, practical, blood-and-flesh task effortless. Nonetheless, Taoism is not only about hard realities. It is a realization that there are no hard realities or that reality is incomprehensible. This is more or less what the ancients were teaching, but we need not turn to inscrutable Chinese mystics to make our own grasp on reality wobble a bit. Hardcore, rationalist, peer-reviewed Western scientists can handle the assignment just fine.

For more than a hundred years now, since about the time Orville Gibson was whittling out his first guitars, Albert Einstein was gluing together a General Theory of Relatively that told us that space and time, the horizon line of the east, and the rhythm that sets the sun to rising, watches to ticking, and feet to tapping are themselves warped and bent like pretzels. This is old news, antique as the gramophone, and still most of us can't muster a sense of reality that matches science's understanding of the nature of the universe. Furthermore, Einstein himself, the man who warped the universe, could never really come to grips with what the subsequent logical leap: the principles of quantum mechanics deduced by his own colleagues, Niels Bohr and Werner Heisenberg, the latter surname now inextricably linked to uncertainty, as well it should be. In his world, electrons, the basic building blocks of all things that exist, do not really exist, or don't always exist, are never in a given place, can't be measured, and oscillate between reality and unreality. This too is old news. The cutting edge is called "loop quantum gravity," an attempt to bridge the mind-numbing complexities of all of Einstein's relativity and quantum mechanics. Physicists still regard both as valid (despite the contradictions), and most of us regard both as incomprehensible, no matter how real.

In a short series of essays designed to reduce all of this to some sort of graspable summary for those of us who are not Einstein or Bohr, the Italian physicist Carlo Rovelli admits none of it makes any sense at all to anyone who has not served "a long apprenticeship," exactly what the Butcher Ding was saying: it takes some practice. But as for hard reality, a real description of the physical world we inhabit, he summarizes what that might be:

> The world described by the theory is thus further distanced from the one with which we are familiar. There is no longer space that "contains" the world, and there is no longer time "in which" events occur. There are only elementary processes wherein quanta of space and matter continually interact with one another. The illusion of space and time that continues around us is a blurred vision of this swarming of elementary processes.

The Tao is not describable. If someone offers a word for the Tao, then what is captured by that word is not the Tao. So how do we find our way? Practice, man, practice. Rovelli's long apprenticeship, Deng's years with a cleaver, or Anders Ericsson's ten thousand hours.

###

That nice round number of ten thousand hours is now a meme, one of those factoids that makes its way into popular culture, passed around, standing on its own, propagating in the collective understanding like a gene in a genome. Given how it came about, it has every right to stand on its own, but it's heartening to see it gaining general currency among musicians as an axiom, an accepted law. For example, slide guitar phenomenon Derek Trucks, interviewed recently in a popular guitar magazine, *Fretboard Journal*, tosses off the following quote explaining how he became a virtuoso by constantly listening to records as a kid and emulating what he heard: "I did that whole 10,000 hours thing, times whatever. I wore those records out."

This is good news for more than Malcolm Gladwell's and Daniel Levitin's literary agents and publishers. Both cited Ericsson's work in their popular books, Levitin in *This Is Your Brain on Music* and Gladwell's *Outliers: The Story of Success*. The latter is not strictly about music, and in fact Gladwell's prime examples attach to computer programmers and people like Bill Gates. But the number itself comes from studying musicians, and it derived from research designed to answer the question that has raged among musicians probably since music began, a specialized version of the more general debate over the role of nature and nurture. The first bit of good news is the research should settle the argument in nurture's favor. It won't, but it should. Before, in magazine articles on people like Trucks, one would be just as likely to see his virtuosity credited to innate talent, a light that began burning brightly just after he climbed out of the cradle. There are whole libraries of mythology celebrating wunderkinder going back to at least Mozart.

In the 1990s the psychologist K. Anders Ericsson set out to test the idea using students of classical violin at the Academy of Music in Berlin. Ericsson asked the academy's staff to group the students based on a simple measure, the brilliance each showed as a musician: Who are the stars, and who are just adequate? Good, better, best. The predictor of a student's ranking was strikingly simple: the number of hours the student had practiced in previous years. Those ranked the best had topped ten thousand lifetime hours of practice. The lessons drawn from this research, now fully developed in further studies and experiments, extend well beyond music. Levitin writes, "The emerging picture from such studies is that ten thousand hours of practice is required to achieve the level of mastery associated with being a world-class expert—in anything. . . . In study after study, of composers, basketball players, fiction writers, ice skaters, concert pianists, chess players, master criminals and what have you, the number comes up again and again."

Even the Butcher Ding. Remember, he himself reported he had struggled with oxen for three years, then things began to come together. Hard to say if ancient Chinese butchers worked a forty-hour week, vacations and such, but at three years he probably wasn't quite there, but close to ten thousand hours. And then nineteen years on one cleaver.

The first lesson here is in the math. Nice round number, but what it really implies is obsession, especially to achieve it as a teenager. Budding musicians set their sights on a practice routine of maybe an hour a day. Good luck. Ten thousand days is twenty-eight years, give or take. Getting the job done in, say, ten requires three solid hours of practice every single day.

Yet this daunting calculation misses a number of more encouraging points wrapped in the body or research, especially for people like me: amateur musicians, parking-lot pickers, and social players. Any one of us would kill to be good enough to be ranked as one of the "good" fiddlers at the Berlin Academy of music. Their number was four thousand hours. Doable.

Yet even a benchmark of four thousand hours misses something most players understand long before they reach it. At some point they ask "When will I get there?" and then suddenly realize there is no "there." We use the term "accomplished musician," but it is a deceptive term that implies a benchmark or bar cleared, past tense. Music is infinite. One never clears the bar. One never ceases practice. Ultimately, this is the real value of practice, this understanding.

There is no end goal, no point of necessary achievement. What we hope for is to get better and the hard numbers from the research provide a clear conclusion: Competence at music, or for that matter, a range of daunting, complex disciplines, is not a matter of raw talent or talent alone. Talent does enter the picture, but not nearly as much as the pure and unbridled obsession that pushes one to devote maybe half of her waking hours to developing the mind-set, ear, and finesse necessary to call oneself a musician. We can get better, but if this were simple, a straightforward linear process of grinding away hours to produce a result, it would not be worth talking about, a machine, set the dial to ten thousand hours and let it grind away.

#

The Taoists were not so much interested in Ding's skill as a butcher as they were his long years of practice as a means of comprehending the Tao, the unseen and incomprehensible order of the universe. The ox is not just a metaphor but a real ox with a complexity and elegance of design that is itself a reflection and manifestation of that order. Complexity cannot be comprehended with a simple mechanistic understanding of the ox, any more than a dance can be danced with only a map of the steps and two feet. Through practice we come to grasp and flow with the unseen order.

This ancient Chinese wisdom is not at all alien to our modern understanding of practice and performance. Physicians freshly minted from medical school, for instance, have all the information they need to succeed, probably more information, certainly more up-to-date information at their command than their colleagues who have already practiced, and that's exactly the word doctors use, the same we use in music: practice. Yet even the newly minted physician will likely admit, and the experienced will certainly argue, that the long-practiced physician is better. It's not a matter of learning new information or even absorbing more. He has spent those years laying on hands, earning a grasp of the complexities.

The same word occurs too, among a set of practitioners even more closely linked to the Taoists and ultimately to music. During the Warring States period Taoism split, with one branch working its way into Confucianism and its preoccupation with form and excruciatingly correct behavior. The more ascetic branch of Taoism, however, became a deep and formative influence on Buddhism, especially as practiced in China, Chan Buddhism, later in Japan where the term "Chan" became Zen. Central to Buddhism, then, now, and in Western forms, is meditation, mindfulness mediation. English-speaking Buddhists call it practice, same word. In this case, because it is the same process necessary in music.

When they meditate, Buddhists are seeking their version of the Tao, some grasp of the ineffable but real order of the universe. Importantly, they are sitting there on that cushion in mind work, but the work is really disengaging the mind. They are not trying to learn lists, check off bullet points, or master any skill whatever. That's why it is so difficult. They are looking for what might be perceived through one's unencumbered senses when conscious thought does not intervene. Neuroscience, of course, has become fascinated by this discipline of the mind and so cannot resist wiring these people up, literally tracking down aging monks who have mediated for far more than ten thousand hours, then hooking their brains to instruments to see what makes their cranial cavities tick. What vibrations attend? Oscillations? There are literally unique vibrations readable, discernible, reflective of the meditative state.

Neuroscientists call our conscious center the prefrontal cortex, chattering monkey brain to the meditators, but this is the principal locus of our conscious minds, the seat of the voices that play out in endless internal conversation, rationalizing, knowing, explaining, whining. The term "neuroscience" has become far more frequent and powerful in popular press and popular conversation as the result of a series of rapid-fire realizations in recent years, but one would not be too far off the mark in arguing that this rising currency is the result of one machine alone, the MRI, for magnetic resonance imaging. An advance on this concept, functional magnetic resonance imaging, fMRI, is even more powerful, giving a snapshot of the brain as it works, recording hotspots, and therefore helping map regions of the brain in play during specific tasks. A snapshot, yes, and nothing as complex as the human brain will ever fully surrender its mysteries in a snapshot. Far too much of the popular press and conversation does not allow for this limitation, so the hand is routinely overplayed. The findings, nonetheless, point in interesting directions.

Of course, someone has thought to load musicians into fMRI machines, just as Buddhists monks have been scanned. These subjects were keyboard players, and they were assigned a couple tasks while entombed in an fMRI machine clutching small electronic pianos. First, subjects played a straightforward musical scale, eight white keys in a row up and down, which is like asking a writer to recite the alphabet. No music here, just an exercise. These subjects, however, were trained jazz musicians, and jazz is certainly music, and improvisation, the very core of jazz requires a thorough command of musical knowledge, maybe not the full ten thousand hours, but something like that. Improvisation is not unique to jazz. It is especially prominent in bluegrass but is the ultimate holy grail of a lot of musicians, amateur and otherwise. It's what happens in a jam session, even in old-time music, the sort of phenomenon I described earlier in this book—social music, when people get together and forget their own pre-learned, rote approaches to a song and instead combine with the force around them to make a collective song, playing off each other. It was the sort of music the old-time player John Hermann spoke of as "an act of compassion."

The experiment's results? When playing the simple scales, the musicians' brains looked like any brain engaged in a normal thinking. When improvising (the activity that requires far greater command of music) their prefrontal cortices, the seat of consciousness and thinking, shut down. Lights out. It is absurd to say musical improvisation requires no skill or learning or accomplishment. It is not free form, a random pattern of notes. It contains unexpected notes, but still ordered and arranged so that the underlying tune is recognizable and musical. It does not follow a set pattern of learned notes but nonetheless is wholly attendant to the unseen, inexplicable order of music. Still, it is not accomplished by our conscious, rational selves.

Charles Limb, the principal investigator in this work, said in a TED talk about it, "To be creative you have to have this weird dissociation in your frontal lobe. One area turns on and a big area shuts downs so that you are willing to make mistakes and you are not constantly turning off all these generative impulses."

Generative, generating creativity.

Effort, mental effort, is a result of our consciousness, the voice that pushes us on or restrains us when necessary. Psychologists speak of this as "executive function," and neuroscience tells us the seat of executive function is indeed that same prefrontal cortex. Furthermore, performance, it would seem, is nothing if not the result of effort, of trying. But the above experiment is telling us just the opposite, that real music only begins to flow when one relaxes effort, why Slingerland titled his book so enigmatically as *Trying Not to Try*. He, in fact, cites the above experiment and one more pivotal bit of information, a translation of some Chinese characters written on bamboo strips 2,300 years ago and pulled from the mud in tombs in Hubei province in 1993: "You cannot try, but you also cannot not try; trying is wrong, but not trying is also wrong."

We postmoderns have an explicit understanding of this riddle, that we often recognize great performances, great artists by the very fact that what they do appears effortless: Fred Astaire dancing, Willie Nelson singing, Barack Obama speaking. It looks effortless because it is and because of years of great effort that came before as practice.

###

Some anthropologists and lapsed students of music labor under the same bad assumptions about practice. The former's arguments, you recall, appeared in broaching this book's prime question as to why music persists as a human cultural universal. Some anthropologists argue that primitive humans would have no use for music simply because they would have no time to practice. Too busy whacking mastodons with stone clubs. That is to say, if Og had not spent enough time woodshedding his bone flute concerto secreted off and alone with a metronome in a soundproof cave, his performance would face a harsh ring of campfire critics. This argument is simply an anthropologist's version of the same blinkers that pinch our common vision of musicianship, that the purpose is performance, that musicians are elite specialists, and that music derives from long hours in solitude on a treadmill of repetitive exercises and endless scales. For some musicians, in fact, this is more or less an accurate description of the process that delivered them to the concert hall stage, so general and severe are our blind spots about this.

This blinkered view at first seems supported by the ten-thousand-hour rule, but even the proponents of this very rule argue otherwise, citing prominent examples, and in Malcolm Gladwell's book these were prominent indeed. He made his case using the early history of the Beatles, who served out a lengthy apprenticeship, performing in obscurity, long hours every day on the stage of dive bars and strip clubs in Germany. They were not individually sequestered, unengaged, or even in a basic economic sense unproductive; they were rowdy young men working in bars, getting paid, and getting laid. None of this sounds like drudgery. If one could have asked them then about their practice routines then, the question would have made no sense. They were just living their lives, and their lives were formed and directed by music. They were not practicing; they were living right, which is the preferred form of practice.

Follow this same idea into the folkier reaches of American music. The path to virtuosity for Earl Scruggs began when, as a young teenager who found a banjo in his hands, learned a couple of rudimentary licks then straightway joined a band and made a living of sorts on what little he knew. He was a professional gigging musician as a teenager and learned on the job. It is the common story of traditional musicians.

One begins as a child, huddled and rapt in a dark quiet corner while a circle of players make music as they do every Saturday night on the screened front porch. Then an old, discarded banjo finds its way to the kid's hands one day, and he pesters an uncle to show him a few notes. Kid plinks in solitude, then come Saturday, sits in his same corner, quiet, but plinks, unheard, then through the years fills in holes between the plinks and moves in imperceptible increments to take a seat in the circle. This is how music comes into a life more often than not, in Og's time and in our own.

The counter example to the idea that musical ability is basically raw talent evident in very young people, practice time notwithstanding, is Bob Dylan. He did indeed form bands and perform as a teenager and played out among the circle of musicians in Dinkytown in Minneapolis as a young adult, but by all accounts his early performance was mostly posturing and his playing was mediocre, if not just plain bad. Same when he showed up in Greenwich Village in December 1960, then nineteen, still young, still performing, still bad and still apparently not past his ten thousand hours. But after a year or so of hustling gigs in coffeehouses, playing all night with friends at parties, playing on the street, playing at Izzy Young's, playing, his abilities exploded, a more or less universal opinion of his friends at the time. One can hear it today, his guitar as it was on his first album recorded in 1961. The kid was really good then, well on his way to guitar wizardry.

Musicians serve apprenticeships, and often as not these include public performance. You don't learn to play and then join a band, you join a band and then learn to play. This is not at all a strange model but exactly what doctors or lawyers mean when they say they have spent years in practice. They had the information before they entered practice; they began amassing the knowledge to be a lawyer or physician by practice, by living the life.

None of this, however, excludes from the mix the narrower idea of practice, of time spent alone in drills, playing songs again and again, even scales set to the deadly ticking drone of a metronome. Yet even practice in the narrower sense is not all that narrow. For instance, the assignment to play a repetitive exercise sounds a lot different if we realize that what happens in practice is indeed exercise in the athletic sense of the word. Our culture's body-mind separation serves us especially poorly in appreciating making music. We have no trouble with the idea of musical genius, blessed with a brain that grasps music. It makes no sense in our blinkered view to call the same person a musical athlete. We have categorized music as solely cerebral, and this is demonstrably wrong.

Oddly, musicians and others who accept this categorization nonetheless use language that undermines it. Earlier, I made the case that one truly learns a piece of music by placing it in a deeper form of memory in one's brain, an unconscious grasp of it. Everyday language often refers to this as "muscle memory," an idea especially common among musicians. When a series of chord progressions or arpeggios flow forth unbidden, we say they come from muscle memory. A blues player I know of teaches difficult licks by advising one to play them until they "come to hand," literally until we grasp them. Madeline Bruser, a classical pianist, is a specialist in learning music and summarizes her expertise in a valuable book: *The Art of Practicing: A Guide to Making Music from the Heart*. In it, she cites a pivotal episode in her own learning. "I could play the piece from memory, but my *hands* hadn't completely memorized it. He [her teacher Menahem Pressler] circled the passage in my score and wrote 'finger memory' on the page, and told me that I must train my hands to know the music."

This is not exactly what is happening here, though; still, I don't mean to completely discount the idea of memory being stored somewhere other than the brain. Our whole body's network of nerves handles a great deal of neural processing, and some memory probably is processed outside of the brain with a series of brain-like structures and chemicals, but I also don't want to steer our thinking to one side of the brain-body divide or the other. Whatever is happening here is not just muscular, muscle memory; it is both muscular and cranial, which is the point. Musical learning smashes the mental-physical divide, which is precisely why it requires practice and why it is uniquely important to the rest of our learning and our lives.

The general case here has been well established by a series of neuroscientists who study locomotion. Among them is the British scientist David Wolpert, who broaches the issue with a fundamental question: Why do we need brains? Not just to think, as we might think. Thinking is a frill biologically and not without its disadvantages. The jury is still out on the question of whether thinking and consciousness confer evolutionary fitness. Brains evolved for locomotion, to move bodies. While that case builds from examining the evolution of all sorts of primitive animals and quasi-animals, it remains valid for humans. Wolpert argues that for computers scientists it was almost trivial to design—as they did long ago—a program that can with depressing regularity beat humans at a mind game, even one that demands considerable intelligence and brain power, say chess. "While computers can now beat grand masters at chess, no computer can yet control a robot to manipulate a chess piece with the dexterity of six-year-old child," he says.

Certainly no computer can finesse the touch of a piano's keys or arc to just the right tension in the heartrending bend in a banjo string, as does that hillbilly over there with tobacco juice spilling from the corner of his mouth.

Finely controlled motor movements of physical locomotion require extraordinary mental capacity and effort, and it should come as no surprise that evolution has provided for building that capacity. The direct chemical link to this process is a chemical called "brain derived neurotropic factor," which stimulates growth of brain cells. The body produces more of it when we make demanding muscle movements, a phenomenon demonstrated not just in short-term experiments with human subjects, but by following physically fit people through their lives. There is, for instance, a strong positive correlation between physical exercise and academic performance. Exercise literally, physically builds brains, and not just the cells governing locomotion. The chemical stimulates growth across the board, enhancing all mental acuity, conscious and otherwise.

The common wisdom attributes all sorts of uniquely human abilities to our large brains, but dexterity and finesse usually don't make it to these lists. They should. Anthropologists have repeated the process of making simple stone tools by chipping flakes from rocks and found the process is not that simple after all. Not every modern human is capable of learning and executing the techniques required. Mastering this fundamental of primitive, stone age life requires practice. Certainly no other animal is capable of this, not a matter of the shape of our hands and the opposable thumb. The skill is fully dependent on the shape of our brains, not just to invent the tool but also to manipulate the hand that makes the tool. Same reason no other species can perform the ballet, sculpt marble, play banjo, or do backflips off a balance beam.

The physical demands of musicianship are the insurmountable barrier to the assertion that musical competence is a matter of talent. One may have an intellectual gift for music like perfect pitch, photographic memory, or a brain seemingly hardwired for grasping the mathematical complexities of music theory, maybe, but one is not born with finesse and dexterity. The hands must be conditioned and trained to dance.

Still, it might appear a bit of a stretch to call a musician an athlete. My examples here are all about what we might call fine motor skills, micromovements. Athleticism also requires finesse, but at the same time requires strength, big movements controlled by large muscle groups. This probably makes not much differences at all as far as the brain is concerned, that control of a runner's quadriceps is not all that different from the curl of a pinky, but music is also about big muscles and whole-body movement.

One of the more valuable guitar lessons I ever had was a one-time session with Scott Ainslie, a virtuoso player and longtime student of blues music, especially that of Robert Johnson. His lesson was called "Blues Give Me Your Right Arm" and was for many guitar players heretical, cut straight across the grain of everything we had been taught before. Guitar players work for maybe the first five thousand of the ten thousand hours to control hand movements and then on the same thing for every hour after, to become precise, fine, and firm. The right hand's technique of fingerstyle players especially—and almost all of traditional blues is fingerstyle—is unusually demanding. Modern teachers and practitioners of the form seem to fully understand that the technique, no matter how earthy it might sound, derived from rural musicians picking up classical guitar techniques, and so many of them teach classical guitar techniques: very little movement in the right hand, and just fingers arching in stokes, the hand itself still and solid to form a foundational platform of stability.

Ainslie disregards all of this. In his style you play with the whole right arm, big gross swings with the beat, like the drive rod of a locomotive wheel. His argument for this is both historical and neurological, and it's hard to see why either has been so steadfastly ignored by most of his colleagues. We take our models from the great players of the early twentieth century, like Robert Johnson, and there are recordings to tell us they were great. There are also a few film clips, not of Johnson but of others, that offer clear evidence. Nothing delicate or airy fairy here. They played exactly as Ainslie says they did, big, full swings of their right arms that would horrify any classical teacher.

Ainslie's neurological argument is even more intriguing and relevant to the rest of us, not just blues players, not just musicians. He was explicit about this in his class, that using a big swinging right arm engages large muscle groups and control of large muscle groups, the gross movements, engage what he calls "the reptilian brain." The primitive brain. The nether brain. He's right. Neuroscientists would agree with the blues player. This is where rhythm lives—that uniquely human ability that allows us to move together—in our primitive, reptilian brains.

Over the years, I have been privileged to watch up close and informally a lot of great musicians, not just blues players but a wide range of performers. It's one thing to hear and appreciate recordings, but in performance the physical presence adds another dimension. Performance, however, is also theater, so we often see staged histrionics designed to arouse the groundlings. Informal sessions strip the theatrics.

For instance, Gillian Welch and David Rawlings one time in a workshop, twenty or thirty people on hand. They mostly sat on the edge of the stage and answered our questions, but when they played a tune they stood, of course. Most great players of this form stand to play. As is the case with Ainslie's big arm, standing to play makes such immediate and dramatic improvements in music that it seems like a cheap trick, because it promotes full body engagement. With Rawlings and Welch, up close, one could see the process. There came an almost magical transformation in a few seconds of silence before they played, that their bodies arched together, heads tipped toward each other, and quietly counted in the rhythm of the tune. We did not need to hear the count, but could see it quietly ripple through each body like a couple of prayer flags catching the beginnings of an afternoon breeze. They became almost literally entranced. I could not avoid the sense that in those few seconds their psyches had been transported to a netherworld. They probably do not know that for most of human time and most of human cultures no distinction arose in language or otherwise between dance and music, but their bodies know it.

###

Madeline Bruser, the pianist, aims her efforts at highly trained classical musicians, teaching them the nuts and bolts of practice. The people she works with are the hyper-trained and hyper-proficient, the very people who have locked themselves away in practice rooms for most of their lives, logging their ten thousand hours chained to scales, exercises, technique, and metronomes. Those of us who play folk music can sometime sound like reverse snobs in speaking of classical musicians, but most of us are not. I am in awe of classical musicians, envious of their skills. The demands of their world are exponentially greater.

So one might reasonably ask how Bruser's advice on their much more demanding practice differs from what got the Beatles, Earl Scruggs, and Son House to their mastery. Endless scales and exercises? Not really, says Bruser. Limited use. Constraining and boring. Metronome? Some. But be careful of overuse. Perfect, rigid form? Good god, no. Perfect maybe, but not rigid. She and Scott Ainslie might get along.

Her book-length compilation of practical advice on practice has almost nothing to do with routines and discipline; it is mostly about body, emotions and breathing. She is constructively critical of the contorted and rigid ways players have traditionally come to relate to their instruments, piano players with hunched shoulders, guitar players with a leg raised by a stepstool, violinists with necks cramped sideways. All of this, in fact, causes injury, especially after ten thousand hours, and she backs this up with advice from physical therapists who specialize in treating musicians. More importantly, though, she believes music does not issue from the instrument and the notes on the page; it flows from the alliance between body and instrument that is only ever wholly successful if it deeply engages the body.

This is simple practical advice, and following it leads almost immediately to better music. She writes:

> For all of us, the impulse to make music is to get our body into it, to use our hands, lips, voice, and breath to create music physically, sensually. But in the midst of our struggles to read the score, execute arpeggios, and shape phrases, we lose touch with the skin that touches the instrument and with the energy that flows through the body as we move. . . . Place your attention on the sensations of touch and movement . . . to help you reconnect with your body and to increase the physical pleasure of making music. The more you enjoy using your body, the better your coordination and sound will be.

Oddly, Bruser seems to have been present in my struggle to learn by ear that I described in the previous chapter, and had I followed her advice, it might have saved me a lot of trouble. She advises classical musicians—the most literate of the lot—to learn by ear, just like hill-billies and juke joint bluesmen do. Her first step in learning a piece excludes her instrument. Instead, she advises players of complex classical orchestra music to learn their parts by first learning to sing them, even piano players, who often have the equivalent of three or four parts or voices happening at once, a right-hand melody against a left-hand bass line. She wants the player to learn by singing first the right-hand and then the left-hand part. This is how to embed music in the brain.

Then play, as I finally learned, slowly, listening to the unique and glowing sound of each note. Then a step further, beyond simply listening to actually feeling each note as a vibration in your body—hands, chest, neck, and knees—how the oscillations propagate as waves. Then a third step: hearing how each note on its own wanders and wobbles into the room you are in, interacting with the physical space. All of this is a prescription for deepening engagement with the music as a means of learning it. Our brains feed on a full range of perceptions channeled through our bodies. The pure sensuality and emotional punch of music urges us to light up the whole network of nerves to take it in.

All of this brings us back to what he Taoists had in mind in the case of butcher Ding, certainly what the Buddhists had in mind as they followed the same strain. For a Buddhist, the center of a life is the practice of meditation, by which they mean a radical form of presence, of being in the moment. That's what Bruser means too, and it is no accident that she is trained in and practices meditation. Recall though, that musicians who know the patterns of music so deeply that they are able to improvise do so by silencing their conscious control, the brain's prefrontal cortex. This is exactly the seat of the chattering monkey brain Buddhists and other practitioners of meditation view as an obstacle to their enlightenment, but, in the Taoist view and in that of many musicians, also an obstacle to their competence, their ability to perform.

There's no need to limit this to music. I've argued here that music is a whole-body experience, a physical activity that shares a lot of ground with other forms of physical exercise and athleticism. In fact, a lot of research in the larger emotional and neurological benefits of exercise parallel findings about the practice of music. The parallels are especially robust and telling among a subset of runners who follow evolutionary rules by running on mountain trails, in natural settings, in moccasin like shoes and on varied terrains. The argument is for a full body engagement of a natural set of surroundings, which has benefits ranging from controlling mental depression to enhanced immune system performance, all of this backed by research. This is practice, yet this is not the way most people run.

Go to any gym and watch someone on a treadmill: a rote, repetitive, and senseless exercise. They may get their heart rate up for a few minutes, and somewhere in the *New York Times* Health section they read some sort of research that said this a good idea, so a timer gets set, steps get measured, data is collected, and a box is checked. This is the trivialization, the imprisonment of our humanity on a hamster wheel.

I have a friend, a physical therapist, who calls this sort of forced labor exercise a full employment act for his profession. That is, he sees the most injuries and therefore gains the most income from people who exercise in repetitive ways like treadmills and even running on flat regular surfaces like roads. The human body is far more sophisticated in its range of motion, balance, proprioception, grace, and agility than any treadmill's design can imagine. Failing to appreciate and use that range of abilities is not only inhuman but causes injuries. It is not practice, but it is checking boxes, and this what we have become.

Wrapped up in all of this is a hollow and false sense of entitlement. We have reduced the range of human endeavors to a set of testable, teachable skills, classes to be mastered, hours to be spent, exams passed. Once we have spent the requisite number of minutes on a treadmill, three days a week, data stored in our Fitbit watch, we are therefore fit and healthy. Says so right here.

I think the reason I am so drawn to music, the reason I persist, is that the practice of it will not tolerate this sort of reductionism. I like it because I have failed. There comes a point—and these have certainly come in my life, I remember every one of them searingly, cringingly—when a student believes they have learned something, practiced it a few hours, and can perform it, but can't and proves it right there in public.

Competence in music cannot be faked. It demands practice, rigor. It is a demanding, harsh beauty.

Yet this is not the ultimate value. It comes in finally realizing that one does not practice in order to perform. Practice itself is the end. I have never met a musician who did not enjoy practicing, guarded practice time, looked forward to it like a guilty pleasure. Not just playing, but practice, working on rudiments, playing slowly.

Abram Chasins, a pianist and composer, was once going to visit Sergei Rachmaninoff at his house, approached and heard him practicing, but Rachmaninoff was playing so slowly that Chasins could not recognize the piece, even though it was Chopin and deeply familiar to both virtuosos. Rachmaninoff himself was by then well beyond his ten-thousand-hour phase. He needed more practice time the same way Richard Nixon needed to read more Machiavelli, and he certainly had no need to play the Chopin piece so slowly.

Danny Barnes, a banjo player, tells a similar tale about John Hartford at a point when Hartford was at the top of his game, a brilliant performer known for his eccentricities, but also blazing fast work on fiddle and banjo. He was a typical traditional musician, having logged his ten thousand hours as a teenager. Barnes called Hartford one day and all the latter wanted to do was talk about a great new model of metronome he had found that he was using to govern his practice time. His long-time habit was to alternate days (he practiced for entire days, days on days) of playing very fast with days of setting his new metronome to make him play very slowly, play that way all day long, everything he played. Very slowly.

Playing slowly puts space between notes. Then, as they amble through the air, I find myself most entranced by that space between them. The sense of depth, of a third dimension appears. The notes are no longer circles of sound, but spheres, and I can begin to hear around their edges. I notice that the sides have a different texture than the face and suspect there is a revelation even more intriguing behind them.

A tune Hartford recorded went like this:

Turn your radio on

And listen to the music in the air
Turn your radio on, have the glory shared
Turn your lights down low
And listen to the Master's radio
Get in touch with God, turn your radio on.

8

I BELONG TO THE BAND

Anyone seeking a religious education should begin with Charles Frazier's admirable Civil War novel, *Cold Mountain*. Frazier frames his story on the most ancient of themes: a lost man returning from war to a woman he loves, an odyssey. Yet Inman's, his protagonist's, long march is set to music playing in the distance, and it is this subplot that promises transcendence, salvation, and even eternal life of sorts, the last of those being the first promise of religion, at least much of organized religion. Fittingly, Frazier's conduit to the divine, his story's prophet and savior, is a loutish drunken bum of a fiddler, Stobrod by name, not a given name but adopted. A stob is a stub, a branch broken to create a backwoods punji, a poke in the eye with a sharp stick.

Frazier is straightforward enough about his intentions for the guy, even giving us the particulars of his religious epiphany. Before the light struck him on his particular road to Damascus, Stobrod was just another no-account, wounded in war and passing his time of recuperation with rote renderings of the few elementary fiddle tunes he knew, but then he played one tune of his own devising, a tune that seemed to come from nowhere, improvised on the spot and played for a dying girl, and in the process he is transformed. Frazier allows the source of his inspiration to be as it was for much of mountain music, from slaves, but it is no ordinary learning that occurs here, rather enlightenment, a transcendence that falls well within the bounds of the varieties of religious experience:

He first spent his attention on matters of tuning and fingering and phrasing. Then he began listening to the words of the songs the niggers sang, admiring how they chanted out every desire and fear in their lives as clear and as proud as could be. And soon he had a growing feeling that he was learning things about himself that had never sifted into his thinking before. One thing he discovered with a great deal of astonishment was that music held more for him than just pleasure. There was meat to it. The grouping of sounds, their forms in the air as they rang out and faded, said something comforting to him about the rule of creation. (295)

The immediate result was Stobrod's desertion; he would study war no more. He returns to Cold Mountain, takes up a life on the lam, and partners with a doltish, fat, mentally defective banjo player (everywhere, banjo jokes, even from novelists), then runs afoul of the home guard, vigilantes who shoot deserters. These devils demand their due, forcing Stobrod and his banjo buddy to play a tune before execution, and they do. "When the song fell closed, Birch said to Teague [of the vigilantes], Good God, these is holy men. Their mind turns on matters kept secret from the likes of you and me."

Then they shoot them, but there is a resurrection of sorts. The banjo player is stone dead but Stobrod only wounded. His hard-bitten, no-nonsense daughter finds him and brings him back to life, but it is Ada—the daughter's pal, Inman's intended, the novel's Mary Magdalene—who dips the water that flows at Stobrod's resurrection and, as she does so, wonders: "She sat and looked at Stobrod, and he lay like a dead man. There was no sign to show that he lived other than a slight movement of his jacket front when he breathed. Ada wondered about his hundreds of tunes. Where were they now and where might they go if he died."

I have no religion. I consider religious questions a waste of thought, consider the phrase "religious education" absurd. Yet here is this question of Ada's, a religious question if ever there was one. I first read it almost twenty years ago, a single simple sentence embedded in an ornate and elegant novel with so much more to it than this. I have read my ten thousand hours' worth of sentences since, and still it leaps to mind. It is this question that made me write this book. Ever since, my nonreligious being, my soulless soul has been haunted and shaken by a religious question. Finally, I must admit I believe what Stobrod, the prophet, believes.

This is deeply unsettling to my lifelong atheism, a term in and of itself I find increasingly inappropriate, not because of any conversion or epiphany; just the opposite. It's simply an odd way to define oneself: a-theism, without god. It implies some sort of relationship with a god the same way a recovering alcoholic goes to the meetings every week, ten years sober, but still suffers an enduring obedience to alcohol. I do not follow professional sports either but would in no way think about announcing my creed as an "a-fan." The question of the existence of a supreme being is not even relevant to my life.

I come by this honestly enough, a matter of heritage and upbringing. I was raised by Bible-thumpers, holy rollers, fundamentalists— "evangelicals" being the anodyne term of our time. I understand fully that my experience was not necessarily the same as that of other people so raised, but mine was inundation in irrationality, willed stupidity, racism, and hypocrisy. From my early adolescence on, I wanted nothing so much as to never see the inside of a church again, and as I became increasingly in charge of my life, I realized this wish. Oddly, my shield against religion became an acoustic guitar. I say "oddly" because this term of engagement that I believed then unique to me was not at all unique. It was common in our time but, more surprisingly still, common through much of the history of civilization, all civilizations, across cultures. Ever since organized religion began, its enemies have been long-haired people with musical instruments.

My initial weapon in this was not even acoustic, but a cheap, sunburst finish electric bass guitar selected on the sole basis that it happened to be shaped like a big violin, that is, shaped exactly as Paul McCartney's was when the Beatles burst into my teenaged consciousness just a couple of years before, although, unlike McCartney's, mine was set up conventionally for right-handed play. I was maybe sixteen years old when I spotted it in Alvin Ash's music shop in Alpena, Michigan, where I took accordion lessons. I persuaded Alvin himself, a pipe-puffing, floppy-mustached sage of a man, to sell it to me for a reasonable fee along with a suitable amplifier. I had no idea how to play a bass guitar or any guitar, but a Mel Bay method book Alvin supplied could fix that soon enough, and I earnestly believed I left the shop clutching the key to the kingdom of my idea of heaven, that I would in no time be fronting a rock 'n' roll band and living a life of licentious abandon. My fundamentalist Baptist parents saw in my new guitar the exact same vision, and all hell broke loose. No matter that it was my own money earned shoveling pig shit that I had handed to Alvin. The guitar was going back or I was going to reform school. Accordions were a separate matter: acceptable in church, Myron Floren played one on *Lawrence Welk*, and Cissy and Bobby danced chastely with big wholesome smiles. The guitar was the devil's box; my parents seemed wholly convinced of this.

If nothing else, though, their stubbornness in this matter parented my own ability to hold a grudge, and it set me on a course bound for a life of music. I thank them for it. Still, if this were simply a personal matter set in my parents' eccentric theology, it would not be worth mentioning here, other than a passing personal footnote. This agon plays prominently in the larger scheme of things.

###

My defiant atheism was eventually an impediment to learning guitar. Not at first, though. The songs I wanted to know and the people I emulate were lefty iconoclasts every bit as areligious as I was. Now and again, I would stumble onto a song that rested in a melody stolen from the Baptist hymnal. Thus, the dull old Protestant drone of "The Sweet By and By" could become in the hands of the wobbly songwriter Joe Hill "The Preacher and the Slave" ("You'll get pie in the sky when you die / That's a lie." Hill wrote it early in the twentieth century, but folkies still sang it in the '60s.) Aside from delivering the most succinct summary of fundamentalist tenets I know, Hill's version was no longer a hymn I needed to avoid but a lovely bit of wry irony I could savor as a private joke. This I could sing.

I was not in this, however, just for jokes. I wanted to learn music so began tracing what I had learned backward to sources, like a lot of players then, back to black blues players, especially the Reverend Gary Davis, and mention of his name almost always included the title, which gets us right at the problem at hand. This book has been following this thread since I began by talking about the song "Delia" as my gateway drug to this obsession of mine and of many others. Now it comes to a head, as it did it my own life. Wildly eccentric as he may have been, a blind, whiskey-drinking, pistol-packing prophet of the Gibson J-200, Davis was altogether serious about the reverend business. He refused to play blues music, only gospel, at least for recordings, at least for singing.

His repertoire, of course, holds counterexamples, "Delia" and "Cocaine Blues" being two. Then there is "Hesitation Blues," a tune I have struggled to play for years, to get it just right in its drive, jolt, and swing, just so I could sing its series of filthy and politically incorrect lyrics, the very sort of jokes that drew me to the blues in the first place, grit and gravel. "I'm up on this wagon tryin' to sell this load of coal / My baby's in the alley tryin' to sell her jelly roll."

But you don't get a tune like this from Davis's recordings. It was widely recorded and performed by the folkies who learned directly and indirectly from him. Same with "Delia" and "Cocaine Blues." He refused to record them, but he would teach them in private, and his students are the sources for the rest of us.

But once I set out on this path I could not be satisfied until I had traced it to the original, to the jaw-dropping, gobsmacked revelation of hearing the man himself. It can still be done, even though Davis himself is long dead. He happened to have performed during the golden age of recording technology when tube amplifiers, big ribbon microphones, and large-format magnetic tape allowed some of the most accurate and alive recording ever. During that period, he laid down an LP under the name Blind Gary Davis, *Harlem Street Singer*. It's still easily obtainable brand new on vinyl. Even in a recording, all these years later, the performance of a single blind man with an acoustic guitar and solo vocals can make walls dance and make birds sing in the dead of winter. Upon hearing it, even the agnostics and murderous vigilantes among us would allow that his mind turned on matters kept secret from you and me, and he was indeed a holy man.

Yet this album is full of gospel, with titles like "Twelve Gates of the City," "Pure Religion," and "Great Change Since I Been Born." I couldn't go there. Could not bring myself to follow Davis into these tunes, could not sing of Jesus effecting my salvation. Would rather sing about jelly-roll. From my beginnings with music, I never once held a song to be just a song but took lyrics as a sort of oath, an affirmation, and, as intoxicating as Davis's music was, as singular and exemplary as his backing guitar made it, I couldn't go there. Especially couldn't go there with an anthem of his on this album *I Belong to the Band*.

> What Band you talkin' about
> Talkin' 'bout the angel band
> I belong to this band, hallelujah.

> I do not belong to this band.

# # #

Ian Zack's biography of Davis is aptly titled *Say No to the Devil*. It is that last word, one Davis used often, that traces a longstanding rift through not just his music but every lick and chord of American roots music. The guitar Davis played is for many the same as it was for my mother, "the devil's box." At other periods in this history, various other instruments served the role, especially the fiddle, but by the mid-twentieth century the guitar became the preferred tool of Satan because of its association with blues music, dance, and riotous living. The opposite pole for most fundamentalists was church music, gospel, or, for some, no music at all. In reality, Davis straddled the gulf between these two poles, but for the record, especially when his wife was within hearing range, he had made a clear choice to join God's band. No blues.

He was not alone, especially among black musicians. Son House, Skip James, Robert Wilkins, and the great Blind Willie McTell all worked both sides of the line, one way or another. The gospel singer identified on his records as Deacon L.J. Bates was really Blind Lemon Jefferson. Zack, who cites these examples, also says: "Even the father of modern gospel music, Thomas A. Dorsey, had a previous blues life as 'Georgia Tom' when he teamed up with Tampa Red on risqué hits like 'It's Tight

Like That' before turning to God and incorporating blues and ragtime forms into his spiritual compositions."

Perhaps all of this crossing back and forth between the two camps gradually wore away the demarcation, but in reality even my benighted Baptist mother could see it had been blurred. There was no clear line. She was like most northern fundamentalists in being every bit as appalled by black gospel music as she was by rock 'n' roll. The line that defined Gary Davis's life would have meant nothing to her whatever. It was all the devil's work. It turns out this blinkered bit of racial prejudice is even more illuminating to our larger point. To begin with, it wasn't altogether racist. Northern fundamentalists then, especially Baptists, could be equally censorious of practices in southern white churches, such as speaking in tongues, dancing, call-and-response, snake handling, and yes, the music. Especially of the dance, the ecstatic display of African American gospel that engulfs and entire congregation in swaying full voice of praise. She saw all of this in her preacher's words as "wild African jungle music." Davis's religious lyrics did nothing to cleanse this spot, in my mother's view. It was the rhythm that these people found offensive, the drive that made you want to dance.

There is a well-documented and thoroughly researched thread that traces the distinctive practices of African American gospel to Africa: African instruments, dance, and ritual, all of it predating slavery and Christianity. Like much of Christian ritual in all cultures, what we regard today as uniquely Christian is simply a veneer over primitive ritual and practice. It is not a matter of race; the exact same tensions and vestigial pagan rituals persist in European churches, both Catholic and Protestant. The conflict here is not between guitars and pianos or whites and blacks, or even Christianity and anything else. It is between doctrine and dance, authority and participation, poetry and prose.

In fact, a standout example of this tension independent of African lineage arises in the case of the Sacred Harp, as the name implies, a form of music that arose deeply embedded in religion. This tradition, eccentric as it may be, has nonetheless given us music that remains vital to all of our culture, hymns like "Amazing Grace," but it began in England, then spread to the isolated and austere corners of Protestantism in the northeastern United States in the early nineteenth century. Forget fine lines of distinction between variously categorized instruments of the devil. The founders of the Sacred Harp believed all musical instruments were devilish and had no place in religious music and so developed a unique form of a cappella singing, and so far this fits with the austere Protestantism, the puritanical streak. But now the story goes off the rails. Puritanism is reflected in the geometry of worship, neat rows of hardwood, uncushioned upright pews, a seated congregation, sullen, stock still, and silent, and in front, elevated above, the stentorian voice of authority holding forth.

Not so with the Scared Harp. There is no choir; everybody is a singer, no separate audience. Everyone sits in a circle and everybody sings. The founders invented a system of musical notation called shape notes that greatly simplified harmonies and the solfege scale. It made reading music readily accessible to all participants, that is, democratized it, the very reverse of authoritarianism of the Puritans. The democratization is emphasized by the circular arrangement of the congregants. The notation system spread widely, in the South especially, and many folk, bluegrass, and country performers, the great harmonizers through the years, began as shape note singers.

There is a leader who sits in the center of the circle, but the job rotates song by song. All participants eventually take a turn leading. This geometry is almost an exact parallel of that which evolved in slave churches. Africans brought with them a ritual called the "ring shout" in which celebrants moved in a circle and practiced an animated call and response. Some musicologists see in this the birth of the blues, but certainly the recognizable patterns of gospel that endure.

And yes, everyone in the case of the Sacred Harp is sitting, not standing, certainly not dancing, so at first glance this might seem irredeemably Protestant after all. But notice the leader, how she is marking time. It's one of the more distinctive traits of the Sacred Harp, what one notices first, and there aren't all that many opportunities for noticing. Sacred Harp music is not performed, not a performance, and so there is no audience. No one just sits and listens, but it is occasionally filmed, and the visuals are striking, especially the leader's wide, full swing of an arm, like a pendulum or piston clipping the notes of the singers to deliver a striking, danceable rhythm. The Sacred Harp is primitive and, like all primitive music, is driven by rhythm. Just one arm dances, but not so bad for white people.

Yet the larger tipoff to where this example leads this story is in what the Sacred Harp has become. This antique and eccentric form of music survives and thrives, not on iTunes or YouTube as archival field recordings but in a living, vibrant, and oddly secular tradition. It is still practiced as one might expect in isolated rural southern white communities but has demonstrated an ability to draw participants from a far broader field, young educated urban people of varied or of no particular religion, atheists, Catholics, and Jews. There are training camps even, places where people can pay to travel to, pay to attend, and burn up a week's vacation time just to learn an archaic form of music that is never performed publicly.

Their rationale is simple enough. They report the experience of sitting in that circle and joining one's voice in harmony and rhythm to those of sixty or so other humans is transformative. Creed and doctrine play no part. They just sing, then feel better.

###

The religious war on guitars and music did not begin with my mother or even her bitterly distilled variety of Protestantism, not with Gary Davis and the Puritans, not even on this continent. Examples of this conflict occur worldwide and through all of historical time. The battle began with civilization, which means with organized religion, or what we choose to define and accept as religion.

Our familiarity with the vibrant traditions of African American gospel as it is practiced today makes it relatively easy to imagine its origins in the ring shout, a boisterous ritual of whirling, singling, and clapping that began in Africa, but in tracing this lineage in her book *Dancing in the Streets: A History of Collective Joy*, Barbara Ehrenreich says, "Nothing like this [ring shout] had occurred in the context of Christian worship since dance was prohibited in European Catholic churches in the thirteenth century." Wait. Is she saying that pre-thirteenth-century Catholicism looked a lot like African American gospel? Emphatically so, yes, she is. At book length and full of evidence. I rely on her work for much of the detail here.

All of the world's dominant organized religions began coincident with the advent of civilization, by which we mean with agriculture. The domestication of plants and animals and cultivation allowed permanent settlements, accumulation of wealth and inequity, and required organized labor, hierarchy, regimentation of time. Civilization required the domestication of humans just as surely as it rested on subjugating plants and animals. Organized religion is a lot of things to a lot of people, but one of its necessary functions was serving as a tool for abetting human domestication. I am not arguing that this is the beginnings of religion but of *organized* religion. Like every other aspect of the human endeavor, religion changed radically more than five thousand years ago, contrary to the character of ritual and ceremony that had existed for fifty thousand years before. So great was the shift that there's plenty to support the argument that what came before was not religion but something else. This is a problem of language and categorization, though, and it doesn't need to be settled here to continue the thought. I'll do so using the separate categories of organized and primitive religion, fully realizing that the language may be provisional.

Primitive religion is rooted in ecstasy, trance, and ritual; organized religion in theology, creed, and law. Primitive religion is a matter of what one does; modern organized religion in what one believes. Aldous Huxley said, "Ritual dances provide a religious experience that seems more satisfying and convincing than any other. . . . It is with their muscles that humans most easily obtain knowledge of the divine." Since the advent of organized religion, people obtained their knowledge of the divine through creed and authority.

Yet to function as religion this form of devotion cannot be hollow ritual, just going through the motions of dance. Its practitioners expect it to be literally a mind-altering experience. Anthropologists have worked out a list of common elements in primitive religious ritual, and it always includes dance, group dance, like a ring shout. It is wholly participatory. Everyone in the circle. It is of course rhythmic, and the rhythm is driven by drums but also other early instruments of all sorts. Music did not exist separate from these circles; they hold the origin of our deep attachment to music. These are the circles that obliterate the distinction between music and dance created by civilization, whereas worldwide ancient languages contained no separate words for these categories.

Further, primitive religious practice includes body adornment, especially face painting and masking. This last seems an outlier at first, but for now mark it as a curious fact. Anthropologists have methods for marking the arrival of humanity based on seeing the preserved physical remnants of a suite of characteristics that emerged about fifty thousand years ago. These defining traits show that humans had evolved to allow the group cohesion, physical skills and language that set us apart from all the other competing species of upright apes that had existed millions of years before. One of the defining traits of humanity is face painting, in particular that about the same time evidence of all of our other traits first arose in Africa, these brainy little apes also began using red ochre as face paint used in ritual dance. The ochre survives as a distinctive marker of human campsites.

But one other trait is common to primitive religion, one we mostly know from contemporary hunter-gatherers and historical accounts of them. It is the trait that tells us primitive religion was meant to be literally mind-altering. Primitive ritual was designed to and often did result in some participants entering a trance, a well-researched and documentable state of dissociation with an experience much like entering another world, often aided by alcohol or drugs.

Yet even participants not deeply entranced still experienced various forms of emotional release, ecstasy, joy, sexual abandon. Primitive religion and ritual were deeply transformative, still are in all of their vestigial practice. These are the roots of our deep attachment to music and dance, and it is this attachment that has historically served as organized religion's most stubborn challenge. This was the clash that sponsored the Catholic backlash in the thirteenth century, but the conflict had arisen much earlier, separate from Christianity. The German philosopher Friedrich Nietzsche gives us the language that still defines this clash in his explosive treatise *The Birth of Tragedy*.

The opening sentences of Rudiger Safranski's book: *Nietzsche: A Philosophical Biography*, are these: "Nietzsche experienced music as authentic reality and colossal power. Music penetrated the core of his being, and it meant everything to him. He hoped the music would never stop, but it did."

It stopped when he went insane. Still, he wrote *The Birth of Tragedy*, while he was still a young man, nominally sane and enthralled with music, especially the music of Richard Wagner, with whom he had a close personal relationship, at least then. He used that mind-set to lay down the analysis of Western civilization that defines the clash between what I have been calling organized and primitive religion, what he called the Apollonian and Dionysian. He was writing about the clash in ancient Greek culture. The Apollonian was the force of the god Apollo at work in organizing Greek civilization, the stern giver of laws. The Dionysian was, well, the Dionysian. Bohemian, libertine, hippie. Needs no definition; we still know it when we see it. Nietzsche himself makes this clear using his terms of "cultural humanity" for civilization:

> Perhaps we shall find a point of departure for our reflections in the claim that the satyr, the invented natural being, relates to cultural humanity, as Dionysiac music relates to civilization. Of the latter, Richard Wagner says that it is annulled by music as lamplight is annulled by the light of day. In the same way, I believe, the Greek man of culture felt himself annulled in the face of the satyr chorus, and the immediate effect of the Dionysiac tragedy is that state and society, the gulfs separating man from man, make way for an overwhelming sense of unity that goes back to the very heart of nature. (38–39)

There's a lot here, but we can begin unpacking by understanding the cult of Dionysius was a real force in ancient Greek society, complete with adherents, rites, festivals, and rituals. Further, these are clear extensions of the outlines of primitive religion in general, especially in the prominent role of women. There's plenty of anthropological evidence that before farming and hierarchy came along, women played a far more dominant role in societies of hunter-gatherers. Much of the evidence for this is written, that early texts of civilizations including Hebrew and Islamic—early organized religions—were dominated by a power struggle, a backlash against women, establishment of patriarchy just as organized religion was dominated by a backlash against music. Both Judaism and Islam, at least in their more conservative reaches, continue to prosecute this war, and when they do, relying on doctrine and texts that arose during this backlash. In Greek society, women also took the brunt of the attack, according to Ehrenreich's account:

> The most notorious feminine form of Dionysian worship, the *oreibaia*, or winter dance, looks to modern eyes like a crude pantomime of feminist revolt. In mythical accounts, women "called" by the god to participate drop their spinning and abandon their children to run outdoors and into the mountains, where they dress in fawn skins and engage in a "frenzied dance." These maenads, as Dionysus's female cult members were called, run through the woods calling out the name of the god, or uttering the characteristic bacchic cry *"euoi,"* they toss their hair and brandish their *thryos*—sticks to which pinecones have been attached. Finally, they achieve a state of mind the Greeks call *enthousiasmos*—literally, having the god within oneself—or what many cultures in our time would call a "possession trance." (34–35)

This sort of display, however, was by no means a universal practice in all of Greek society, rather a source of conflict and at times actively suppressed as counter to the organizing imperative of civilization, counterproductive and subversive to activities like governing, making war and spinning. None of this makes the Greeks exceptional. Similar rites existed across humanity and art depicting similar ritual is in evidence in China, Mesopotamia, and Palestine. The Hebrew word for festival *hag* also means "to go in a circle," and Hebrew literature testifies to central tensions with hard-drinking, orgiastic dancing cults throughout its history. The stern rule-giving Yahweh is forever competing for attention with local deities like Baal and Anat, who were Dionysian.

Even early records from Oaxaca, a Zapotec and Mixtec urban center in preconquest Mexico, show a similar tension. So does Islam, with tensions the Dionysian side represented to this day by the music-loving, whirling dervish dancing poets that are the Sufis.

Indeed Dionysus had counterparts in early history in a region spanning five thousand miles, from the Iberian peninsula on the West to India, known variously as Bacchus, Pan, Minotaur, Faunus, Priapus, Liber, Ammon, Osiris, Shiva, and Krishna, generally a long-haired nature lover, musician, immoderate binge drinker, and sexual libertine, or so described by the forces of civilization, that is, those who wrote history. Ehrenreich calls Dionysus himself the "first rock star."

Further, Christianity itself arose in this environment and some early Christians were Dionysians. In fact there is a credible argument that Christ himself was modeled on Dionysus, long-haired nature-boy socialist who marked important events with feasting and drinking. There's a long history of comparison of the two, but also a case to be made as Ehrenreich does, for social pressures steering early Christianity toward the Dionysian, regardless of the character of the man himself. Decades passed between the death of the Christ before anyone began writing a history of his life and doctrine. The people who eventually did so were largely Jews who spoke Greek, some of whom knew of and approved of Dionysius. Some Jews during the same period were already linking the Hebrew god Yahweh to Dionysus and incorporating ecstatic dance in worship. The whole business was popular, and adopting elements of Dionysian practices gave Christianity a competitive edge, especially among women and the poor.

For whatever reason, ecstatic dance, drinking and participatory ritual became firmly established in early Christianity. Some of the evidence for this comes from the Romans, who had already engaged in their own backlash against Bacchus, the Roman version of Dionysus. Roman historians writing in this period describe early Christian practices in the same terms they used to condemn the Bacchic.

All of this combined to infuse early Christianity with many elements of primitive religion, a process that continued as it spread to the pagan reaches of Europe. Christian holidays such as Christmas and the practices attached to them were largely cut and pasted from indigenous pagan celebration, a plagiarism that continues into modern times with Catholic adoption of Native American practices in the New World.

Yet in the earliest days of Christianity there was not that much distance between the church's practice and the pagans. We know this from the condemnations of the early Christian leaders who were attempting to herd their congregations in more dour directions. For instance, in the fourth century, this edict issued from one of them, Gregory of Naxianus: "Let us sing hymns instead of striking drums, have psalms instead of frivolous music and sing . . . modestly instead of laughter, wise contemplation instead of intoxication, seriousness instead of delirium." If early Christians were not doing these things, he wouldn't have had to tell them to stop. Another, an archbishop, condemned similar practices with this: "For where there is a dance, there is also the Devil." My mother believed the same and said it in similar words.

Still, by all indications, these guys were fighting a losing battle then, and the early church remained dominated by primitive, ecstatic worship for another eight hundred years or so. The more successful backlash against ecstasy erupted in the thirteenth century, was still being waged intensely in the nineteenth, and has never really ended. Before the eighteenth century, churches didn't have pews—that is, were not set up for audience. Rather congregants stood and milled about, the better for dancing and participation. This is the geometry of the ring shout, the shape of primitive religion.

By victory over the primitive, though, the bishops had to settle for something well short of eliminating dancing, music, and festival. These practices were simply too popular and too ingrained. They settled for moving these practices out of the church and onto the streets, and so was born the tradition of carnival, widespread throughout Europe beginning in the thirteenth century. The religious roots of carnival were and are abundantly clear. Festivals meshed with the church calendar, triggered by various holidays and saints' days. That is, events that were once periodic celebrations within the church simply changed venue. But from their beginning, carnivals shared the very same elements that had vexed early church leaders, before that, the Apollonian Greeks and before that, defined primitive ritual for fifty thousand years. Central to these celebrations were frenetic, participatory dance and music, feasting, drinking, masquerading, and ecstasy.

One imagines the institution of carnival endured because it was adaptive in the evolutionary sense, served a real purpose in European society: a stabilizer. Life otherwise was drudgery, but carnival offered a release valve, a respite of joy from stoop labor. This role surfaces as a remarkable trait shared among carnivals across the continent and prefaced by similar practices in pre-Christian cultures. Part of the masquerading, the shape shifting of carnival was a lampoon of social status and hierarchy. Peasants dressed as nobles and vice versa. Carnival, even in thirteenth-century Europe, held hints of subversion.

The cakewalk fad spread through late nineteenth- and early twentieth-century America, and that the specific dance itself was rooted in the plantation South. It arose as a satire by African slaves on masters dancing the minuet. This bit of theater would have been right at home in thirteenth-century France.

Church leaders, however, finally escalated, especially when Protestantism came along, especially its most severe form, Calvinism, the strain that laid the foundation of American Puritanism. Thus began a war of carnival itself, especially in Protestant regions, but the intensity varied with time and place. For instance, Martin Luther, the founder of the Protestant movement, was not himself opposed to dance and carnival. Octoberfest could endure in context of his Lutheran Church. John Calvin was more single-minded from the beginning, and eventually so were the Lutherans. But in varying degrees, Protestantism stamped out carnival where it could. For a long period, so did the Catholics.

Yet strains endured, even in the New World. New Orleans still maintains carnival in the Mardi Gras, a direct descendant of European pagan practices preserved through the French Catholic tradition unique to this region of the United States. No accident then that this hotbed of ecstatic dance, resting as it does at the hub of the nation's most important transportation network of the eighteenth and nineteenth centuries, the Mississippi River and peopled by Creoles, a hybrid culture, was particularly well placed to serve then as the incubator of America's music. Jazz and blues are not just simply roots music but grew rooted in primitive ecstatic ritual, both African and European.

Yet it would be altogether shortsighted to view this, not just New Orleans, but all of this, as a conflict between dancers and religion. Indeed this is precisely the way organized religion would have us view it, and because organized religion—that is civilization—controlled writing and the recording of history, an obvious bias. Thus we associate the Dionysian rituals with hedonism, a matter of placing pleasure above principle. Pleasure is very different from ecstasy and joy.

At play here is conflicting view of theology, or maybe even rejecting the idea that religion is theology, the knowledge of a god. Organized religion is contractual, and, under its terms, access to the deity is granted through doctrine, law. Primitive religion delivers access to a larger sense of the creation in the here and now through practice, manipulation of body and brain. It is not a matter of pie in the sky but of obtaining a widened state of consciousness that opens an immediate connection to and awe of the creation and of our shared humanity.

Peter Matthiessen, one of our best writers and a lifelong Buddhist, titled his last novel, published just when he died in 2014, *In Paradise*. Set in a former Nazi concentration camp, the story faces up to the worst aspects of humanity, but its title and its message wrap around one of Christianity's defining moments, when a crucified and dying Christ promises a thief crucified with him that he will soon enter paradise. The meaning of that moment as regarded by Christians today rests on the translation from the original Greek, but there is a school of thought that argues the accepted version is in fact a mistranslation. In the original, Christ was not talking about the future. The present is all there is; if there is a paradise, then we are in it. Whether or not we enter paradise depends on our ability to perceive it in this world of ours, in Matthiessen's story, even in Auschwitz. The position you take on this depends on whether you are, at your core, a bishop or a dancer.

###

By now it may appear as if I am building a case for some sort of resurrection of primitive religious practices, yet no such case needs to be made.

These practices need no resurrecting. They never died. Nor is there a clear and dichotomous line that would sort the varieties of religious experience into one camp or another, even though throughout the course of organized religion, people have tried to do so. Poles yes, pure types we can pose for the sake of argument to channel thought to desiccated abstraction. The Dionysian endures because it is a necessary facet of our existence. It is an element of all human endeavor, not a dividing line between humans but a line that defines dehumanization.

Nor is there a good way to parse the various elements of primitive religion to pick one or another as explaining this endurance. I have entered this discussion through music, and certainly this is a workable path, but we don't get very far along it before we begin talking also about rhythm and dance and finding we, like our forebears, need no separate words for dance and music, so closely do they mate. Likewise with ceremony and ritual, likewise with ecstasy. Easy enough to see how these lump rather than split into separate categories.

Yet the anthropologists bring us up against a couple of traits that may seem, from our perspective in this present, weird, ancient, alien, maybe even vestigial and unnecessary to the core idea. The first of these is trance. The record is clear enough, that a point of primitive religious ritual was to send not everyone, but someone, the select, the shaman off into a mental state that most of us might label delusional or mentally ill, the sort of behavior we would today expect from a bum sleeping under a bridge, these places being our modern version of mental wards. Or a stoner, and a lot of shamans got there just this way—ayahuasca, peyote, marijuana, alcohol. We believe we don't do trance anymore. But we do.

There's even a literature of sorts on the topic, and some of it is as quirky and undisciplined as one might expect. The idea takes us naturally into crystal gazing, unseen energy fields and no small amount of snake oil. But not all of it. Some writers and researchers have taken a serious, disciplined look at trance. One of these writers, Dennis Wier, makes the case that trance is a lot more common than we think. A daydream is a sort of trance. So is successful practice of meditation. Hypnosis is well established and researched, as are conditions like ecstatic trance that results from modern practices such as Gregorian chants or whirling around at a Grateful Dead show. Falling in love is becoming entranced. His evidence, though, is the most widespread and successful use of trance is in television and the internet. Advertisers, especially political advertisers, thoroughly understand and use the technique. There are even patents on researched trance inducing methods, some of those in use, deployed and proven effective by the US military during the Iraq wars.

The common denominator in all forms of trance is what psychologists call "dissociation." This is a mental state that of a sudden places one outside of usual patterns of thought and habits of mind, often dramatically enough to produce an out-of-body experience, as if viewing oneself from a distance. Often a dissociated person has a gap in memory, to recollection or awareness of the period of entrancement, like an alcoholic blackout, an effect easily produced with hypnosis or simple meditation techniques. Easier still with some repetitive and hyperrhythmic forms of music. Other markers are suspension of logic, critical judgment, and self-control. All of this is a setup for doing really stupid things: joining a cult, following a führer believing in magic. Our habits of mind protect us, and breaking them is dangerous. Yet also necessary. Our habits of mind restrict us and channel us into our solipsistic and tunneled vision. Trance lies at the center of primitive religion because the dissociative state allows us to imagine the vast and unfathomable complexity of the creation Easy enough imagine how this is true.

The science journalist John Horgan comes at this for a number of angles in his book *Rational Mysticism: Spirituality Meets Science in the Search for Enlightenment* but finds the dissociative state we call trance as a common element. For instance, he looks at the research of two neuroscientists, Andrew Newberg and Eugene D'Aquili: "The common element in all spiritual experiences, Newberg and D'Aquili contended, is a sense of deeper unity than that conveyed by ordinary consciousness. The sensation can range from the mild communion that a congregation feels while singing a hymn to the 'state of absolute unitary being' in which you lose all sense of self, of subject-object duality."

This mental state is dissociation.

But what of the red ochre? Why do we see evidence from the very dawn of humanity of face painting and disguises, masquerade that winds through this story worldwide universally persistently, right on up to the masked revelers in Mardi Gras, Halloween and New Year's Eve. Friedrich Nietzsche and Bob Dylan both have something to say about this. Ehrenreich introduces and expands Nietzsche's case drawn from her examination of the role of primitive ritual:

> First because such rituals serve to break down a sufferer's sense of isolation and reconnect him or her with the human community. Second, because they encourage the experience of *self-loss*, that is, a release, however temporary from the prison of the self, or at least from the anxious business of evaluating how one stands in the group or in the eyes of an ever-critical God. Friedrich Nietzsche, as lonely and tormented an individual as the nineteenth century produced, understood the therapeutics of ecstasy perhaps better than anyone else. At a time of almost universal celebration of the "self" he alone dared speak of the "horror of individual existence" and glimpsed relief in the ancient Dionysian rituals. (152)

Arguably, Dylan is of a time even more mired in "a celebration of self" and was a far more Dionysian character than Nietzsche. He appeared in concert in whiteface, masked in white paint. The superficial interpretation was that he did so as an imitation of mimes. The somewhat more historically aware interpretation was that he was mirroring blackface performers, the source of his music and much of American roots music. But it was a clearly a religious observance, tracking through time not only to blackface but also to redface, to ochre. That he would a few years later issue a work called *Masked and Anonymous* repeats the message. Donning a mask is at once the act of becoming someone else, of empathy, but at the same time, taking the necessary corollary step of hiding one's own self. It's no accident that best evidence of this transformative ritual emerges at the very beginning of the human experience, evidence of an evolutionary leap that enhanced our survivability as a species.

The neuroscientist Walter Freeman says: "Dance is the biotechnology of group formation." This is a restatement of something Freeman told us toward the beginning of this book about music: "Here in its purest form is a human technology for crossing the solipsistic gulf. It is wordless, illogical, deeply emotional and selfless in its actualization of transient and then lasting harmony between individuals."

My progress in playing guitar was not and is not linear, not a matter of each day getting a bit better. It comes in fits and starts. When it happens, it feels more like transformation than progress and is signaled by strange signs, sometimes upsetting, alien, unexpected. The best example was the day I came to believe my own guitar, the same instrument I had held in my hands for years, had suddenly become physically smaller, a couple of inches shrunken in all its dimensions, so small I barely noticed as a separate object. There was a jump cut in my perception. At the same time, I seemed to lose all consciousness of the fingerboard, that grid, that minefield of notes I had so patiently and painfully committed to memory. Lost track of my fingers. In these times, I began playing music, not notes.

And then this sudden mind shift would as suddenly correct itself, but over time I found I could more and more easily reproduce the effect, even predictably by playing for a long time, hours, repetitively, and then the music would return, coming from my suddenly small guitar.

Then one day I found I could make it happen with a Gary Davis tune, one of his gospels, one I had in earlier years avoided. As I learned more and more about my guitar, I was more drawn back to Davis and found his blues tunes, the ones I loved to sing, limiting. As I learned more about music, I found more to grasp in his gospel, and of course there would be. That's what he cared most about, and he invested these religious tunes with a power and drive he thought they deserved. They are technically harder, fuller, richer, but also use techniques that make the music rise and soar if one gets it right. It took years, but I studied them for the musical techniques, just wouldn't sing them. But then there was the shape shift. My guitar got small, and I found myself singing words of devotion and praise I had long detested, yet irresistible now for the power Davis gave them. I found myself singing, "I belong to this band, hallelujah."

9

SECOND MIND

Best to have a guide during a visit to Louisiana's bayou country, not to avoid hazards but to discover its inner workings. Mine that sunny May day was Paul Anastasio, not a Cajun, not a local, but a newcomer, moved to the place only a couple of years before drawn by the music and fleeing high housing prices in his hometown of Seattle. Anastasio is of retirement age, but the term makes no sense whatever to a professional musician. They live to play and play until they die or are too addled or bent and broken. Anastasio is none of those yet. He is one of the world's best jazz fiddlers, for a long time the fiddler in Merle Haggard's band, then with Asleep at the Wheel, Larry Gatlin, Loretta Lynn, and Mel Tillis. He got his start in bluegrass and studied as a young man with the jazz great Joe Venuti. With such a star-studded career, he is blessed but, like most such musicians, not rich. But he and his wife, Claudia, found a friend in bayou country, and the friend offered a place where they could set up a secondhand Katrina cottage they found, which is a long manufactured home the size of a semi trailer used for emergency housing after Hurricane Katrina wiped down this same landscape. They plopped it onto the friend's land and next to it a retired shipping container that Anastasio uses as a climate-controlled warehouse for his 6,500 vinyl recordings and manuscripts. Claudia plays old-time fiddle and some Cajun music. Paul teaches fiddle camps in summer, a few Skype lessons, plays gigs here and there. He says he really doesn't play Cajun fiddle.

I've only a couple of days to spend with Anastasio, so I leave our itinerary to him, and he has decided the Saturday morning jam at Marc

Savoy's as just the ticket. Savoy's shop is an industrial looking steel shed of a building just outside of Eunice, Louisiana, not so much a music store as a workshop. The front is stacked high with boxes of Peavey amplifiers and mixers. There's a long glass counter at one end for CDs, cables, and such and a long back room that is mostly warehouse. But the front end's floorspace is open, and on this Saturday morning it is set up with folding metal chairs to accommodate an audience of twenty or so locals, sitting. Then there is some open floor for dancing.

Savoy himself is behind the counter, head down tinkering with an accordion. He builds them and will create to order a custom Cajun button accordion that sells for about $5,000. He doesn't say all that much, and Anastasio has already warned me not to try an interview. It's not what he does. Mustached, round face, flat affect that occasionally breaks to a wry smile, Savoy is nonetheless friendly enough, and when his few words come, they flow in the murmuring lilt and easy cadence unmistakably Cajun.

Meantime, a half dozen or so musicians have filled a circle of chairs around the ancient upright piano, a liberal smattering of guitars as with any amateur jam session, but even as the group begins a few tentative warm-up tunes, even the untrained ear can hear that the accordions and fiddles are in charge, especially the accordions. They drive the melody with gusts from the bellows, pumping abrupt accents to articulate phrases. This pulls dancers to the floor.

This sound of Cajun music took some time to evolve, but it began with a fiddling tradition separate from the Irish and Scottish lineage that infected Appalachia and ultimately the rest of American roots music. The word "Cajun" is a corruption of the term Arcadians, labeling the French people kicked out of what is now east coast Canada by the Brits in the mid-eighteenth century.

The accordion came later, but this is not the piano accordion of the upper Midwest, the mother-of-pearl cliché of polka bands. It is the older and simpler diatonic button accordion common throughout Europe. The first ones into Louisiana were of German manufacture, and they were good enough for a start, but the Cajuns eventually learned that the timbre they wanted came from the reeds—the thin vibrating plates that are the source of the sound—in Italian accordions. So they tinkered and made their own accordions based on the German design with Italian reeds. This lineage founded the craft of Marc Savoy, but he is not just a builder. He is a prominent player. His most famous and lasting collaboration has been with the great Cajun fiddler Michael Doucet, who founded the band BeauSoleil. Savoy and Doucet played the mother of all folk festivals, the Newport Folk festival.

But this morning Savoy stays behind the counter tinkering and talking with a string of visitors, his neighbors, the locals. This weekly gathering is not so much a performance as a social ritual with music at its center. A few kids play on the concrete floor. There's an urn of coffee and plates of sugar-soaked food. Some sit and listen to the rising wave of music and some ride it on the dance floor, kids dancing with kids and old ladies with old ladies.

I am expecting to be musically perplexed by this exotic music, my first direct exposure, but as I listen to the guitar players, I realize it is bone simple. Three chords, and those don't change all that often. Key of G. The people's key. Waltzes and two-step. There's a vocal line, high and keening, and I understand not a word of the Cajun French, but then begin to hear the notes as the old-time fiddle tune of "Red Wing." It's also "You Are My Sunshine." The lyrics would translate to something altogether different, but there it is. Ancient borrowed melodies, Italian reeds, German accordions, French fiddles, and C.F. Martin's guitars.

Simple it may be, but the music entices. It's just a jam, but a good one. No one is using it as platform to show off licks, to stand out. It's a collective. The melody lines pushed along by accordions ride on an easy bed or rhythm laid down by three or four guitars. Yet the whole business doesn't cross the line into ethereal territory until the vocals kick in. The singer causes me to stare off into the distance, maybe a century or so away from the place it seems to be coming from, then notice that I am standing right next to the vocalist, a couple of feet away perched on a steel folding chair. He's an old man, tall and rail thin, weather-beaten and haggard-looking. He's got a lap full of harmonicas he's been blowing. There's a fiddle propped next to him, and every now and again it comes into play, its butt end resting on his chest in the primitive rural style.

I wait for the long pause between songs when the musicians nod and murmur to each other and then catch the singer's attention. Coz Fontenot tells me he has been playing since he was four years old, first fiddle then harmonica. Always sang, as near as he can remember. All this in a sentence or two of lilting Cajun accent. When he was a boy in this place, the prairie bayou country north of Lafayette, one chose to play music the same way one chose to breathe the air. Fontenot never stopped, but there's a catch, a common enough side effect of music, and I am tipped off to this by a series of jarring moments. Fontenot is only a couple of sentences into telling me about his start in music when I notice him break up, tears running down his face, weeping. I look down, avoiding his eyes and then notice one of his legs is prosthetic. But then I notice a box of CDs at the base of his chair and try to distract both of us by asking him if I can buy one. His photo is on the cover and it shows a man only a couple of years before who was a good sixty pounds stouter than this cadaverous husk sitting before me in tears.

Paul Anastasio is not playing but holed up in the back room with his laptop working on a wickedly complicated arrangement for twin fiddles he is to perform that night in concert, but I interrupt him for the backstory. Fontenot is dying. He has liver cancer and a rack of complications, most of them traceable to his long history of alcoholism and tobacco addiction. He's not seventy-five, as he looks. He's in his early sixties. He lived the life of a musician and now it is killing him young. Anastasio has spoken with him about this at one of these Saturday morning jam sessions at Marc Savoy's accordion shop. Fontenot never misses one of these sessions, even though he is dying. He told Paul, "I wish every day was Saturday."

Frankie Lymon, Prince, Whitney Houston, Amy Winehouse, Hank Williams, Michael Jackson, Jay Bennett, Townes Van Zandt, Ike Turner, Howie Epstein, Dee Dee Ramone, Carter Stanley, Allen Woody, David Ruffin, Brent Mydland, Steve Clark, Paul Butterfield, Mike Bloomfield, Tim Hardin, John Bonham, Lowell George, Sid Vicious, Keith Moon, Elvis Presley, Tim Buckley, Nick Drake, Gram Parsons, Kurt Cobain, Alan

Wilson, Dinah Washington, Jim Morrison, Jimi Hendrix, Janis Joplin, Charlie Parker.

It is the most cursory of lists, barely a beginning, just a few of the musicians dead of drugs. Nor does it include the walking wounded, drunks and addicts who kicked or struggled to kick their addictions. Some relapsed, some died early. To begin: Steve Earle, Shaun Colvin, Bonnie Raitt, Johnny Cash, Ozzy Osbourne, Miles Davis, Eric Clapton, Yoko Ono, David Bowie, Keith Urban, Neil Young, David Crosby, Jerry Garcia, Elton John, George Harrison, Ringo Starr, Ray Charles, Brian Wilson, Chet Baker, Ginger Baker, Billie Holiday. Most anyone can add to either list off the top of her head. There is a strong association between famous musicians and drug and alcohol addiction. Becoming a famous musician is a bit like becoming a logger or bomb defuser, a hazardous occupation carrying high risk of winding up badly damaged or dead. A problem for musicians, but also for the thesis of this book, which is founded on the assertion that music persists because it makes us better. Addiction and overdose argue the opposite. Music in our time has a body count. The evidence, at least the circumstantial evidence, says playing music kills people. Where's the fitness in this?

There are a couple of facile counterpoints, valid, true enough and beside the point. The first is purely biological and useful not so much for illuminating the larger point, but in telling us something important about the pitfalls of purely biological arguments. Biological fitness is not about survival of the individual but survival of the individual's genes, the realization expressed in the term "selfish gene" popularized by the evolutionary biologist Richard Dawkins. Some of the early and narrow arguments about biology and music focused on sexual selection, that music was a form of display behavior that demonstrated intelligence, accomplishment, and fitness to potential mates, like a peacock's tail or a bull elk's big chest and antlers, allowing musicians attract more mates. The biologists went on to support this case with examples like Bob Dylan, rock stars who have had a truly enormous number of sexual partners and have in fact fathered a large number of children. One of the more famous examples appears on one of the lists above. Jimi Hendrix had a surfeit of sexual partners and fathered children but died young of a drug overdose, bringing home the point that in biology, dying young is not a failed life, as long as one leaves a string of genetic copies in the next generation. So in this narrow sense, music confers fitness.

The reader is forgiven for not finding this argument as satisfying as do the evolutionary biologists and can probably just as quickly knock it down by pointing out that a number of people on the above victims list are women. Addicted women make lousy mothers and produce unsuccessful offspring. Further, many of the men were difficult, eccentric, near psychotic humans, unfit for any sort of role as a parent and mercifully fathered no children before the needle in their arm slipped them into the grave.

In less censorious terms, the stark biological argument fails to realize that some evolutionary biologists have moved beyond stark and myopic biological arguments, laws of the club and the fang and that sort of thing. Ideas about group selection have led us to some understanding that passing on human genes demands more than copulation and gestation; it requires successful rearing of offspring to adulthood, which requires reasonable stable and well-adjusted adults, group cooperation, and cohesion. Hence, arguments about community stability, empathy, and pair bonding enter the picture, and we need to consider music's role in these larger necessities.

Pop psychology offers its rationale for the high correspondence between musicians and addiction, and it's no more satisfying than the narrow biological argument but worth mentioning. It steers us to a deeper discussion. A list of reasons might look something like this: Pop music, especially forms like rock 'n' roll and its various derivatives, but also country music and antique forms like blues, even old-time Appalachian music, are served up in atmospheres of general licentiousness. Of course they are. Always so. Recall the Dionysian roots of music. So if one's workplace is a bar with a back alley for drug deals, one indulges. Further, famous musicians are rich, so they can afford drugs. Celebrity status grants them license to buy and use drugs in public, life on the road is tedious and unsettling and begs to be alleviated with drugs. Iconoclasm and counterculture create peer pressure. Pop stars are young, and the young believe they are invincible, immune to such matters as overdose that plague mere mortals. Drugs and alcohol fuel rebellion. And on and on.

All of these matters are true enough, and I don't mean to exclude them as factors, but settling on these explanations keeps us from some larger issues and more importantly falls into exactly the same trap that has plagued much of the scientific research about musicians. All of this reasoning applies to professional musicians, especially those in the bizarre, historically unique and exceedingly remote—to most people—culture of fame, fortune, and celebrity. People who aren't musicians but live in this same vortex—actors, for instance—have a record of addiction every bit as dismal. Musicians who aren't celebrities, the people I have been writing about here, the amateur, the back-porch picker and stalwart of the local symphony orchestra, don't have this profile. They are musicians, just not famous. Much of the long-established addictive tendencies of famous musicians can be written off as a function of fame, not music.

Yet the not-so-famous are hardly drug- and alcohol-free. I know stories. We all do. They are commonplace enough to be not worth telling. The problem can easily be overstated by focusing on celebrity but doesn't go away if we move away from it, and I don't mean to sidestep by going that route. Yes, these are facile and unsatisfying answers. There must be more to it than this, yet the deeper answers are in some ways no more satisfying but open the way to fuller grasp of what is going on in our brains when we make music or, for that matter, deal with the complexities of human existence.

If one is looking for clues about drugs and music, a good tactic would be to follow Steve Earle. Or looking for clues about wives for that matter; he's had seven, a number that speaks to a life unsettled. Nonetheless, he's still on his feet, more than just surviving. He is by any measure an extraordinarily successful songwriter and performer, has branched into an acting career with David Simon vehicles like *The Wire* and *Treme* and is a published author. Earle set himself up for turmoil early on when he decided to become a songwriter, ran away from home, and signed on for his first apprenticeship with Townes Van Zandt, a notorious drunk, a character one might be tempted to write off as pathetic were he not one of the finest songwriters of modern times. He drank himself to death. Earle would not settle for such a pedestrian path. He was a heroin addict and did prison time as a result.

Earle's work is very much in the vein of Van Zandt's, true first to Texas, but also to the rural Southern rebels, the outlaw yarn spinners, men in black and boots and big hats. This hardly seems the heroin crowd, but the better journalism now about the status of rural America, especially the South, says otherwise. Not so long ago, alcohol was the drug of choice here, but supplanted in Johnny Cash's time and even in Hank Williams's by prescription drugs, of late oxycontin, for a time known as "hillbilly heroin," which, it turns out, is often merely a brief stop on the road to the real thing. Hillbilly heroin today is heroin. Earle was just precocious.

If one is tracking this history musically, the omnipresence of heroin in hayseed habitat is an odd jolt. Bebop. This is where heroin belongs. Chet Baker, Charlie Parker, Miles Davis, and many others among a whole generation of jazz greats was marked by needles in their arms, and some of them died for it. One can make this case, it seems, by picking paragraphs at random from Miles Davis's autobiography, but here's an example describing the jazz world in the 1950s:

> There was a lot of dope around the music scene and a lot of musicians were deep into drugs, especially heroin. People—musicians—were considered hip in some circles if they shot smack. Some of the younger guys like Dexter Gordon, Tadd Dameron, Art Blakey, J. J. Johnson, Sonny Rollins, Jackie McLean, and myself—all of us—started to get heavily into heroin around the same time. *Despite* the fact that Freddie Webster had died from some bad stuff. Besides Bird (Charlie Parker) Sonny Stitt, Bud Powell, Fats Navarro, Gene Ammons were all using heroin, not to mention Joe Guy and Billie Holiday, too. They were shooting up all the time. There were

a lot of white musicians—Stan Getz, Gerry Mulligan, Red Rodney, and Chet Baker—who were heavy into shooting drugs. (emphasis in original)

Yet they were the jazz sophisticates musically, producing a burst of musical creativity. They were urban, urbane, hip, mostly black, in all ways polar opposite to hillbillies.

Earle himself once offered a clue that helps resolve the contradiction. Just after his prison time, Earle recorded an album that was a departure for him, *The Mountain*, a collection of hardcore bluegrass songs all written by him but true to the traditions traceable to Bill Monroe. His band for this project was Del McCoury's, hardcore bluegrass as they come, high, lonesome and fast. Earle explained all of this is his own way, that some years before he had gotten interested in bluegrass music for a curious reason, just because he began hanging around with bluegrass players. He did so not out of any musical curiosity, he said, but rather because he couldn't help noticing at music festivals that bluegrass players always had the best drugs.

It is tempting to assume Earle's hypothesis here caused the strait-laced, dictatorial Bill Monroe to spin at 78 rpm in his grave, but Monroe probably knew better, even in his time, certainly by the midpoint of his time when bluegrass infected California and attracted such people as Jerry Garcia, John Hartford, and Tim O'Brien. It became the stomping grounds of a bunch of stoners and still is. Yet there is in this otherwise unremarkable fact a bit of news that is useful to advancing my story. Get it from Sam Bush, like Monroe a hot mandolin player and a giant of the genre, but unlike Monroe, very much of the new grass tradition.

Like bebop and all the other forms of jazz that flourished through the mid-twentieth century, bluegrass is wildly improvisational. It's a bit more formulaic than jazz, but nonetheless revolves on key members of the band riffing their way through "breaks," solos improvised on the spot. The core competency of a bluegrass musician is improvisation, just as with jazz.

Sam Bush is famous for teaching workshops and seminars on mandolin improvisation by advising students to advance their cause by smoking marijuana. The same sort of advice issued from jazz musicians but was rooted in stronger stuff.

It seems from all of this is that these accomplished musicians are telling us something about how music works or maybe how music culture works, at least for these two highly improvisational forms. They are telling us how our brains work, and not just in the case of music.

Recall now the neuroimaging studies I mentioned earlier in the book, that the neuroscientists Charles J. Limb and Allen R. Braun of the National Institute for Health and Johns Hopkins performed brain scans on trained musicians improvising and compared them to scans of the same musicians playing routine rote musical exercises, scales. Scales require technical musical ability but no creativity. The differences were remarkable, that during improvisation the regions of the brain associated with self-control, the prefrontal cortex, the smart part, conscious control, shut down, down regulated in the terms of brain science. Just the opposite when the same people were playing rote exercises.

"This unique pattern may offer insights into cognitive dissociations that may be intrinsic to the creative process: the innovative, internally motivated production of novel material (at once rule based and highly structured) that can apparently occur outside of conscious awareness and beyond volitional control," the researchers observed about this phenomenon.

What catches the eye first in the stilted language of academics is that phrase "beyond volitional control"—exactly the state one achieves in inebriation of any sort. We have controls in our brains, useful, necessary controls that keep us from bad decisions and bad behavior but at the same time prevent spontaneity and creativity. This is not to suggest that to make music one needs to surrender to general licentiousness, although plenty of people believe this. Ever been to a Grateful Dead show, or even to the local open-mic night at the local bar to hear a soulfully rendered drum solo best described as noise? People tend to forget the idea stated here by the scientists that pleasing improvised music is "rule based and highly structured." If that sounds like a contradiction, it is. Most interesting matters in our lives are conundrums.

Music arises at the point of creative tension between these opposing ideas, but in our rule-bound, literalist, frightened society of overachievers, it is difficult for most of us to achieve the abandon that frees the mind to wander the creative process. Many improvisational musicians have learned to do this unassisted by chemistry. Those players entombed in the neuroscientists' fMRI machine with electronic keyboards were not drunk or high. Still, drugs provide a shortcut, a cheat. Get the dosage right, and the player can quickly find himself in the zone of just the proper surrender of control to access the magic of music, freed, but still able to remember the rules and the structure. It's a delicate dance, in the case of heroin, with the devil. Some people get it right until they don't, and we all know of such cases.

This is not just a matter of music but one of those areas where what is pronounced and obvious in music applies to the whole of our lives. Indeed this is the very matter that drew one researcher into his investigation of ancient Chinese realizations expressed in Taoist traditions. Edward Slingerland, in his book *Trying Not to Try*, indeed uses musical examples to make his case, but also more common experience, such as falling down. It's a common insight among his undergrad students, he says, but not just his, that kids new to drinking sometimes stumble into childish acrobatics, footraces, and tumbles and are quick to figure out that those properly inebriated fall, roll, and giggle, then stand again unharmed, while the stone cold sober among them suffer injuries. It's a matter of control, that the sober use their executive function, their control brains to prevent injury and so override the body's subconscious and hardwired abilities to protect us better than the conscious brain can. We don't trust our instincts to guide us, and reason is a poor substitute in many situations.

Slingerland quotes an ancient Chinese Taoist text, the Zuangzi, as being ahead of the undergraduates in this realization: "When a drunken person falls out of a cart, although the cart may be going very fast, he won't be killed. His bones and tendons are the same as other people's yet he is not injured as they would be."

Yet even before Taoists began falling out of carts, this was far more than a matter as simple as falling down. For all of human time, even before religion became religion, people have been using drugs to effect a crossing, a journey across a great divide. The job description of shamans was to travel to a netherworld, which they did by a state of trance, a brain state, a surrender of the conscious, controlling, rational brain to access more capacious and revelatory sections of cortex, to access the way, the Tao, the nether brain that keeps us from injury when we fall, call it what you will. Just recall that for as long as this has been going on, the shaman's journey has been assisted by drugs: ayahuasca, cannabis, alcohol among the Dionysians. The early Taoist monks favored hallucinogenic mushrooms.

In my own mind, though, I have come to believe this is the exact journey necessary for musical improvisation, a hunch of mine that seems bolstered by the neuroscience that says improvisation is marked by a shutdown of the rational, controlling, chattering monkey brain. We cross into that land of magical creativity, where music flows, and we cannot know where it is coming from by learning to fully inhabit an unseen portion of our minds. As long as I have been playing guitar, now half a lifetime, I have been in awe of ordinary everyday pickers—truck drivers, accountants, PR executives, foresters, and teenagers—who magically cross this great divide as effortlessly as if it did not exist. And I cannot. I am stuck playing only the notes I learned one by one.

This is why I have finally sought out Paul Anastasio, who is nothing if not a master of crossing, a shaman, not only a gifted improviser but a teacher, a shaman who teaches shamans. I had met him in Montana through friends of mine, a pickup band that he joined. Then we sat and talked in a pleasant kitchen in Livingston just before he and the others headed off to a gig, a house party at Tom Brokaw's ranch. He was then bright, friendly, and engaging and seemed open to a longer conversation, so I flew to meet him in Louisiana.

We're en route to Marc Savoy's shop in Anastasio's Prius, and I finally get around to asking him about drugs, alcohol, and improvisation, giving him the Sam Bush story about marijuana. It's bullshit, he tells me, doesn't even bother to engage it. This, remember, is a serious road musician, a side man, and every side man has seen careers wrecked by alcohol, and he offers an example. He did a stint as a fiddler for the country star Mel Tillis, toured in his band, and Tillis is an alcoholic but decided to get sober. He went into treatment and learned that the alcoholic's family must also go through the process, and he considered his band as family so the whole band took the cure. Tillis paid. "We learned a ton," Anastasio says. I'm with Anastasio for three days. He drinks nothing but soda water. That's the rule of thumb for all the amateurs I know. Jam sessions, festivals, back porch pickings. Alcohol is rare, drugs wholly absent. Some have a very different past, but that's the point: It has passed, and they prefer it that way, having seen the needle and the damage done.

So what about improvisation? How does Anastasio teach people to do magic without drugs? Oddly, this question of mine triggers a long, involved lament of the state of humanity and amateur musicians in particular. There is in this nation an intricate and evolved network of both competitive fiddling and summer camps where both children and adults attend for weeks on end to learn to play better. Anastasio is deeply involved in both, a judge at contests and an instructor at the most prestigious of camps.

As a judge, he's learned to ask competitors, often the winners—technically skilled practitioners of lightning fast arpeggios, intricate fingerings, precision—what key they are playing in. Often they don't know. He tells me the response he gets is something like: "I dunno, but the first two notes are this one and this." This is much like asking a painter what colors are in her palette and she doesn't know.

At camps, Anastasio has learned that the same students are back year after year and they get no better, that he can teach the same tune he taught the year before to the same students and still it's new to them, that the camp itself is a sort of ritual, a box to be checked, which is how our literate society believes it learns: go to a class and get a certificate, not knowledge. Certainly no rigor or practice between. Rigor? Practice? I thought we were talking about improvisation?

But then he drops his lament. I think he understands I am not like these people, that I sincerely want to know how to cross over. You want to become a musician? Here's how, he tells me. And it turns out this is not original to him, that he was holed up in a small town one time on tour and happened across an old instruction book for jazz trombone, which he could, of course, not avoid reading, and it delivered the key to wisdom and enlightenment. To become a musician, you need four things: a mirror to judge one's physical engagement with the instrument, a metronome to enforce fidelity to rhythm, a tuner to stay in tune, and a recording device to hear yourself. That's it.

Fundamentals. Rudiments. This is where the magic lives. Anastasio's answer is not substantially different than the one I have gotten through the years from whomever great improviser I have asked: How do I learn to improvise? Play scales. Just those two words, again and again I have heard them. Play scales. Boring, mundane, rudimentary notes, eight in a row or five in a row, up and down, through the keys, major and minor, cowboy keys, flat keys, jazz keys, up and down, over and over, play scales. The exact same exercise the neuroscientists used to show a brain locked in its logical conscious self, the prefrontal cortex, that in playing scales it stayed there. And then in improvising it crossed over, went to its nether reaches. This is the paradox. We learn magic by mastering the mundane. Rigor is the foundation of creativity.

###

I spent only a couple of days with Anastasio, but unexpectedly our time together had a profound effect on me, and it didn't seem to come from what he told me or what I saw. Our conversations were long and involved, the scenes and characters novel and engaging, but nothing to augur a sea change.

The effects began with pronounced and stubborn insomnia, or so I thought, at first. Now I would bet that it was the sleeplessness of a particular sort that researchers in the field know well. A subject reports being awake the whole night but was in fact asleep, locked in endless, wakeful dreams. Yet my dreams that night, if that's what they were, weren't composed of images but sound, more to the point music, realized, fully formed intricate and engaging music, but notes set in a synesthetic matrix of colors and lights, hallucinatory like a mescaline trip. I didn't mind the insomnia; I was loving the music and colors. None of it I had ever heard before. Not earworms. These were not tunes I had heard Anastasio play during those few days before. There were original compositions, as far as I could tell.

This sort of event has happened to me before, maybe four or five times. In every instance, the experience seemed provoked by listening to music for an extended period, but not recordings of music. Live. I had tagged along with Anastasio to a series of rehearsals and concerts and then one morning's performance of several hours when he and a woman named Albany, a gifted young jazz guitarist who often accompanies him, sat in the living room of an ailing old lady, a neighbor, and played. So few of us ever hear music this way, not Marshall stacks in an arena or hypercompressed MP3s through earbuds, but unmediated by electronics, a straight line transmission of organic, unadulterated sound waves from wood and steel strings to brain. So few ever hear it crisply and precisely rendered by virtuosi, each note pitched and placed perfectly, beginning and ending in rhythms not wobbling even a nanosecond, music in a pure, distilled shots, 180 proof. Such music moves the brain, and mine had been moved.

But then just a day later, another trip, another dream, but before it, a real and awake experience that provoked it. That night, I decided to learn a new tune on banjo and so was doing what has become a standard practice, and not just mine. I went to YouTube to search out videos of various players doing the tune. Appalachian fiddle tunes evolve and shape-shift according to time and place, once a regional signature on the music, but with festivals and now recordings and now YouTube, less geographically defined, but still variation. I happened on a video of a well-known fiddler in a circle of musicians at a festival playing that tune, and was immediately drawn to the version, a good sign, but then as instantly drawn away from the tune and to a particular fiddler in the circle, gobsmacked, really, stunned. She was fairy-tale beautiful, seemingly of another place and time reachable only through a fiddle. I became obsessed with her like a teenager entranced with a centerfold model and forgot about learning the tune.

And then I slept and fell into a vivid cinematic dream, a classic, really. In my mind I was young and found myself at a series of funerals for relatives, old school funerals just like I remember from growing up in traditional, rural Midwest. But as I stared in terror at the corpse in the coffin, an old gray lady, powdered and rouged, my grandmother, or so I thought, I suddenly realized it was not, but a young woman, beautiful, not dead but made up to look like my grandmother. And then I discovered that Granny herself, indeed dead, was stuffed unceremoniously in the back room. The woman in the coffin was a stand-in, an actor, supplied by the funeral home as a consideration, a euphemism, a surrogate stiff, in deference to prevailing sensibilities in our time that are unable to look death and grief in the face. This new wrinkle to our funereal practices was the logical result of our alienation from our lives.

Aside from the Coen brothers film *O Brother, Where Art Thou?*, sirens make their most famous appearance in *The Odyssey*, in which the poet Homer uses them to great effect. He was riffing on a common trope in the ancient world. Throughout the whole prehistoric Mediterranean region, mythology is fully populated with a series of irresistible women who often took bird bodies, or part bird bodies, and sang in voices that surpassed birds and sometimes played musical instruments. They lured men to their deaths, so irresistible were their charms. Throughout the region, though, even before Homer and the Greeks, they were associated with the netherworld, funereal characters, their songs luring men to cross over to the deeper and dreamier mysteries beyond.

###

This matter of playing musical scales attaches to an odd little factoid that I now am finding difficult to ignore, a curiosity really, but one deeply embedded in the whole consideration of drugs and brain-altering substances. Most music, especially simple music such as American folk music, gets by on the vanilla notes of the major scale, spiced with the pentatonic scale, the offbeat, Africa-derived intervals that deliver the punch of the blue notes, the flatted thirds, fifths, and sevenths obvious and distinctive even to those ears that have no idea what a flatted third is. Yet the better-trained musicians, the jazz sophisticates and Julliard grads, are thoroughly versed in an array of scales called modes. These come into play in modal music, logically enough, the ethereal sounding strains from Ireland or the Middle East. It's an easy enough concept. Take a C-major scale, for instance, which is a series of eight tones beginning with the note C, stepped up on a piano by playing white keys in order. No blacks. No flats or sharps. It turns out, though, that those exact same notes, just white keys, white-bread keys of the white-bread major scale, produce radically different effects, radically different emotional content, depending on where one begins. Play the same white keys stepping up in pitch in order, but begin with the second note, the D, and suddenly the effect is darker and deeper, otherworldly. Same notes. Same order. Different beginning point. These are called modes, and each has a name: Ionian, Dorian, Phrygian, Lydian, Mixolydian, Aeolian, and Locrian. If it sounds like Greek, it is, and not by classical pretense that reached for Greek names. The Greeks knew the modes and named them.

The neuroscientist Walter Freeman believes that three of these modes—three that were important to the Greeks—work on the human brain through separate pathways, separate specific neurotransmitters, in parallel to how different addictive drugs stimulate those same neurotransmitters. He writes:

> Phrygian music was martial and served with trumpets to incite action in battle. Emotions of fear and rage are associated with intracerebral release of norepinephrine. Similar forms of aggressive and terrified behavior in modern times are induced by cocaine and amphetamine, which mimic some of the central effects of norepinephrine. Lydian music was solemn, slow, plaintive, and religious, with reliance on flutes instead of trumpets. Contemplative and relaxed moods induced by Muzak-like music are associated with release of serotonin in the brain. Similar effects were induced by ingestion of mushroom hallucinogens, which preceded LSD, and are now gained by Prozac, which blocks endogenous serotonin reuptake and prolongs its action. Ionian music was convivial, joyful, and according to Plato, effeminate, relying heavily on drums to induce dancing. Pleasurable states are now associated with intracranial release of dopamine and endorphins. Then as now they were induced by alcohol and tetrahydrocannabinol

[cannabis], which serve as adjuvants to facilitate the passive onset of such states at modern rock concerts and rave dances. (417–18)

Long before I understood the pathway drawn by modes, I followed a separate line into understanding the brain, a more conventional line for a journalist, a series of sources, scientists I interviewed. One led to another. More often than not, discovery begins as happenstance. Through an odd series of coincidences, I got to know Bessel van der Kolk. He's a psychiatrist, Harvard-trained. The work he is known for began with treating veterans of the Vietnam War suffering what in earlier wars was called shell shock. Van der Kolk helped label it posttraumatic stress disorder, a term now so ubiquitous in common discourse that it's hard to think of it as a coinage. Now, though, he is far better known for applying that line of thinking to children, and his efforts have spawned a national, federally funded network of researchers and an enormous and shocking body of knowledge. We learned, for instance, that child abuse is epidemic, largely from the effects of poverty, also widespread, and that sexual and physical abuse of children and a range of deprivations permanently warp developing brains to lock them in fear. As a result, those same children as adults develop a predicable set of life-threatening problems like alcohol and drug addiction, which you might expect, and lung disease, heart disease, diabetes, obesity, and suicide, which you might not.

Also as you might imagine, this has spawned a burgeoning industry in "treatments" all manner of psychological counseling, and dizzying array of talk therapies, medications, and a full-blown lexicon of psychobabble. Van der Kolk himself has had a hand in many but is now, late in his career, cynical, skeptical and dismissive of much of this. He happens to be the sort of scientist one finds rarely, but the very sort my experience in interviewing hundreds of scientists has taught me to seek. He is brilliant and eclectic, bombastic and iconoclastic. He is blunt and does not undermine his thoughts with the usual weasel words and qualifications.

I had known him for years and had heard him lecture therapists in groups of hundreds, sometimes for entire days, holding an audience's full attention all the time, but I finally got a chance to sit him down for a conversation in his office on the first floor of a stately old townhouse in Boston, a chance to ask what I had long been meaning to ask, that here is a man who has experimented with and seen the results of literally dozens of interventions for posttraumatic stress, a severe and epidemic injury of our brains. Everything from computer controlled electronic neurofeedback to Prozac to yoga to talk therapy. So tell us, Bessel, what works. He didn't hesitate but delivered an answer in plain English.

"Moving rhythmically together," was his exact phrase.

Like dancing. Yes, dancing. But together, moving with others in rhythm.

Recall now that this places him squarely in the agreement with writer Barbara Ehrenreich but from a completely different direction, from the experience of abused children and battle-worn soldiers. Ehrenreich's book *Dancing in the Streets* traces the path of music and dance from the Greeks through a series of tensions with Christianity. Recall now that she argued the Greeks, the Dionysians, used ecstatic dance as therapy and understood it just that way. She writes of a tradition in Greece preceding even Dionysus when healers or priests called *orpheotelestae* traveled the country healing mentally ill people with dance:

> Dionysus arrives in the city of Thebes in the form of such a traveler, and when Dionysian worship comes to Rome about two centuries after Euripedes' time, it is brought by a wandering magician-priest. As a healer, the itinerant charismatic cured by drawing the afflicted into ecstatic dances—which well may have been effective in the case of psychosomatic and mental illnesses—suggesting that he was a musician and a dancer as well as a priest. It was probably his arrival, announced by the beating of the *tympana*, that drew the women out from their houses and into the "madness" that was also a *cure* for madness. (40–41, emphasis in original)

Van der Kolk did not mention Ehrenreich's work, but nonetheless the correspondence goes further. For instance, he uses and endorses and odd form of therapy that uses Shakespearean theater, but he told me modern Western theater has lost much of its power to heal, compared to its predecessor, Greek theater. The former was far more participatory for the audience and always featured a chorus either chanting in rhythm, singing or dancing or all of these. Greek theater was rooted in Dionysian ritual, a linkage revealed by many paths of etymology. For instance, our word "tragedy" is a Greek compound word meaning "goat song," invoking an animal often linked with Dionysus.

Ancient societies were violent. Frequent devastating wars are at the center of Greek literature for a reason. The ancients certainly knew trauma, probably more than we do. Of necessity they developed ways for dealing with it in mass ritual of movement and song.

But one thing leads to another, and my conversation with van der Kolk led then to a colleague of his, an equally iconoclastic scientist he knows well doing research in Raleigh-Durham. So I traveled there to visit Stephen Porges in North Carolina. Porges's claim to fame is a conjecture of his that he named the "polyvagal theory." It's a description of our body's most socially important physical mechanism, which allows humans to be human. It is a firm and measurable answer to a question raised by anthropologists, best framed by the anthropologist Sarah Hrdy in an observation of hers, an experiment she suggested. She said that if we loaded an airliner with any species of wild mammal, a hundred or so individuals seated for a coast-to-coast trip, even highly social chimpanzees, even our closest relatives, that by the time the animals arrived at their destination, all of them would be dead. They would kill each other. The human species is only mammal with eusociality, the hyperevolved ability to control violence through social graces.

The root of the term *polyvagal* is the vagus nerve, a primitive but seminal nerve that wraps around the organs of a human's chest cavity and abdomen. Tellingly it is the only nerve that connects directly to our primitive limbic brain, because it regulates background functions like digestion, heart rate, and respiration, unconscious acts. But it is intimately wrapped up in every mammal's fight-or-flight response. This is the axis, the hot wire of trauma, of PTSD. A fear response is a normal evolutionary response to danger. It protects us by shutting down digestion, accelerating respiration and breathing, in short, steeling us for a fight. Fear sends us automatically to hyperarousal, an alarm state when our logical brains shut down, and we trigger the literally visceral responses necessary to survive existential threat. We lash out and kill our enemy. And then the threat disappears and we stand down. That's modulation, the very skill that allows us to get along and not kill each other, at least not all of the time, on fully loaded airliners. The simple explanation of why abused children suffer all those health consequences is through a long history of abuse, the body more or less locks into fear mode and is unable to modulate. Van der Kolk is fond of saying "trauma lives in the body," and this is what he means by that, often why talk therapies don't work for PTSD victims. They literally do not hear what is being said to them. The primitive brain has taken over.

But what does work to calm these same people is even, rhythmic breathing, and Porges's idea gets to the heart of this, literally the heart. He has detected and measured a subtle little quiver in heart's rhythm that signals relaxation, an arrhythmia he calls it. Not heart rate, although that plays in all this, but a little jiggle in rhythm that seems to be driving the process, but it is the question of what is driving that makes this most interesting. Our brains? One might think so, a central command that evaluates threat level and signals the heart and lungs to stand down when threat has passed. Makes sense. Here's the rub. Porges has demonstrated that cause and effect works just fine in the opposite direction. If one simply and consciously forces slower, controlled, rhythmic breathing, the whole arousal system of nerves and organs responds and relaxes. Then our brains follow on by going to the relaxed and rational place where it becomes possible to get along with others and not lash out in fight, flight, or fear. In this observation, we now have an explanation for something long observed, even by Porges himself, who is a musician, a French horn player. Horn players breathe in rhythm, but so do others. For instance, Gregorian chanters of the old school suffer less anxiety and depression when they are chanting regularly, compared to when they are not practicing. Both maladies are markers of traumatized people. Likewise the controlled, relaxed breathers of various meditation schools.

But none of this works on a conscious level. It nonetheless works, and all rests on rhythm. Now we should recall that humans are unique among species in more than our ability to survive an airline flight across the country without killing each other. We are unique in our ability to embody rhythm. Rhythm lives in the limbic section of our brains, where the vagus nerve connects.

Porges wanted me to know one more thing in our conversation, even after we had spent some hours discussing his work, and he does consider it groundbreaking and seminal but, like most wide-ranging scientists, wanted to direct me to another idea. He asked me whether I had heard of Iain McGilchrist.

In one of our conversations, van der Kolk answered a question of mine with one of his blunt sentences that will stick with me forever because it altered the way I thought about myself and everyone else. We were talking about radical differences in basic human behavior across generations and I asked him how this could be true. He said: "The brain is a social organ." By this he meant something like what neuroscientists mean by one of the discipline's axioms, that neurons that fire together wire together, the literal pathway of habits of mind. Patterns of behavior get hardwired in the brain, physically modifying the organ. Events in a child's upbringing play out later in life as behavior, but also in the physical shape of the brain. Brains are not predetermined by genetics so much as they are a recording of life history, shaped by our social interactions. They are social organs.

McGilchrist's case is that for two thousand years now, Western civilization has been warping our brains in massively debilitating ways. His case, laid out in great detail in his 2009 book *The Master and His Emissary*, is based in the brain's bilateralism. You have heard about this, and McGilchrist acknowledges that what you have heard about this is probably not helping his argument. Bilateralism is based on the differences between the right and left hemispheres of our brain, which a generation ago was all the rage in pop psych. Being right-brained meant you were creative, a poet; left-brained, an accountant. Like most pop psychology, the idea became clichéd and ridiculous and at the time was based on some spurious science.

Nonetheless, bilateralism is a fact evident in most animals' brains, birds and mammals especially. McGilchrist argues this is because all living things have two contradictory tasks, so contradictory that animals must be of two minds to make it work. He illustrates this with the example of a chicken, which has a markedly bilateral brain. A chicken needs to focus narrowly to forage, pick out bits of grass seed and bugs among the gravel and chaff, a survival skill that requires a precise and close command of a narrow plot of ground, along with categorizing and deciding. But a chicken also needs to have a broad focus on its entire surroundings to take in everything at once. No telling where the hawk or fox might come from. The left hemisphere handles the former, the right the latter.

Over time, this bilateral relationship has evolved and developed to wholly separate and identifiable sets of behaviors by each hemisphere, a case McGilchrist develops in reams of neuroscience, experiences of stroke victims with damage to one hemisphere or the other, but also through the philosophy of Plato and Nietzsche, the poetry of Goethe, and the music of Schopenhauer and Mozart. The pop psych version of this from a generation ago looks like a caricature drawing of his case, but nonetheless the lines are there. The left brain is logical, the right brain holistic and wise. In no way does he argue it is better to be one or the other, but rather that to be a functioning human we need to be both and are both. Specifically to our subject here, to music, the brain scans are clear enough. Music is an activity of both hemispheres. And that is, in McGilchrist's telling, precisely the root of the problem.

The title of his book is taken from a fable about a master, a ruler, a king, who appoints an emissary and in time the latter becomes puffed up with his power and believes he is in charge, is, in fact, the king. McGilchrist says the demands of hyperrational, commercial, hierarchical society over the course of two thousand years has rewired our brains to place us in this position, that our right brains, the seat of wisdom, have been usurped by our left, that we live so firmly in our left hemispheres we have lost access to wisdom, beauty, spirit, and music.

McGilchrist's case is eccentric among neuroscientists, which doesn't of course, make him wrong, but there are in his case some fundamental points that align completely with the broader direction of our understanding of the human brain. His dichotomy divides left from right, and the shape of the organ, the sheer structure obvious to anyone looking at a brain in a bottle, signals the importance of his analysis. There are, however, other lines of demarcation, and I've used them throughout this book, as does McGilchrist. The brain is also split front to back, prefrontal and frontal, the former representing later stages in evolutionary development. And top to bottom, again the former representing later stages. There have been a lot of assumptions and unwarranted conclusions through the years that uses whizbang technologies like magnetic resonance imaging to isolate certain functions in one of the areas of the brain, conclusions that speak to the function of a piece of cranial geography, but, as the science has progressed, we have come to understand the brain as more complicated, that disparate regions of the brain work together (or sometimes, more revealingly, work against each other) to handle tasks like music. But there is an even more intriguing conclusion emerging from neuroscience.

The great blues icon, my hero, Mississippi John Hurt ended his version of "C.C. Rider" with this verse:

If I had listened
To my second mind
I wouldn't be standing here
Wringing my hands and crying.

This lament agrees with the science. For instance, the biologist and neurologist Robert Sapolsky took on the enormous task of summarizing the current understandings of neuroscience in his important book of 2017 *Behave: The Biology of Humans at Our Best and Worst*. At the center of his case is an argument aimed straight at the common assumption of Western thought about who we are. The whole idea of free will rests on the assumption of a command and control brain with a central seat of power, a decider, an autocrat that mediates among the competing and contradictory impulses to set a course for an individual. The science says otherwise, that the brain is really a coalition of the various separate, independent parts, and they emerge in various combinations, depending on the moment, depending on how we have been molded and shaped by our lifetime of social interactions. But there is no central command, no decider. No one is in charge.

Which is where McGilchrist becomes really interesting. Our lives do in fact have a storyline, a narrative that tells us who we are, rationalizes, in the psychological sense of the word. Exactly. This is the left hemisphere talking. Through some herky-jerky combination of impulses, the various elements of the brain launch us on a course of action, then the left hemisphere makes up a story that lets us live with it. The emissary is there to make up a story that accounts for our behavior after the fact. It's not making the decisions that guide that behavior. The left hemisphere like the emissary is notorious for overrating its own importance in the coalition. As such, it is the seat of self-awareness, of narcissism. McGilchrist writes: "Too much self-awareness destroys not just spontaneity, but the quality that makes things live; the performance of music or dance, of courtship, love and sexual behavior, humor, artistic creation and religious devotion become mechanical, lifeless, and may grind to a halt if we are to self-aware."

That's McGilchrist's bottom line, a fear that civilization has so truncated our thinking that we no longer have access to wisdom, the larger view. We are stuck with the emissary's self-serving illusion. He makes a case for subversion of civilization's control of our brains, which is why I play scales—a paradox because this is demonstrably an act of the left brain. But someday it will slip. Someday I will so internalize those notes and patterns that I will slip the leash of the left brain and cross over to the netherworld, the other side, to that capacious area of wisdom and creativity that allows magic to happen, into my second mind. Music is an act of subversion. I began this book by asking why we humans persist in making music. Here's one answer: because it opens a pathway to our larger selves.

10

LOVE AND THEFT

The interstate highway that threads from Houston northeast along the Texas Gulf Coast is a dystopian hellscape, an oppressive roar of tractor trailers and hot-rodded monster pickup trucks smeared in confederate battle flags and NRA cant. Nothing in the passing scene invites a traveler to leave the truck-grooved highway and explore among the refineries, dollar-store strip malls, payday loan storefronts, and barbecue stands. Unless of course one knows about the Blanchette Cemetery. Until just a few years ago, no one did.

Blanchette was once a town separate—segregated, more accurately—from the city of Beaumont, Texas, but now has been absorbed into the whole, more or less. One gets there winding along Beaumont's surface streets south of the tracks, apparent wrong side, among shotgun shacks and narrow, quiet lanes without curb and gutter. A few pedestrians are abroad in midmorning of a hot early summer's day, all of them African American, but mostly the streets are quiet and empty, the houses modest, curtained, and quiet. The pace is relaxed.

As recently as 2007, no one could find the Blanchette Cemetery, at least not on the ground, where it had been lost to tangles of brush and undergrowth. Then, it was evident only in abstraction, on paper in a few obscure city records, platted somewhere down on Hegele Street among a bevy of churches like the House of Prayer and the Greater Little Zion Baptist Church. Yet two researchers, seekers, Anna Obek and Shane Ford, used the records and found the actual cemetery hidden in the weeds, crumbled rudimentary headstones, aboveground crypts common to the swampy region and here and there the odd unearthed casket that had slipped its bounds. Paupers' graves mostly and in Jim Crow south, "pauper" was another way of saying African American. Graves uncared-for in the afterlife just as the bones there resting had been uncared-for in life.

Being fans of early twentieth-century blues, the two researchers were here seeking the grave of one person in particular. Until they went looking, the world's only evidence of Blind Willie Johnson, other than awed respect universal among any who had heard his music, were recordings of thirty songs laid down in a series of five sessions in Dallas, New Orleans, and Atlanta between 1927 and 1930. That, and the bit of him NASA shot into space as irrefutable demonstration to space aliens of the value of our planet's humanity. In 1977 the astronomer Carl Sagan headed a project to develop a recording that would be included with the deep space Voyager mission, just in case it ever encountered intelligent alien life. Sagan included Johnson's "Dark Was the Night, Cold Was the Ground." There are no serious students of American roots music who have not heard that recording, thunderstruck. The music makes the case that Sagan and his colleagues were only returning it whence it came.

Just from sound alone, we know Johnson played slide guitar, but not much more about his technique. He roared and rumbled his vocals in a rasping chest voice of a street singer, which he was, or more accurately, a street preacher. All his tunes are gospel. Most accompanied by a high-pitched keen of a female voice as wildly eccentric in the high registers as his was in the low ones, a gospel shout, then moans and wails in wobbling synch with a slide guitar. On the earliest series of recordings, the moan was Willie B. Harris, his wife. Other women's voices appear later, and it is said the later women were also his wives, and all of this may have been true. Marriages at the time among poor black people of Texas often went unrecorded, so there's no way to look it up.

Johnson was paid fifty dollars a side for the thirty recordings, probably more money than he ever made before or after, and then like many musicians of the period, white and black, faded back into obscurity when the Great Depression sank record sales to near zero. The recordings were for a time greatly successful, but then forgotten until Harry

Smith selected one for the seminal *Anthology of American Folk Music* in the 1950s, and then the Great Folk Music Scare took up his cause in the '60s. The Reverend Gary Davis was a champion and recorded versions of his songs, the very songs that later landed on records by Peter, Paul and Mary and made Davis enough money to buy his first house. Davis, another blind, black musical genius street preacher, got the writing credit for the songs.

After recording, Johnson continued to preach in Beaumont, but his house burned down. This blind man nonetheless continued to live in the charred ruins until exposure aggravated his malaria. He died in 1945 to claim his pauper's grave. Unmarked, no one knows really where it is, but Obek and Ford used a series of written records and interviews to get as close as they could. They cleaned up the whole cemetery, restored markers and crypts, reburied caskets, and then set a new marker to honor Willie Johnson in 2009. I found it easily enough. Read it. Photographed it. Then headed back to the roar of the I-10 a few miles north, then lost in the roar of diesel kept entertaining a question Johnson himself laid out in lyrics. We don't know if he wrote them, but he sang them clearly enough:

> I want somebody to tell me
> Answer if you can
> I want somebody to tell me
> Tell me what is the soul of a man

In any other time, this trip of mine might have been regarded as homage and pilgrimage, but lately it takes on a new description, an accusation really, an act of cultural appropriation. I am guilty. A little bow at a grave, and then I am on my way, listening again to his recordings and trying my best to pull off a passable version of "You're Gonna Need Somebody on Your Bond" or "Keep Your Lamp Trimmed and Burning." In the '60s, there was a joke, made at the expense of anyone who tried to pick up a slide and play bottleneck guitar the way Johnson did. "You're trying to play bottleneck? Funny. You don't look Jewish." The tradition of American roots music, by and large, was a candle flame tended by white musicians, in the '60s, by a preponderance of New York City Jews and red diaper babies. Accordingly, the folk tradition has been one long string of cultural appropriation because, some would argue, this music belongs especially to the African Americans of the Jim Crow south. Many of them, not just Blind Willie Johnson, wound up in pauper's graves and the white guys got record deals and mansions.

I have my doubts that space aliens ever will cash in on the opportunity learn about humanity from listening to Blind Willie Johnson. This is unknowable. Be that is it may, we, the earthlings, could stand to learn a great deal about our own humanity by listening to him, or appropriating his culture, if you insist.

Theft of culture is not a new argument or idea, which is perhaps why it seems to make sense to me now to consider this music in context of an experience I had in Ethiopia once. That African nation is among the world's poorest, a fact everywhere in evidence in both countryside and city streets of Addis Ababa, the nation's capital. The country straddles the Great Rift Valley, which the paleoanthropologists tell us is the wellspring of all humanity, the site that held the oldest fossil evidence of our lineage. Indeed while I was there in the late '90s I was able to slip into an empty old building that reminded me then of an old-fashioned one-room school in the rural US and stand before a simple unguarded glass case that held the bones of Lucy, then regarded as the earthly remains the oldest fossil in our line, our own ancestor. Sagan's job in that space shot was to summarize the totality of Lucy's descendants, the issue of this very rack of bones.

The argument among the people I met in Ethiopia, however, was not about Lucy, was more current, although my sample of sources was oddly skewed. I was interviewing agronomists, plant breeders, and geneticists, all cooperating in a broad international effort to bolster Ethiopia's food supply to give its people some chance of avoiding poverty and starvation, both starkly evident everywhere I went. At the base of this was a fight over what these specialists, the gene jockeys, call germplasm, and it is one of Ethiopia's most powerful resources. The country is a center of origin, albeit it a minor one. All of humanity today exists on plants grown by agriculture, and all of agriculture in turn rests on a handful of crops first domesticated in four or five major centers of origin, places where evolution and conditions aligned to over ten millennia produce a unique series of plants that could be domesticated, wheat in the Mideast, corn in Mexico, rice in India and China. Ethiopia gave us coffee (not a trifling matter, not at all) but also a number of lesser known and unique crops like teff, a cereal grass that is today the foundation of the country's diet.

This legacy was more than a matter of pride, but of stubborn insistence for the Ethiopians I met. They believed their germplasm is a property right, not of the region or the people, but of the nation state, the borders of which were laid down long after human evolution dealt its hand. They argued that the unique botany somehow corresponded with the arbitrary border lines, and use of that germplasm elsewhere was theft, cultural appropriation. Oddly, many of the international band of agriculturalists working there agreed with the Ethiopians about this, and the Swedish government paid for a state-of-the-art gene bank to allow the government to collect and protect its property, then dole it out to the highest bidder. The screaming irony of this development was that at the same time the same plant breeders laboring to stave of starvation were actively deploying a full range of DNA, of germplasm, from throughout the world delivered free to Ethiopia to enhance crops there by leaps and bounds.

This is not an isolated case, not even close, but teases out the tension that lies at the very heart of all of human development and civilization. Jared Diamond, in his landmark book *Guns, Germs, and Steel* makes the important argument here. He says that Europe and Asia were so overwhelmingly powerful compared to the New World, Africa and Australia by the beginning of the nineteenth century for simple reasons of geography, more specifically the shape of geography. Europe and Asia were contiguous, arrayed on a very long east-west axis, while the rest of the world stretched north to south, or was isolated, like Australia. That alignment led to an early and robust exchange of food crops among the people on the Eurasian landmass, because of alignment of the major centers of origin along a given line of latitude. Plants move easily along latitude, but with difficulty along longitude. Crops from Beijing could be readily adapted to grow in Turkey and were. Crops from Mexico City could not be readily moved to the Andes, but both are centers of origin. Along with crops moved ideas, fabrics, art, technology, and yes, music. That exchange sponsored a hybridization that was the root of creativity and technology.

Through much of this process, but especially in the twentieth century, especially in agriculture, that word "hybridization" is of monumental importance. I am wandering back and forth a bit here to stray from the technical meaning of the term to analogy, but in crops, in food, that word has a specific technical meaning, and is the most important idea I know of for human survival. I mean this literally. Hybridization is why there can be seven billion of us on the planet today. In biology, hybridization is defined as a wide cross, that is, crossbreeding individuals that normally would not breed, often across species lines. Mostly it applies in this technical sense to the plant world, but examples of hybrid animals include mules, a cross between donkeys and horses. At its root is a phenomenon called "heterosis." Mules are bigger and stronger, more robust than both horses and donkeys. Hybridization is not an averaging process. Something about a wide cross creates a whole greater than the sum of its parts. Heterosis is explosive in plants. Early in the twentieth century, horticulturists found that wide crosses, especially between wild progenitors of our domestic crops like corn and domestic corn led to bigger, more productive crop plants, lots more food. All of agriculture today is based on hybrids, and all of humanity exists because of the explosive increase of productivity in our main food crops that was the Green Revolution, which at least doubled food yields. And all of this was dependent on a broad exchange of germplasm among plant breeders working in various parts of the globe. Theft and cultural appropriation? Not really. Creativity and innovation are not zero-sum games.

Yet agriculture is the root of culture to a degree our modern society ignores, but as Diamond pointed out, ideas follow the plants, and while it is indeed analogy and not technically heterosis, something like heterosis occurred with ideas, memes, not genes. We can make this case with a simple plate of red beans and rice, and idea that first occurred to me while headed up a canal in Costa Rica in a wood dugout canoe with a bunch of biologists braving an alligatored swamp to seek out a weirdly colored wild rice. Only the rice we were after wasn't really wild, not even a particular variety, but a patchwork array of plants with seed heads drooping and plump with grains of red and brown, cream and cinnamon. Most agronomists would regard these plants as weeds, the plant world's version of ne'er-do-wells, miscreants, and bums.

The nags of cultural appropriation have extended their arguments to food, and so the truly authentic experience only applies in, say, Louisiana, along the Gulf Coast, maybe to Mississippi and Beaumont, Texas. Certainly a seminal plate of the Deep South: Red beans, as domesticated and given to the world by Aztec Indians. (We should pause here to acknowledge the degree to which Aztec and Inca crops support our lives: corn and potatoes, two of the four crops that are half of all human nutrition on the planet, but also the red beans, tomatoes, and chiles, a special case. Chiles were such a success that they were imported and widely used in the highlands of Tibet within the lifetimes of the conquistadores who found them in what is now Mexico, high-speed cultural appropriation in the sixteenth century. And chocolate.)

In the case of red beans and rice, it is the latter that tells the more interesting story, and because we are in Louisiana, the more musical story. The beans are easy to place here, right at home really on the Gulf Coast. Aztec corn-bean agriculture extended as far north as what is now Quebec before the Spanish invaders imported guns, germs, and steel to devastate the indigenous population. The more twisted tale is in the rice, which was first domesticated, of course, or so we once thought, in Asia. The first clue is the name of the crop, rice, or *arroz* in Spanish, clearly related words, but both seem rooted in older Indian and Iranian terms. Yet in this way, the rice is probably African in just the same way the banjo is. Arabic traders working the Silk Road into Asia first brought rice into the Middle East, traded it into Europe, but also introduced it through their extensive trade networks into Africa, where local people adopted it into their already thriving local agriculture. Likewise, the Arabs may be the source of the weird pentatonic scale that came to signify African music, and the banjo was a hybrid bred from Arab stringed instruments. And for a long time, rice's story stopped right there, but researchers—anthropologists but also geneticists—teased out a more interesting subplot.

The British colonies in what is now the Southeast American states began as rice-growing plantations largely because they are tropical and wet, as were the corresponding places in West Africa where slaves were seized and sold. Those people brought with them a set of skills and knowledge for growing rice, for a long time, assumed to be the rice they had learned to grow from Arab traders. It was. But it wasn't. It turns out that there had been a separate domestication of rice in Africa by Africans, a separate species called *glauberima* that has a clear genetic footprint. It was grown widely throughout the American Southeast, the Caribbean and Central and South America, mostly because slaves knew how to grow it, preferred it, and needed it to survive. In the Caribbean for instance, slaves were commonly left to subsist on whatever food they could grow on their own. Plantation crops like sugar were cash crops for sale elsewhere.

Those geneticists in the canoe on the canal in Costa Rica were looking for that genetic signature of African rice, but there was a lot more in the mix. The Asian varieties, yes, indeed, but Costa Rica also harbors native grasses closely related to Asian rice, a remnant of when today's continents were all mushed together as Gondwana, so old is the evolution of this plant. All of these had bred together in a dizzying profusion of creativity painting the rainbow of seed colors and in a way, the glorious mashup of genetics was the point of the trip. The colors signal the presence of all sorts of micronutrients and phytochemicals, many of which figure in some way in human nutrition. The chemical responsible for reds and browns, for instance, are sometimes cancer fighting agents. Our vision of rice as white can be attributed to the Chinese. Early in the domestication, the Chinese began equating white with civilization, refinement, and purity and so selected for white varieties, breeding all the life out of the crop. The epithet "white-bread" comes into a new meaning here, as humans suffer quite literally from a white-bread diet.

But those Costa Rican researchers were also looking for traits that emerged as a result of hybridization. They were thoroughly plugged into the network of international researchers that shared germplasm across the globe learning of new ways to take advantage of hybrid vigor. A few months after I was in Costa Rica, I interviewed a geneticist at Cornell who had discovered that wild relatives of rice were even more important in hybridization than domesticates, producing phenomenal gains in yield by simple crossbreeding. And a couple of months after that, I met some researchers in Beijing who had read of the Cornell researcher's work, tried it on Chinese varieties and realized those gains to the point that Chinese peasants were no longer starving. When I spoke with them there, they indicated that they thought the Cornell researcher—her name is Susan McCouch—was some sort of goddess and were stunned that I had been able to interview her.

So the trail of this rice runs from India, Japan, and China through Africa bridged by the Silk Road and Arabs, then on slave ships to Central America, then to Cornell and an international network, literally a network of genetic information compiled by people working together around the globe, DNA sequencing, then back to rural China again, which is a lot of agricultural appropriation. And whose culture is all of this anyway? The Chinese and Indians never lost the original rice and the knowledge that went with it. The Arabs did not take their rice and wisdom away. That's why appropriation is the wrong word here. Theft did not occur. This is not a zero-sum game, yet there is culture in the larger, musical sense of the word pulsing through the whole story.

The tale becomes most intense in places like South Carolina, Louisiana, Costa Rica, Brazil, Jamaica, places where rice is sacrosanct, but also diverse and hybridized. In exactly those same places so is music, and it has a marker: the weird pentatonic scale that is the genetic signature of African music that hybridized so profusely with Celtic modal music to now travel the world as jazz, rock, bluegrass, and blues. Heterosis—hybrid vigor—is a technical term that does not apply to music, language, art, yet it is nonetheless true that centers of creativity spring up along trade networks, where cultures come together and hybridize. Maybe it should apply after all.

###

Every white, educated, privileged acoustic blues player—and most players are—has a dirty little secret about the songs we sing, or more importantly, the songs we can't sing. We revel in, obsess over, even worship the work of long-dead, poor black people who were musical geniuses. Earlier generations of players sought them out while they survived, literally sat at their feet and copied them note for note, lick for lick. Some spent long days dropping a needle over and over again on the same spot on a scratchy 78 disc trying to figure out two or three notes, decoding a weird little harmony that was the hook of the tune. Some mined the trove in archives and libraries. Appropriation is a lot of work.

Yet much of what we heard and learned we deliberately ignored and forgot. And not just the lascivious material. Truth is, most of us were first drawn to the blues by this very delightful bawdy character of the genre, only to find that the deeper we dug, the filthier the material became, much of it too overt and dated to be performed with a straight face today. Much of this became an inside joke but no cause to shy away from this, for reasons that tie together the other facets of this argument. Southern rural black culture in the early twentieth century, indeed well before, was overtly and unabashedly sexual. Bowdlerize this, and you erase a bit of understanding and grasp of our history.

Beyond, though, a lot of the material is racist, forms of layered discrimination that may have been explicable in the time and context but are something of an embarrassment today. Lyrics often tell of a singer's preference for various shades of dark-skinned sexual partners. Blind Willie McTell taunts his girlfriend with a threat to run off with other women: "I might take my fair brown, I might take one or two more." High browns, yallers, categories of sexual fantasy ranked on skin color, common enough stuff. Meat-shakin' women, big-legged women, funky butts.

More disturbing still is the violence, many violent songs, knife fights, shootings, and beatings, but often enough disturbing stuff served up as threat or accounts against a particular woman, beatings mostly. Skip James sings:

You know, I wanna buy me a pistol

Wants me forty rounds of ball
Shoot Crow Jane, just to see her fall

Or Mance Lipscomb:

Went downtown, got me a line
Whupped my baby 'til she changed her mind

Nor was this exclusively African American. From Appalachia comes "Little Sadie":

Late last night I was makin' my rounds
Met Little Sadie and I blowed her down
Went back home, went to bed
.44 smokeless under my head

You can maybe try to write all of this off as a joke if this sort of thing didn't happen so often, then and now. Most of us wouldn't use these lyrics today, at least not in performance, but that doesn't mean we ought to ignore the violence or pretend it didn't happen. Not just the blues, but all of American roots music is full tunes about violence, just as was English folk ballads centuries before. People die in them, but it is of particular importance that we not turn our heads away from this in the African American blues tradition. Spend some hours listening to the original recordings of Son House or Bukka White moaning tunes like "Parchman Farm," an account of the notorious Mississippi prison that was nothing so much as a hard time concentration camp for black men through much of the twentieth century. Listen to Charlie Patton sing "High Sheriff Blues" in his ethereal moan and know by this that Black Lives Matter stands in a long tradition of protest against police brutality. Yes, to try to take these songs, for a white guy to take them to a coffeehouse stage, is indeed cultural appropriation, but that doesn't argue against knowing them. As the composer Berlioz said about his suffering at a concert: "Are you under the impression I came here to enjoy myself?" Our impulse is to look the other way, but there's something to be gained by staring straight at titles like those from Appalachian fiddle music: "Run Nigger Run" and "Shaving a Dead Nigger."

The long stream of American roots music draws disproportionately on tunes from the South, but also there are an inordinate number of tunes that trace to the late nineteenth and early twentieth centuries. This wholly matches the arc of the larger culture, a great upheaval that was the Civil War followed by chaotic and sweeping changes in demographics, economy, industry, creativity. At the core in our long experiment in hybridization was the countertension of racism and discrimination and at the core of that was slavery, but layered on genocide against Native Americans, exploitation of Hispanics, internment of Asians and Italians, discrimination against the Irish. It's all in the music, there for the reading, and to know it, to sing it, is to own it, as in own up to it. At the very least, it allows one to exit the argument raised by the better-paid pundits of cable news that this nation is not racist with a single word: bullshit. Our music is the living counterpoint.

Our music is simply a deeper reflection of who we are, and there's a better chance of us believing the evidence of song. Biologists have been for some time now offering a surprising statement based on gleanings from the deeper code that runs in parallel to music, the human genetic code. On the genetic level, there is no such thing as race. There are plenty of good arguments to the contrary, ideas we need, for instance, that certain diseases tend to track certain ethnic groups, a genetic marker. This is true enough, but the important qualifier here is "tend to" a matter of probability, of odds. There well may be a genetic base for sickle-cell anemia, but that doesn't mean it is present in every person identified as African American, no certainty at the individual level. But the real basis of the statement by biologists is far more interesting, that there is very little variation in the human genome. We may dwell on inherited traits like skin tone, but this is like dwelling on a single pixel on a stadium-sized screen to describe the whole picture.

That lack of variability is in sharp contrast to most other species. Other species show lots of variation, but our pattern of little variation is common to nomadic species. The same pattern appears in the American bison, for instance, simply because the great herds wandered the length and breadth of North America, mixing it up and leveling the field. Likewise, humans have mixed it up.

This whole idea has been common among biologists for a generation or so but is now showing up in common ken thanks to the growing popularity of genetic testing to reveal one's ancestry. A lot of people are shocked by the result, lots more Indians, slaves, Slavs, blue bloods, Caucasians, and aborigines in our family trees than we might have imagined. Of course there are. It's right there in our music.

Clint Watts is a spook, a spy, who pops up on MSNBC from time to time, but his knowledge spools out in greater detail is his 2018 book *Messing with the Enemy*. It is, like a lot of books that year, an earnest and urgent attempt to analyze how America became such a political mess, especially vulnerable to political manipulation by enemies of democracy, domestic and foreign. Only unlike a lot of people, Watts, an intelligence analyst, had been watching this cancer develop globally, especially as bad actors like Al Qaeda and the Islamic State became expert in propaganda techniques matched to the more sinister possibilities of the internet. To Watts the issue boils down to what he calls "preference bubbles," by which he means the internet has played to destructive tendencies already in our brains, greatly enhanced and amplified by lifetimes of commercial advertising that have convinced us happiness is a matter of satisfying our every single whim. Thus ordering a cup of coffee now often involves several minutes of display behavior while the person at the head of the line spiels out in minute and excruciating detail the specs of the only cup of coffee that will do, their special needs and whims, worn like badge of honor. Where this becomes insidious is in the self-sorting to preference bubbles with social space, both real and virtual, where our social engagements are fully governed by the same set of whims, and we only engage with people who match. A subset of this is the information bubble, which needs no explanation.

There's nothing new about this, at least not in principle, just in degree. One can't help but notice that popular conversation is making more and more use of the word "tribalism," an old concept. This is one of those rare examples of popular conversation selecting and buzzing with exactly the right word. The human brain has always been programmed to fear the other, and now the other comes in a wide assortment of shapes and sizes. The countervailing tendency is our rationality and our finely tuned social skills that allow us to relax and accept, engage with, learn from, and even enjoy the other, a process that has greatly enriched and enlivened all of civilization. Losing this ability threatens to destroy civilization, and raising this prospect, recent years has taught us, is not alarmist.

Recall now that early in this book we encountered the neuroscientist Walter Freeman, who concluded that over the long haul of human evolution music has always been necessary as a means "to bridge the solipsistic gap," the means of pulling us out of our fear-enforced shell, our protective bubbles to engage the world around us. Recall also that the means for doing so was empathy.

#

There's something very odd about Blind Willie Johnson's tune "Dark Was the Night, Cold Was the Ground." It is preserved in one famous recording, and every single slide player from rock to roots to swing, every one, I would wager, has heard it like the voice of god at some point or another. Yet almost no one plays it. Not so with his other tunes, "You're Gonna Need Somebody on Your Bond," "Keep Your Lamp Trimmed and Burning," "Motherless Child." These we play. But not "Dark Was the Night." Even the great and eclectic slide player Ry Cooder only offered up his own version, his haunting piece that became the theme for the film *Paris, Texas*. Cooder said this was indeed his version of "Dark Was the Night" but an homage, not a cover. The thing is, the original is too good, too much Willie Johnson. It cannot be appropriated. But in the end, no song can be.

Every one of us has heard roots music players who sound like caricatures, as if performing in masks or blackface. They get the tune and the notes right, know the lyrics, but somehow never succeed in pulling off the song, in owning it. Some even make good livings at this, but they still look like clowns and mountebanks in the process.

The better teachers of blues music, the scholars of the craft, people who have given their lives to this work, almost always offer an important piece of advice to students: Don't try to copy it note for note. Instead, make it your own, which appears like a prima facie case of appropriation, more theft than love. But this is not so. To sell a song, to own it, one does not replicate the original, just the opposite. One reaches simultaneously into the original and into one's own self to wire together common human emotions and experiences. Songs live on this exchange, a reach across a gulf of a personal divide, a cultural divide.

Roots music is forever plagiarizing itself, so much so that there are recognizable floaters in the tradition, common verses and lines that show up in widely disparate songs. Here's one we've all heard: "Corrina, Corrina, where'd you stay last night / Come home this morning, clothes didn't fit you right."

I never knew Corrina or Leadbelly or any of the other dead black men who howled these lines, but somewhere each of us can plum our own painful depths to find an emotion to match. Each of us knows jealousy well enough. That's why these things endure. They conjure the specters that haunt all of us.

In this conjuring, we have woven our own story into those angry men, or into Dink's lonely lament after she was abandoned pregnant on the Brazos River, or the Irish teenager fresh off Ellis Island and issued a blue uniform and a rifle in the Union cause:

These days will be remembered by America's noble sons
If it hadn't have been for Irishmen, what would your Union done
Hand to hand we fought 'em all in the broilin' sun
Stripped to the pants, we did advance at the Battle of Bull Run

In singing these lines, we own more than the song. We peer into our history, our common story. Somewhere along the line we got the wrong impression that the grasp of history is a matter of gaining information, education. It is, true enough, but insufficient to the urgent cause of sustaining our humanity. Book learning is the bias of a literate people. Music gives us access to its emotional content, a far more necessary bridge beyond ourselves.

In the preceding chapter I offered an answer to book's prime question: Why music, why do we persist? The answer was that it allowed internal access to the regions of our brain otherwise abandoned and atrophied. Now comes another answer: because music grants us access to everything external, to the wider wonder of the human condition.

11

WEISER

I have arranged to meet my friend Dillof at Lost Trail summit, where there's a parking lot perched on the divide between Montana and Idaho. We each have a two-hour drive to that point, but I'll leave my Jeep there, and we'll travel together in his rig. Then I drive the six full hours of winding mountain roads southwest to Weiser, Idaho. No way I'm letting him drive, not even his own SUV, not a single mile.

He's late, but then he always is. There's not much cell phone coverage in the canyons and curves climbing to the pass, but he gets a call in to let me know what I already assumed, so I wait. It's vexing, but I am about to get even. I'm wearing my best boots, custom handmades, underslung inch-and-a-half bull-dogging heel, leather-lined, tooled uppers stove-piped at fourteen inches, a fashion statement in their own right, but the rest of me is in faded raw denim, including a red tab, pearl-snap-button Levi's denim shirt, a high plains tuxedo, all topped by a Stetson summer straw with a Gus crown. The boots crunch gravel in the parking lot. Then I spot his vintage gray Toyota Land Cruiser topping a rise, and it winds into the parking lot, towing a pup of an aluminum teardrop camper trailer behind. Dillof is grinning. It's been months. We shake hands, and then he looks down and his face falls. "Geez. I should be wearing my boots. I've got nice boots right in the trailer. This isn't right."

He's in flip-flops and khakis, a lapse bordering on ethical collapse in our small world, and I knew he would be so dressed. What I've done is the rough equivalent of pranking a friend by convincing him it's a masquerade party when it isn't. I do this to him every year, and every year he forgets. Like a tape loop, and loops are a theme in the world of Dobro Dick Dillof. He's mentally ill, or at least that's how the polite society might label his state of mind. Literally. A lifelong handicap of Tourette's syndrome. But then anyone who might think less of me for duping a man so burdened should know he has made a near second career out of practical jokes far more elaborate. He gives as good as he gets.

I grab a couple of cases, a banjo, a guitar, a duffel, and a tent from my Jeep and pile them onto the far more substantial collection of weathered vintage guitar cases that stack like cordwood to fill the back of the Land Cruiser. Then I drive and he talks, mostly continuously for six hours. I've brought a stack of CDs, tunes I want him to hear, chops to admire, licks to steal, but mostly he talks, and it is a loop, recursive, cycling chatter folding back on itself. Every now and again, though, he pauses long enough to play a few bars of a tune he is exploring on his harp guitar, his small one. He has several. A harp guitar is more or less what it sounds like, an archtop guitar with a sidebar of long harpish drone strings. They were popular at the beginning of the twentieth century, and Dillof is plucking a ragtime tune from that era, that era where his head mostly seems to live.

None of this I mind, not a bit, especially not his chatter. Unlike a lot of us, he has some stories to tell. He's nearing old manhood now, both us are, both born in the same year, both boomers, but Dillof did a lot more booming fueled by equal parts zeitgeist and Tourette's. Like a lot of mountain men, hobo-buckaroos, he came by his hat and boots and yarns by way of Long Island. He was raised a New Yorker who came of age at the height of the Great Folk Music Scare living near enough to its epicenter to become contaminated in the blast. He says now this was mostly a result of the Tourette's talking. Ragtime guitar is among the most devilish of disciplines to be warped onto the instrument, an attempt to duplicate the sound of a barrelhouse piano on six strings stretched across a few ounces of Sitka spruce and mahogany. Dillof did not begin guitar by strumming "Michael Row the Boat Ashore" but rather by teaching himself as a teenager to play ragtime, which would be a bit like noticing your toddler laying out a play block structure by using a slide rule and trigonometric functions.

The lure of ragtime was simple and explicable, he says now. It was the syncopation, the offbeat and herky-jerky jump that pushes it along by pulling it back every now and again. Syncopation was a little rhythmic joke that exploded into American music in the Gilded Age, but he says it helped to control his Tourette's, the ticcing that is the most disruptive symptom. Which is why the idea of mental handicap is a nonstarter for Dillof. "I consider my Tourette's a gift," he told me once.

There's a finer point to be put on this that makes a bit more than the power of magical positive thinking. Tourette's sufferers can, for instance, accomplish such feats such as snatching a flying insect out of midair, and action too fast for most of us to even see, let along duplicate. The syndrome has the odd effect in their brains. They can perceive in slow motion. That's a gift for an improvising musician about to snatch a lead in a rapid-fire bluegrass break. He gets more time than the rest of us. Dillof confirms the research: this is how it works for him.

But then, about the same time he taught himself ragtime, while he was still a teenager, someone showed him a banjo, a weird open-back, primitive clawhammer banjo, and he was smitten, still is. Old-time banjo music is nothing at all like ragtime, far simpler, more a drone, ethereal and repetitive, a loop, but nonetheless broadly syncopated, often strung out in weird modal scales that Dillof believes is an emblem of its "negritude," a term in his lexicon that signals approval. Musicologists agree, although they might use a different word to describe the distinctive harmonic shadings of Africa. Nonetheless, he finds the repetition seductive and will get lost for whole days in a single set of sixteen bars, meditative like a Zen chant.

"I can't help but play it over and over. Like meditation," he tells me. "And if it doesn't work for mediation, at least you get your tune down." This is why Buddhists call meditation "practice."

Dillof tried a conventional middle-class path to the university, Kent State in Ohio, but it didn't work out. So he hit the road, as in "on the road," in the fashion of the day, hitching, bumming, and finally hooking trains, guitar case in hand, literally so. He tells me, though, that the real lure was not the road itself. The music that interested him came from a long line of hard travelers, to invoke one of Woody Guthrie's song titles. Dillof wanted nothing so much as to make his music authentic, and he believed doing that entailed direct experience. He lived a lot of years as a hobo, Guthrie-esque, Ramblin' Jackish. When he finally got a more permanent residence, it was a sheep wagon, a common vehicle in the west, the summer residence of mountain sheepherders a century ago and now. They look like mini Conestoga wagons with barrel arched tops of canvas and are about the size of a small bathroom, just room for a bunk and a place to sit out of the weather. Dillof's was parked for years on the Montana property of the writer Richard Brautigan. Brautigan, also a notorious prankster, liked having him around.

Now that same sheep wagon sits on one of the world's most beautiful pieces of land, forty acres Dillof owns racked up against the Absaroka Mountains in Montana's aptly named Paradise Valley. A gentle little creek, cold and clear, runs past the wagon, a modest old craftsman farm house where he mostly lives, and a caboose, fully refurbished to museum grade. I bunk in the sheep wagon when I visit.

Early on, he became fascinated not just with syncopation but with the endless possibilities of slide guitar and took to the Dobro, the version of slide guitar separate from Blind Willie Johnson's blues that migrated first into country music, then bluegrass, hillbilly styles, but also into western swing, Bob Wills and the Texas playboys, that sort of thing. The lineage of the Dobro is something like Brother Oswald, Tut Tylor, Norman Blake, Cindy Cashdollar, Jerry Douglas, and Dobro Dick Dillof. He's a master. The instrument warbles and pitches like the human voice, so can stand in ensemble in places usually occupied by fiddle or mandolin, but has that high lonesome quality that supplies a plaintive whine to most any sort of roots music, so Dillof was in demand. For a while, he was a sideman for Ramblin' Jack Elliott. Elliott stories are a big part of our conversation loop as we wind through Idaho, stopping every now and again for silence and awe in spots like Stanley, where the Sawtooth Mountains sculpt a vista close to religious.

It's nearly dark when we finally pull into the expanse of clipped green grass behind the ballfields at the high school in Weiser, Idaho, to park the Land Cruiser and Dillof's teardrop trailer in our assigned plot. The spot is marked by Bruce Stanger's camper parked parallel, the shade tarp stretched taut, and under it a circle of players with mandolins, banjo ukuleles, archtop guitars—vintage Martins and Gibsons—hats and boots all around. Only a couple of a years ago I was an interloper in this circle and still feel that way a bit, but this feeling is only my well-worn case of imposter syndrome speaking.

This circle defined by four people has made me nothing if not welcome, even though I have entered it for only a couple of years. Nonetheless, I park the teardrop to rest against its chocks and feel as if I have come home. It is only well later that I am struck by the irony of this moment. Earlier in this book I reported that I could mark the beginning of my descent into the netherworld of music when I was in a campground in Idaho, that the row of campers then struck me as a marker of a regimented and normal life I wanted nothing to do with. And here I am backing a trailer into an assigned slot in Idaho. The difference is, no one here could be mistaken for normal or regimented.

###

The town of Weiser holds five thousand or so mostly red-state citizens of the sort that makes Idaho politics retrograde, even by modern standards. It lies out along the undulating plain that smacks up against the Rocky Mountains to the east. This is cow country broken here and there by orchards and beet fields, all irrigated by Idaho's beaten slave of a river, the Snake. As with most such towns, there was an annual rodeo stretching back as far as anyone can remember and, almost as far back, a fiddle contest, where the locals demonstrated their chops with music made for the boot-stomping revelry attendant at midsummer rodeos. One thing led to another and then not. World War II so hobbled such gatherings that the fiddle contest ceased but then revived anew just after, just in time to become thoroughly infected with Texas swing fiddle styles then popular. It grew, and today the contest, still dominated by the same style, draws thousands to hear a full complement of contestants at the high school for a week of competition. The fiddle contest is wholly irrelevant to everyone in the general vicinity of Dillof's camper at that moment. These are not contestants or even observers but a hodgepodge of several hundred musicians in tents and campers surrounding a row of ancient and crumbling concrete buildings that look depressingly institutional because they were an institution once, a county "normal school," the archaic term for degree mills that in bygone days used to turn out schoolteachers. All irrelevant because all of these campers have come to Weiser especially to not attend the festival. Most arrive the week before it begins and leave before it does. Most loathe fiddle competitions as rote exercises that have nothing to do with music.

In the '60s or thereabouts, the staid festival began drawing a slightly more licentious lot to the revelry surrounding rodeo and fiddle contests, which led to masquerade parties, folk music, naked swimming, and other varieties of shameful behavior. The sideshow evolved to a sort of counterfestival but one still centered in music, still centered, oddly, in the performing version of Texas contest fiddling which is western swing, jazz for people with big hats. That form of music is still at the center, but then spread around those old partly refurbished concrete buildings are discrete sets of recognizable tent and camper communities with highly porous boundaries. The most recognizable subset of the whole is the football-field-sized collection behind the buildings named Stickerville in honor of the thorny weeds that dominate when tents don't. In full swing, it holds sixty or seventy camper trailers and tents, a hundred or so people, a younger crowd, twentysomethings dominate, but a full complement of the age chain, mostly playing old-time Appalachian fiddle music, guitars, banjos, mandolins, and fiddles. No performance center or stage, mind you, just dozens of circles of players, forming reforming, shifting coalitions from dawn till dawn.

Then off to one end—more upscale, more campers, big campers surrounded by big people, older and fatter, bluegrass reigns. Dillof says this quarter is recognizable because trailers, stomachs and belt buckles are bigger, while dogs are smaller. Then separate, but the apparent center of the whole, there stand a couple of big shade tarps where three circles of six or eight musicians seem assembled 24/7, stand-up bass, archtop guitars, resonator guitars, Dobros, lap steels, fiddles, and now and again a saxophone or mouth harp. Here the music is mostly western swing but also jazz standards, blues, snaky convoluted jazz chord progressions.

Dillof and I anchor to this greater whole in our own small circle where I am the interloper. There are pods like this all around and most are like ours, a circle of friends, each of whom knows where he will be the second week in June every year, because they have been doing this every year for thirty years. Our particular circle is anchored by four men, all about the same age, all musicians and seemingly with nothing else in common. Bruce Stanger is a big guy, with a ready string of patter, boisterous, always a summer straw hat, usually boots, big truck, looks like a rancher because he is one, from Bone, Idaho, a burg in the foothills of the Rockies on the eastern edge of the state. He can talk cows and fences, is a Bernie Sanders Democrat and a Jack Mormon, a term for lapsed Mormons, a species one encounters frequently among musicians of the region. He became infected with the folk music in college, and life has never been the same since, a life history that has more than once put the Jack in Jack Mormon throughout the West. Music is subversive.

He sits in a folding chair in the shade picking a ukulele but also wields banjo and guitar. Still, the image of the ukulele sticks best, a big, fat man in an outsized hat threading ham-sized rancher's hands into an instrument that looks like it was made for a preschooler.

Jim Weaver sits next chair over playing guitar and usually carping about how lousy he has been playing lately. I listen and this perennial assessment of his seems to me wholly false. Weaver is trim with gray hair, thoughtful and internal. He is playing a guitar he made himself, a copy of the prewar Gibson model favored by blues players. It is an impeccable instrument and would find favor in even the most expert of hands. Weaver is a lawyer or was a lawyer but in midlife decided he'd had enough of the law. He lives in Boise and works as a wilderness pilot flying supplies and dudes in light planes into the remote grass airstrips the size of suburban lawn in central Idaho's vast wilderness. And he is a professional luthier.

Then there is John Stein, known mostly as Doc, because he is an MD, a career-long emergency room physician from Portland, Oregon, slight, intense, glasses, head topped by the remnants of a Jewfro. He is a direct product of ground zero of the folk upheaval, hung around Greenwich Village as a teenager, and was pals with Woody Mann, a great guitarist in the tradition who was a student of the Reverend Gary Davis. Stein went to medical school at Saint Louis University and discovered the library had a world class collection of old 78 recordings, so spent his spare time deep in those stacks absorbing grooves as intensely as he absorbed human anatomy. He has recently retired from practicing medicine but has picked up a new role as sideman playing Dobro and guitar at concerts with Jim Kweskin and Geoff Muldaur of jug band fame, two icons of roots music.

These four personal profiles only seem eccentric in the larger context of modern life. In Weiser they are commonplace. The next camp over, for instance, holds a retired English professor from Kent State, a nuclear power plant engineer, and a clinical psychologist. I met another who was a professional chess player. There is, only slightly hidden in this statement, a simple and true answer to the book's fundamental question: Why music? Because the people who play it are the most interesting people I know.

###

I had first heard about this gathering many years before from friends in Montana—most of those very same people are here now as they are every year—and finally decided to make the drive on my own long before I met Dillof, expecting to find a friendly collection of circles of parking lot pickers, little jam sessions where three chords would credential me, and then I could make easy music flow. So years ago I packed a tent and went, but that first year was anything but pleasant. I camped in Stickerville and wandered around, guitar case in hand, looking for a circle where I could fit in, as I had in other such festivals, grab a line of bluegrass, and go. But then I heard the music, saw what people were actually playing, and hid my guitar case in my tent so no one could suspect I played. It was monumentally depressing, and I could stand it for only a day, then packed up my tent and drove the six hours home, tail between my legs. It only gradually dawned on me what was on display there as I got to know a few people and heard more of the music. Imagine several hundred professional and semiprofessional musicians of the Pacific Northwest and northern Rockies decided to take a vacation from playing music on stage to play music under tarps for a week every year. That's Weiser.

But in the years since, I've learned a few more chords and licks and stories, and also finally figured out this is not what really matters here. It's worth braving the embarrassment for the stories and characters. Ray Wood, for example. A couple of years ago, Dillof and I were in the same camp, maybe listening to a Stanger yarn, they are endless, when the conversation was broken by the annoying stutter of unmuffled internal combustion. An old man, he looks eighty, is piloting a miniscooter, the sort of affair with a lawnmower engine bolted to a homemade frame, into our camp. He parks it, stubs out his cigarette and lights another and greets the group all around, then matches Stanger yarn for yarn, detailed accounts of driving the back roads of Arizona. This is Ray Wood, a jazz guitarist from Seattle who was a jazz guitarist as a teenager, a working jazz guitarist all his life. Later that day, I would hear him play, see him arch his body out over the neck of the guitar as if cradling a child, and then effect the illusion that his old wracked frame had somehow absorbed the instrument, and they were one. He did not play the music so much as he emitted it, walking his fingers up the fretboard like a ladder to the heavens, an enlightened master with a cigarette dangling from his mouth.

Wood was but a pinnacle of an assembly of musicians and in a crowd like this, reticence and sound judgment told me to remain a lurker, listen and learn but leave the guitar in its case. I didn't want to embarrass myself, and these folks were dealing out a class of music that was better and way beyond anything I knew to play, three-dimensional chess when I played checkers. The fallacy of this attitude was believing complexity equaled better.

I should have known better. There were hints. For instance, my friend Greg Boyd—he was at Weiser, is always there, sets up a remote music store in one of the old school buildings and does a brisk business—introduced me to another of his customers one time, a crusty old character in a ball cap, a retired electrician from Idaho. Right away I sensed an odd set of leanings in him, odd for Weiser, but not odd for Idaho or retired electricians. My suspicions were reinforced by learning he came from an area of the state known as a redoubt of white supremacists, Trumpists, and tinfoil hatters. He looked the part. But Boyd was undaunted and said to me, "Go ahead, play something for him." Okay. Let's have this out. I launched into the blackest and most primitive version of an old Mississippi John Hurt tune, in my mind, a deep rumble of rebellion and rage against Jim Crow. The redneck sat down and stared, fascinated. "I love John Hurt," he says. "Wish I could play it. Play some more." And then a few other folks gathered to listen to music plain and simple.

But still, there were all around me plenty of examples where complexity and sophistication ruled, like one I didn't see but heard about repeatedly. It turned out to be a pivotal moment in the whole week of music that every one spoke of in almost hushed tones. That I had not seen it myself was most vexing because it involved my friend Dillof, whom I take to be a great musician, but he almost never plays with others, not even at Weiser. He often says he's going to. Takes out his Dobro even or a lap steel, but then he launches into loops of conversation about a new banjo he wants to try or a slide or an amp or a guitar he covets and will sit for hours tweaking the instrument in repetitive four-bar licks. Seldom does he sit in a circle and play.

Then one afternoon I saw people coming from the area that holds the central jam session, the hot stuff, and to a person they are shaking heads in amazement. I see Jim Weaver, Dillof's longtime friend, whom he has known for thirty years, head down almost thunderstruck and ask him what happened. "Dillof tore it up." That is, Dillof had sat in a circle of world class musicians playing the cowboy version of hot jazz and had improvised pyrotechnical feats of creation that caused everyone present—every one of them a skilled musician—to believe him to be some sort of a space alien. And then he stopped, put away his guitar, and went back to obsessing over some banjo he wanted to buy. The feat was not repeated through the course of the week.

It was about then that I met a Paul, a luthier, tall, fit, and chiseled looking guitar-maker from Oregon who was a central player in all of this. His display of guitars he has made usually centers that main jam area, and he is a player in that inner circle of the most sophisticated. He's also a nice guy and asked me why I didn't play more. I told him I don't know jazz chords or western swing, but I like lurking to listen to what real players can do.

So he told me a story. He moved out west only a few years before from Upstate New York and had heard about Weiser, so made the drive, six hours, and pitched his tent in Stickerville, ready to play. He made the rounds, listened for a bit, ready to find a circle where he'd fit, but realized he didn't, outclassed and outgunned on all sides. So he packed his tent and drove straight back home, tail between his legs, six hours. But during the course of a year, determination got the better of his depression, and he drove back to Weiser the following June and met Ray Wood, who asked him why he didn't play more. And Paul told him it was because he couldn't handle the western swing chords, so Ray sat him down right there and showed him the chords.

Then Paul commanded me to show up at his tent the next morning for a lesson, and when I didn't, he came to our camp and got me and he sat me down and showed me the contorted set of moves that had defeated me for years. They're not that hard, like entering a familiar room through a new door. It's like having the secret to levitation revealed, and it turns out to be nothing more complicated than walking backward while touching your nose.

###

It's a fine Idaho morning toward the end of the week at Weiser, clear blue and clean, and the five of us are shuffling about, lighting propane stoves to boil water for morning coffee, talking, political, technical, musical. Then Stanger announces without preamble: "John Hansen called. Said he'd stop up from Boise this afternoon."

I absorb this for a second, knowing Mormon country well enough to know that the name John Hansen seems to belong to about every fourth adult male in the state, but then this gathering is about musicians, so maybe. It could be. This could be exactly the same guy I last saw almost forty years before, my musical idol, the guy I used to go hear play at every opportunity but was too starstruck to get to know him, until my guitar teacher then, Tenley Stephens, the beautiful woman who died of brain cancer, sent me to Boise to buy my first Martin guitar from him. I had been too embarrassed to play in front of him and so tucked it into its black worn case and drove back home. It could be that same guy.

It was. He walked into camp that afternoon, still tall as a I remember, but, if memory serves, he was thinner back then. He now had an old man's round, fleshy face, but he was in there. Stanger introduced us, and I mumbled something about my first guitar and that he had caused my problems, fanned the flames of an obsession that more or less ruined my life, and he laughed at this, having lived fully a life even more given over wholly to this wonderful obsession of ours. I caught up on news of his old guitar partner at the time, a scary good player, Rich Brotherton, who went on to become and remains lead guitar player for Robert Earl Keene. Hansen and Brotherton are still in touch.

Then John sat down in our humble little circle and pulled out his Martin, custom made for him in Nazareth, Pennsylvania, and I sat back waiting to hear what he had become. Hansen's fingers had walked these frets a full forty years since I last heard him and now, he like Dillof, would sit in the circle of hot players and rip it up. But he didn't. Not a bit. What came from his guitar were simple songs in three chords, the same songs I had heard him do all those years ago, most of them songs I had forgotten about, but some I still played and now realized had learned by listening to him. Songs that would come to mind from nowhere years later and for some reason I would feel compelled to learn. Or songs like "Shady Grove," an old Appalachian tune that everyone plays, but everyone plays differently. I had learned it from Tenley, a quirky version I have heard nowhere else, and now here was Hansen playing it the same quirky way, which means Tenley learned it from him or vice versa. Thus it had passed hand to hand.

During the couple of hours he played, I never once requested a particular tune, but as I sat there on a folding camp chair in the Idaho sun, my whole musical and personal history came pouring out as if reeling off a spool, forgotten events, friends, association, passions, failings, regrets, and grievous errors.

Once I was introduced to a parking-lot picker on the way to a jam. Someone told him I was a guy writing a book about why we play music. He took this in for a second, then looked straight at me and said, "Because it saves your life." Then he grabbed his case and walked away, five words that held the answer I had been seeking for months. But more. It only later occurred to me the response had a second meaning beyond the self-help sense of rescue, saves it like on a hard drive of stored memories.

Still Hansen never ventured much beyond the simple chords and melodies, but he held a circle of hot shot musicians in rapt attention for hours, because he sat back stroking that Martin and let it drive his fine singing voice to the depths of where music comes from. The man knows how to tell a story. The man knows how to sell a song.

Dillof was there, quiet. Didn't have much to say, but he unpacked his Dobro case. He'd heard of Hansen over the years but had never met him, and he figured he had something to add and he did. He played along the whole time, taking his Dobro breaks just where Dobro breaks belong, clean, clear, simple sliding phrases and ornaments that echoed the plaintive depths of Hansen's songs. No pyrotechnics, just music. He told me later that he loved every second of it, felt as if he had come home. We pickers, we players, that's where we have been headed all this time, all these years, to home.

###

It is dead of winter, late 2018, and a resolve that arose in Weiser has propelled me to an alien but altogether familiar place, never been but nonetheless feels like home. I'm in an upgraded frame house unremarkable and common as rain in its place, Seekonk, Massachusetts, a bedroom town that is a lean-to tacked on the edge of Providence, Rhode Island. The tenant here, a renter with roommates, has the run of the first floor. The potters live upstairs, but this first floor is the musician's nest, no need to guess. It's a clutter of instrument cases, dozens of them, stacked and stashed all around a living room and hall, guitars mostly, but also National resonator guitars, banjos fretless and fretted, Cajun accordions, fiddles. The tenant is a master of all of these. There's a rack of fiddle bows on one wall above a work desk with hand planes and tools for restringing bows, his cottage industry. The guy lives like a grad student—rented housing, make-do furniture, roommates—although plenty old enough to know better. He's in his sixties but doesn't have much in mainstream measures of success to show for it.

"I have accumulated nothing that society says I need. Nothing. I'm a fucking computer or a blown engine away from homelessness," he tells me. "I look around and I see I have very little to show for what I have done over the past fifty-odd, years and it scares me. It makes me panicky and fills me with regret."

It was the merest of coincidences that caused me to meet him that first time at the beginning of those fifty-odd years at a folkie venue in Ann Arbor in 1973, an encounter that opened this book and sent me on this odd obsessive journey of my own. Other than a brief chance encounter in Boston a few years before, I had no contact with Martin Grosswendt between, but now it seems right all these years on the check back in with the guy part of me always wished I had become. It'd time we had a serious conversation.

When I first met him in Ann Arbor, he was a cool, cocky, hip kid; now he's old, overweight, divorced. That was an old man's word he used just a minute ago, "regret." It was a lapse. It only popped up once or twice in two days of conversation and music, and in the end, no more than anyone our age might use it, no more than I do. Grosswendt may still be the guy I wish I had become, but that's my own old man's non-sense and is irrelevant here. What matters is it seems to me that he became the guy he needed to become, and not many of us can say that or understand that this is the proper measure of a life well lived.

I have no doubt his life has been well lived; I heard it for myself. It only takes a few seconds for instant recognition, nothing flashy, no pyro-technics or fretted acrobatics, just a solid right hand, the dead-on flaw-less rhythm of deeply schooled fingers ranging across six steel strings of a vintage acoustic guitar, the total command of the nanoseconds and microtones of music that cause it to flow as effortlessly and seductively as wind in the trees. If lucky, one hears such sounds up close and per-sonal maybe a handful of times in a lifetime, a half dozen players among thousands. No mistaking it when it arises half a living room away.

When I met him, he was eighteen years old and already a seasoned professional musician touring with the folk legend Utah Phillips, the golden voice of the great Southwest. He got there by being a troubled kid alone in a big farmhouse in eastern Massachusetts that happened to hold a stash of two hundred even-then-ancient 78 rpm records that he listened to obsessively as only a thirteen-year-old can do. He then taught himself to play guitar with the help of an old instruction book he found in a piano bench. It detailed how harmonies are embedded in chord families, and he figured out the rest, much of it that same day. At the same time, he taught himself to drink. The combination of guitar and beer was his escape hatch from an abusive father and a family that foundered. He fled the farmhouse and school.

"I left the tenth grade in May of '71. By January I was in Saratoga playing music and drinking and meeting people and washing dishes at Cafe Lena and stealing everybody's repertoire if they were there for more than one month," he says.

That cafe in Saratoga Springs, New York, had legendary status in the outwash from the Great Folk Music Scare, and it fostered a hotbed of folk music thereabouts that gave rise to a series of collectives and enterprises, notably, Philo Records, a prominent folkie label. Utah Phillips recorded for Philo, and Grosswendt became a studio musician for the label, hence the tour. He had also become by then a precocious alcoholic or in plainer terms, his own, an "asshole."

So I tell him I think this is a part of the story of music, that alcohol that seems to flow in close harmony in musicians' lives.

"Here's my instant take on that. It's a matter of being able to express yourself. Some of us are so driven by pain to express ourselves, but we have been so conditioned to not express ourselves that it really takes some chemical help," he says.

He can be more direct about this, that his father's particular form of abuse demanded his son's silence along with everyone else in the family. Realizing this connection to voice came late for a guitar player, but he finally understood that all of instrumental music is really a poor attempt, a struggle, to re-create the nuance, pathos, and passion of the human voice. We play guitars to finally learn to sing, and we need to sing to get better.

"It's all about trying to re-create the human voice or to speak with something other than the voice you've got in here," he says, laying a trained right hand on his chest and spreading those educated fingers. "I was not encouraged to speak. None of my siblings or my mother were encouraged to speak for many years."

Grosswendt was as precocious in his sobriety as he was in his alcoholism, abandoning alcohol forever when he was twenty-one. He straightened up, got a place to live, a day job cleaning houses or painting them, played in bands, got a GED, earned a "bogus" undergrad degree from Brown, decided to go to law school, did that, failed the bar exam in Rhode Island but passed it first try in Massachusetts, then immediately ask the Massachusetts bar to place him on its inactive list. He wanted no part of practicing law. So he played in bands, country bands, top-40 bands, taught guitar classes, recorded some, worked odd jobs, got married, raised twin daughters, got divorced. He's still a working stiff musician: tours the folkie circuit, records CDs, teaches at music camps, one of the handful of skilled musicians one notch below famous who carry the flame of quality acoustic music.

We are sitting at his dining room table all the time he is telling me this story, digressing now and again to anecdotes and meanders in cul-de-sacs of musical history, the lore of folklore that so engages both of us. He's affable, funny, and articulate, schooled deeply in the arcana of our music, in the biographies and the power of the right hands of long dead black men. Propped a few feet away is a gorgeous 1957 Gibson J-185 that has been his main squeeze of a guitar since a friend commanded him to buy it in the '70s. No accident here in the instrument's proximity; no matter where he has been, this guitar has never been all that far away. As we talk, I have a sense he may have used that guitar just as blind man uses a white cane, to feel his way in a world otherwise dark and unknowable. So I press him on a line of questioning that consumes me, a big part of what sent me on this quest in the first place.

Grosswendt and I are both rapt in the core of American folk music, and it flourished not in a steady, measured beat, but all of a sudden, a big bang that coincided completely with the national upheaval tracking industrialization and Reconstruction. Further, it arose especially, especially the branch of it that so captivates both of us, among the former slaves and descendants, whose personal stories intertwined directly, brutally with matters like sharecropping, poverty, forced labor concentration camps, lynchings, Jim Crow, and various sadistic forms of wholesale slaughter at the hands of white-sheeted thugs who were the direct progenitors of many of the present day's more popular Republican politicians. Amid the upheaval of 2020, our time, this earlier period of troubles is more than analogy. There's too much continuity. Not separate, but the same national stain, an introgression in our collective DNA that never leaves, only waxes and wanes, like a herpes virus. So what does this mean for the music? How did these poor people cause an exquisite and refined art to arise from sadness, oppression and violence? What is it about these troubles that sponsored creativity? I need to know what happened then to serve as some solace against what is happening now.

I ask this imponderable in a variety of vague and stammering questions, but Grosswendt doesn't want to talk much about this. It's not that these are irrelevant questions or that he is politically apathetic. Like most musicians I know, he is not. The problem is, there are no good answers to my questions and too many hollow academic answers that in the end tell us nothing valuable. He thinks the origins of our music are more or less inexplicable, a mystery to us much like the music itself.

For Grosswendt, the cause of our attachment to the music, his and mine, is at once much simpler and simultaneously more profound, a matter of the fundamentals of sound, vibrations, frequencies, rhythms primal and deeply encoded. When these sounds arise, the effect is life-changing. For him, it began while he was still a teenager and heard for the first time his first blue notes, first flatted thirds that moved his comprehension beyond the standard major scale, then grew and blossomed in watershed experiences like hearing Robert Johnson, Flaco Jiménez, and the great and largely unknown mountain banjo player Reed Martin, who by happenstance was one of Grosswendt's teachers.

"It's culture, but it's more than that. It's stuff that grabs you at the deepest possible level of your psyche. It's a conversion experience. You see something or hear something that is just so alien to you and yet it's native," he says. "It's like getting hit in the head with a hammer. It's an amazing experience. I can't imagine being alive and not having had it. It would be like walking around dead, as far as I'm concerned."

Both of us in this conversation are advanced enough in age to realize we will be not walking around but otherwise dead soon enough, a topic that emerged in a strange way as we talked. I've brought a guitar with me, a fine instrument, and I am hoping that after we have done business Martin might give me an hour's lesson. He agrees, so I play and can't help but notice his face fall in disapproval. The truth is, it isn't my best. Nervous. But something more sets him off. I play with fingerpicks, bits of metal on two fingers and a thumb of my right hand to get a sharp rhythmic quack from my guitar. Lots of players do so, but Martin does not approve. Says the touch and control gained from playing with bare fingers is the magic of his music. This method gives him better control of the sounds but more importantly of the silences. I need to learn his way, and I know what this means. I take off the picks, and it feels as if fingers have been amputated. I am a stumbling novice again, as if starting over. The truth is, I came hoping for approval, acceptance, the blessing from a particular saint. I longed to be told that as a musician, I had arrived. Instead, I am told to start over. He sees this register in my face.

"Don't worry. You can keep doing what you already know. It's not like you have to start over. Besides, you don't have enough time left to start over."

I think that last bit stuns both of us, and we let the oppressive truth of it sink in, but I leave his house, guitar in hand, determined to do as he said.

I did, and it wasn't all that hard. It opened up whole new possibilities in my music, and Martin and I continued lessons. He became my teacher. There is no such thing as an accomplished musician, no end. You never arrive. Understanding this hard fact is the only way to become an accomplished musician.

From Grosswendt's hometown to Manhattan is an easy train ride, so I left him and took the opportunity to do a little business, meet an editor in the city. The train I took from Providence pulled into Penn Station a bit late, so there was a scrum of suits slamming laptops, crowding the door, punching text messages, angst all around. I caught a cab and gave the driver an address that meant not much to me, then fretted my schedule as we crawled and stammered in gridlock. Then a few blocks from my meeting's place, I noticed where we were, down toward the Village, Sixth and Bleecker. I had the cab driver let me off there to walk the last bit, a head trip more than a walk. I didn't care if I was late to my meeting. I knew this to be ground zero of the Great Folk Music Scare, Greenwich Village.

I travel light, because I like to walk, just a backpack and my guitar case, generic, plain, flat black. I walked east on Bleecker to MacDougal then cut north to Washington Square Park. A long-haired guy in jeans with backpack carrying a guitar toward Washington Square Park. There is ample precedent for this behavior on this spot, but I presented the only such example this day, in these times. No matter. I was not walking in the present tense, so I didn't notice much the people all around. They were all droids, freaks, aliens. No home for me in this world anymore. Nor did they notice me, and especially they failed to notice the over-whelming spectral presence. No one seemed aware of walking on sacred ground, but I was. I was walking among ghosts of people, actual, real-ized people, and every one of them carried a guitar.

ACKNOWLEDGMENTS

As with all works of nonfiction, my primary debt here is to works of nonfiction. This book builds on foundations laid by others. I have tried to acknowledge that debt throughout by standard journalistic practices, which happens to be my bias and is also my preference to avoid clutter in the narrative. Instead of using extensive source notes and footnotes, I try to make clear in the text the source of my material and quotes. The bibliography gives more complete information on those sources. I include the bibliography, though, for another reason: a hope that the reader might use it as a guide for further explorations. I make the argument in the book that tracing the music to its origins can assemble an alternate and enriching version of the American story that we humans happen to need just now. Further reading can also populate that story with a lot of interesting characters. This is a backhanded way of inviting the reader to explore the lives of people like John Hurt, Gary Davis, or even Dylan in the biographies listed in the bibliography. It's worth the trip.

Still, this does not go quite far enough in acknowledging the book's debt. There are a couple of sources that, while quoted in the book, nonetheless loom far larger in framing my thinking. I mention here Barbara Ehrenreich's *Dancing in the Streets* and Iain McGilchrist's *Master and His Emissary* as particularly important works that played in constant background during the years when I wrote this. Also of outsized importance was the anthology *The Origins of Music*. Having encountered this book now, I fail to understand why it is not seen as more important and is not more widely read. It truly is a service to our culture.

As with printed sources, I also try to credit and identify all personal sources in the text. It was an honor to do so. But know now that all of these people I name in this book are far more than just interviewees. They are friends and mentors, many of them, lifelong friends, decent humans, every one. I am in their debt not just for this book, but also for my continuing musical education. In the book, I am driven along by the question of why I persist in making music, and I also give away the game a bit by saying music allows one to meet interesting people. That's the story really: I do it for the people I meet.

This book also got some help from people who aren't musicians. It began as my books often do with my last book, an investigation of human well-being and evolution. During the process, I kept tripping across all sorts of interesting references to music, ideas I quietly filed away until they formed a big enough pile to launch this effort. My co-author on that earlier book, *Go Wild*, was John Ratey, and conversations with him helped me see this idea. Likewise, my agent then, Peter Matson, saw the value in this book and helped greatly in urging me toward it.

It found its way to print as many books do these days, through a circuitous path, but a chance meeting with its editor, Joey Paxman of PM Press, sealed the deal. I thank him for his confidence and guidance through the process of publication.

Rick Bass also gave this project a great boost when he did me the honor of providing a foreword. I suffer some guilt over this knowing he sacrificed perfectly good hours in wilderness in Montana to turn out his essay, so the debt is doubly deep.

Know also that a couple of people vital to my musical life were unnamed in the book. Throughout the unwinding of this story and now well after, I played in a band. We call ourselves Raised by Wolves and do indeed play out every now and again. Matt Bugni, the fiddler, and Bill Lombardi, a talented and tasteful lead guitar player, have become my most valuable musical partners. They've taught me a lot, and some of it shows up in this book. All of it plays into my life.

The fourth band member, however, is the most important, a subjective and biased opinion of mine, but one I will hold forever. She is my wife, Tracy Stone-Manning, our band's singer and my life's true north. I will follow her anywhere and sing with her as long as I am able.

BIBLIOGRAPHY

Brock, Pope. *Charlatan: America's Most Dangerous Huckster, the Man Who Pursued Him, and the Age of Flimflam*. New York: Three Rivers Press, 2008.

Bruser, Madeline. *The Art of Practicing: A Guide to Making Music from the Heart*. New York: Harmony Books, 1997.

Byrne, David. *How Music Works*. San Francisco: McSweeney's, 2012.

Carlin, Bob. *Banjo: An Illustrated History*. Milwaukee: Backbeat Books, 2016.

————. *String Bands in the North Carolina Piedmont*. Jefferson, NC: McFarland, 2004.

Carter, Walter. *Gibson Guitars: 100 Years of an American Icon*. Los Angeles: General Publishing Group, 1994.

Conway, Cecelia. *African Banjo Echoes in Appalachia*. Knoxville: University of Tennessee Press, 1995.

Dubois, Laurent. *The Banjo: America's African Instrument*. Cambridge, MA: Belknap Press of Harvard University Press, 2016.

Dylan, Bob. *Chronicles: Volume One*. New York: Simon & Schuster, 2004.

Ehrenreich, Barbara. *Dancing in the Streets: A History of Collective Joy*. New York: Metropolitan Books, 2006.

Erdbrink, Thomas. "Rebirth of Cool: American Music Makes a Return to Iran." *New York Times*, February 24, 2015, A6.

Garst, John. *Delia*. Minnesota: Loomis House Press, 2012.

Gioia, Ted. *Delta Blues*. New York: W.W. Norton, 2008.

Gladwell, Malcolm. *Outliers: The Story of Success*. New York: Little, Brown, 2008.

Gura, Philip F. *American Transcendentalism*. New York: Hill and Wang, 2007.

————. *C.F. Martin and His Guitars: 1796–1873*. Chapel Hill: University of North Carolina Press, 2003.

Gura, Philip F., and James F. Bollman. *America's Instrument: The Banjo in the Nineteenth Century*. Chapel Hill: University of North Carolina Press, 1999.

Haberman, Clyde. "Grappling with the 'Culture of Free' in Napster's Aftermath." *New York Times*. 2014.

Hrdy, Sarah Blaffer. 2011. *Mothers and Others: The Evolutionary Origins of Mutual Understanding*. Boston: Belknap Press.

Janata, Petr. "Electrophysiological Studies of Auditory Contexts." PhD dissertation, University of Oregon, 1996.

Klein, Joe. *Woody Guthrie: A Life*. New York: Alfred A. Knopf, 1980.

Krause, Bernie. *The Great Animal Orchestra: Finding the Origins of Music in the World's Wild Places*. New York: Little, Brown, 2012.

Krist, Gary. *Empire of Sin: A Story of Sex, Jazz, Murder, and the Battle for Modern New Orleans*. New York: Crown Publishers, 2014.

Kytle, Ethan J., and Blain Roberts. "Birth of a Freedom Anthem." *New York Times*, March 15, 2015.

Levitin, Daniel J. *This Is Your Brain on Music: The Science of a Human Obsession*. New York: Penguin, 2006.

Limb, Charles, and Allen Braun. 2008. "Neural Substrates of Spontaneous Musical Performance: An fMRI Study of Jazz Improvisation." *PLOS One* 3, no. 2: 2008. https://journals.plos.org/plosone/article?id=10.1371/journal.pone.0001679.

Lomax, Alan, dir. *The Land Where the Blues Began*. PBS, *American Patchwork* series. New York: Association for Cultural Equity.

Macdonald, Helen. *H Is for Hawk*. New York: Grove Press, 2014.

Marcus, Greil. *Invisible Republic: Bob Dylan's Basement Tapes*. New York: Henry Holt, 1997.

Mazor, Barry. *Ralph Peer and the Making of Popular Roots Music*. Chicago: Chicago Review Press, 2015.

McGilchrist, Iain. *The Master and His Emissary: The Divided Brain and the Making of the Western World*. New Haven, CT: Yale University Press, 2009.

McMahon, Darrin M. *Divine Fury: A History of Genius*. New York: Basic Books, 2013.

McNally, Dennis. *On Highway 61: Music, Race and the Evolution of Cultural Freedom*. Berkeley: Counterpoint, 2014.

Nietzsche, Friedrich. *The Birth of Tragedy*. New York: Penguin Books, 1993 (1872).

Oliver, Paul. *The Story of the Blues*. Boston: Northeastern University Press. 1969.

Palmer, Martin. *The Book of Chuang Tzu*. New York: Penguin Books. 1996.

Papanikolas, Zeese. *An American Cakewalk: Ten Syncopators of the Modern World*. Stanford, CA: Stanford University Press, 2015.

Pareles, Jon. "A Solo Spotlight for a Powerful Voice." *New York Times*, Jan. 25, 2105, AR1.

Petrus, Stephen, and Ronald D. Cohen. *Fol City: New York and the American Folk Music Revival*. New York: Oxford University Press, 2015.

Petrusich, Amanda. "Hunting for the Source of the World's Most Beguiling Folk Music." *New York Times Magazine*, September 24, 2014.

Porterfield, Nolan. *Last Cavalier: The Life and Times of John A. Lomax*. Urbana: University of Illinois Press, 1996.

Ratcliffe, Philip R. *Mississippi John Hurt: His Life, His Times, His Blues*. Jackson: University Press of Mississippi, 2011.

Rovelli, Carlo. *Seven Brief Lessons on Physics*. New York: Penguin Books, 2014.

Sacks, Oliver. *Musicophilia: Tales of Music and the Brain*. New York: Alfred A. Knopf, 2007.

Safranski, Rudiger. *Nietzsche: A Philosophical Biography*. Translated by Shelley Frisch. New York: W.W. Norton, 2002.

Slingerland, Edward. *Trying Not to Try: The Art and Science of Spontaneity*. New York: Crown Publishers, 2014.

Stern, Lew. "Dwight Diller's Recipe for Pairing Banjo and Fiddle." *Banjo Newsletter* 43, no. 10 (August 2016): 20–21.

Stringer, Chris. *Lone Survivor*. New York: Henry Holt, 2012.

Szwed, John. *Alan Lomax: The Man Who Recorded the World*. New York: Penguin Books, 2010.

Thomas, Elizabeth Marshall. *The Old Ways: A Story of the First People*. New York: Picador, 2007.

Wade, Nicholas. *The Faith Instinct: How Religion Evolved and Why it Endures*. New York: Penguin Press, 2009.

Wald, Elijah. *Dylan Goes Electric! Newport, Seeger, Dylan, and the Night That Split the Sixties*. New York: HarperCollins, 2015.

Wallin, Nils L., Bjorn Merker, and Steven Brown, eds. *The Origins of Music*. Cambridge, MA: MIT Press, 2001.

Wier, Dennis R. *The Way of the Trance*. New York: Strategic Books, 2009.

Wilentz, Sean. *Bob Dylan in America*. New York: Anchor Books, 2011.

Wilkinson, Alec. "A Voice from the Past." *New Yorker*, May 19, 2014, 50–57.

Yates, Michael. "Cecil Sharp in America: Collecting in the Appalachians." *Musical Traditions*, 1999. http://www.mustrad.org.uk/articles/sharp.htm.

Zack, Ian. *Say No to the Devil: The Life and Musical Genius of Rev. Gary Davis*. Chicago: University of Chicago Press, 2015.

Zwonitzer, Mark, with Charles Hirschberg. *Will You Miss Me When I'm Gone? The Carter Family and Their Legacy in American Music*. New York: Simon & Schuster, 2002.

INDEX

"Passim" (literally "scattered") indicates intermittent discussion of a topic over a cluster of pages.

ABOUT THE AUTHORS

Richard Manning is a lifelong journalist, the author of eleven books. He is a contributing editor for *Harper's* magazine, was a John S. Knight Fellow in journalism at Stanford University, and has received many awards, especially in environmental journalism. His book *One Round River* was named a significant book of the year by the *New York Times*. His work was featured in *Best American Science and Nature Writing, 2010* and *Best American Travel Writing of 2017*.

Rick Bass is a writer and environmental activist. Bass won the Story Prize for books published in 2016 for his collection of new and selected stories, *For a Little While*. He was also awarded the General Electric Younger Writers Award, a PEN/Nelson Algren Award Special Citation for fiction, and a National Endowment for the Arts fellowship. His other books include *The Lives of Rocks*, *The Traveling Feast*, and *Why I Came West*.

ABOUT PM PRESS

PM Press is an independent, radical publisher of books and media to educate, entertain, and inspire. Founded in 2007 by a small group of people with decades of publishing, media, and organizing experience, PM Press amplifies the voices of radical authors, artists, and activists. Our aim is to  deliver bold political ideas and vital stories to all walks of life and arm the dreamers to demand the impossible. We have sold millions of copies of our books, most often one at a time, face to face. We're old enough to know what we're doing and young enough to know what's at stake. Join us to create a better world.

PM Press
PO Box 23912
Oakland, CA 94623
www.pmpress.org

PM Press in Europe
europe@pmpress.org
www.pmpress.org.uk

FRIENDS OF PM PRESS

These are indisputably momentous times—the financial system is melting down globally and the Empire is stumbling. Now more than ever there is a vital need for radical ideas.

In the years since its founding—and on a mere shoestring— PM Press has risen to the formidable challenge of publishing and distributing knowledge and entertainment for the struggles ahead. With over 450 releases to date, we have published an impressive and stimulating array of literature, art, music, politics, and culture. Using every available medium, we've succeeded in connecting those hungry for ideas and information to those putting them into practice.

Friends of PM allows you to directly help impact, amplify, and revitalize the discourse and actions of radical writers, filmmakers, and artists. It provides us with a stable foundation from which we can build upon our early successes and provides a much-needed subsidy for the materials that can't necessarily pay their own way. You can help make that happen—and receive every new title automatically delivered to your door once a month—by joining as a Friend of PM Press. And, we'll throw in a free T-shirt when you sign up.

Here are your options:

- **$30 a month** Get all books and pamphlets plus 50% discount on all webstore purchases

- **$40 a month** Get all PM Press releases (including CDs and DVDs) plus 50% discount on all webstore purchases

- **$100 a month** Superstar—Everything plus PM merchandise, free downloads, and 50% discount on all webstore purchases

For those who can't afford $30 or more a month, we have **Sustainer Rates** at $15, $10, and $5. Sustainers get a free PM Press T-shirt and a 50% discount on all purchases from our website.

Your Visa or Mastercard will be billed once a month, until you tell us to stop. Or until our efforts succeed in bringing the revolution around. Or the financial meltdown of Capital makes plastic redundant. Whichever comes first.

The Explosion of Deferred Dreams: Musical Renaissance and Social Revolution in San Francisco, 1965-1975

Mat Callahan

ISBN: 978-1-62963-231-5
$22.95   352 pages

As the fiftieth anniversary of the Summer of Love floods the media with debates and celebrations of music, political movements, "flower power," "acid rock," and "hippies", *The Explosion of Deferred Dreams* offers a critical re-examination of the interwoven political and musical happenings in San Francisco in the Sixties. Author, musician, and native San Franciscan Mat Callahan explores the dynamic links between the Black Panthers and Sly and the Family Stone, the United Farm Workers and Santana, the Indian Occupation of Alcatraz and the San Francisco Mime Troupe, and the New Left and the counterculture.

Callahan's meticulous, impassioned arguments both expose and reframe the political and social context for the San Francisco Sound and the vibrant subcultural uprisings with which it is associated. Using dozens of original interviews, primary sources, and personal experiences, the author shows how the intense interplay of artistic and political movements put San Francisco, briefly, in the forefront of a worldwide revolutionary upsurge.

A must-read for any musician, historian, or person who "was there" (or longed to have been), *The Explosion of Deferred Dreams* is substantive and provocative, inviting us to reinvigorate our historical sense-making of an era that assumes a mythic role in the contemporary American zeitgeist.

"Mat Callahan was a red diaper baby lucky to be attending a San Francisco high school during the 'Summer of Love.' He takes a studied approach, but with the eye of a revolutionary, describing the sociopolitical landscape that led to the explosion of popular music (rock, jazz, folk, R&B) coupled with the birth of several diverse radical movements during the golden 1965-1975 age of the Bay Area. Callahan comes at it from every angle imaginable (black power, anti-Vietnam War, the media, the New Left, feminism, sexual revolution—with the voice of authority backed up by interviews with those who lived it."
—Pat Thomas, author of *Listen, Whitey! The Sights and Sounds of Black Power 1965-1975*

Silenced by Sound: The Music Meritocracy Myth

Ian Brennan
with a Foreword by Tunde Adebimpe

ISBN: 978-1-62963-703-7
$20.00   256 pages

Popular culture has woven itself into the social fabric of our lives, penetrating people's homes and haunting their psyches through images and earworm hooks. Justice, at most levels, is something the average citizen may have little influence upon, leaving us feeling helpless and complacent. But pop music is a neglected arena where concrete change can occur—by exercising active and thoughtful choices to reject the low-hanging, omnipresent corporate fruit, we begin to rebalance the world, one engaged listener at a time.

Silenced by Sound: The Music Meritocracy Myth is a powerful exploration of the challenges facing art, music, and media in the digital era. With his fifth book, producer, activist, and author Ian Brennan delves deep into his personal story to address the inequity of distribution in the arts globally. Brennan challenges music industry tycoons by skillfully demonstrating that there are millions of talented people around the world far more gifted than the superstars for whom billions of dollars are spent to promote the delusion that they have been blessed with unique genius.

We are invited to accompany the author on his travels, finding and recording music from some of the world's most marginalized peoples. In the breathtaking range of this book, our preconceived notions of art are challenged by musicians from South Sudan to Kosovo, as Brennan lucidly details his experiences recording music by the Tanzania Albinism Collective, the Zomba Prison Project, a "witch camp" in Ghana, the Vietnamese war veterans of Hanoi Masters, the Malawi Mouse Boys, the Canary Island whistlers, genocide survivors in both Cambodia and Rwanda, and more.

Silenced by Sound is defined by muscular, terse, and poetic verse, and a nonlinear format rife with how-to tips and anecdotes. The narrative is driven and made corporeal via the author's ongoing field-recording chronicles, his memoir-like reveries, and the striking photographs that accompany these projects.

After reading it, you'll never hear quite the same again.

"An interesting and important project."
—Noam Chomsky